Italian Horror

ZOMBI 2
LA ISLA DE LOS MUERTOS VIVOS
con IAN Mc. CULLOCH - TISA FARROW - RICHARD JOHNSON
al cliver - auretta gay - y con OLGA KARLATOS
producido por UGO TUCCI y FABRIZIO DE ANGELIS por la VARIETY FILM
Dir. LUCIO FULCI - TECHNICOLOR

ITALIAN HORROR

by Jim Harper

Luminary Press
Baltimore, Maryland

ISBN 1-887664-55-6
Library of Congress Catalogue Card Number 2005923718
Manufactured in the United States of America

First Printing by Luminary Press, an imprint of Midnight Marquee Press, Inc., September 2005

Dedication
My heartfelt gratitude
to my wife,
without whom this book
would never have been written

Italian Horror

Table of Contents

Acknowledgments

First, thanks must go to Gary and Susan Svehla for their consideration and support during the creation of this work. Thanks also to my mother, father, sister and brother for their unfailing support and optimism. Thanks to Carl, Marc, James, Charles and Dominic for being subjected to more Italian horror films than they would have liked.

Author's Introduction

This book is intended to cover Italian horror films released between the years 1979 and 1994. Why choose those years? Well, primarily for convenience. They mark the release dates of Lucio Fulci's *Zombie*, the film that instigated the last great wave of Italian horror, and Michele Soavi's *Dellamorte dellamore*, the last great Italian horror film. After the release of Soavi's film, relatively few new Italian horror movies were made; the trend had run its course, and such films were no longer seen as commercially viable.

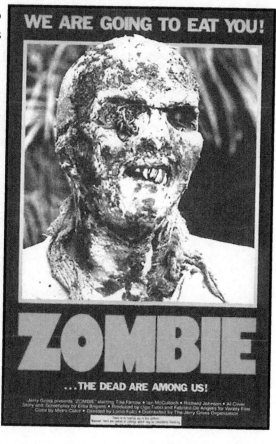

This period has attracted relatively little serious study, with the exception of the works of certain high-profile directors—Dario Argento, Lucio Fulci and Ruggero Deodato. More often than not, the 1980s are passed over as a time when Italian horror was bogged down in derivative sequels or toothless made-for-television efforts, before fizzling out in the early 1990s. There is some truth in this assertion, but it blithely ignores the decent films made during that period. Lamberto Bava may be forever cursed to be compared with his father, the great Mario Bava, but in the early 1980s he released a handful of stylish and energetic films that confirmed his own talents. Sadly, it's not hard to find critics churlishly condemning *Demons* (1985) and *Demons 2* (1986) as mere splatter movies, or criticizing *A Blade in the Dark* (1983) for being a *giallo* in the traditional vein instead of something more adventurous. *Demons* is nothing but a splatter movie, but it aims to be over-the-top gory fun, and it succeeds. The concept that extreme gore needs to be balanced by some form of *message* is

both obsolete and pretentious. In short, there were more good films made in Italy during the 1980s and early 1990s than the critics would have us believe. It's just a question of finding them.

The aim of this work then is to guide the unfamiliar viewer to the best films of the period while hopefully steering him or her away from the dross. Obviously films do not exist in isolation, so an account of the origins and development of the Italian horror film is provided. This will help the reader place the films reviewed in this book in the appropriate historical context. I also describe the trends that have developed over the years. I have included a brief discussion of the decline of the Italian horror film, hoping to shed some light on the demise of a genre that had been in existence for over three decades. Placed throughout the main section of the book are a series of biographies devoted to important figures in the world of Italian horror. They include directors, producers, screenwriters and special effects technicians.

I should devote some space to the conventions used in the book. Films are reviewed under their most common title. In many cases this is the English one (e.g., *The House on the Edge of the Park*), but occasionally it is more appropriate to use the Italian title (e.g., *Dellamorte dellamore*). If the Italian title is used, it is either because the film is more widely known under that name or because no English title has ever been devised (*La casa del buon ritorno*). Definite articles (*the, la, le* or *l'*) and the indefinite article have been ignored when arranging the films into alphabetical order (e.g., *La casa del buon ritorno* is listed under "C," not "L." When listing alternate titles, only ones in English or Italian are given. Character names appear in parentheses following names of actors. Names followed by square brackets are pseudonyms, while names given in between the square brackets are people's real names. Titles followed by an asterisk indicate a film I was not able to view. For such films I have included whatever cast and crew details I was able to find, as well as any important facts. Since I was not able

to view those films, I cannot vouch for the accuracy of the cast and crew details. As far as I know, they are correct.

I hope this work proves useful to movie fans. If I have made any mistakes or if you have any queries you wish to present, feel free to contact me through Midnight Marquee Press, Inc. If there *are* any mistakes in the text, they are of course entirely my fault!

—Jim Harper

vas an international success and the first *bona fide* talian horror classic.

Producers were quick o recognize the commer-:ial potential of the Italian 1orror film and began :ommissioning their own Gothic terrors. The re-vards were enough to empt Riccardo Freda back o the horror genre; he re-eased *L'orribile segreto del lottor Hichcock* (*The Hor-ible Secret of Doctor Hich-:ock*) in 1962. A grim tale of murder and necrophilia,

Barbara Steele in Freda's *The Horrible Secret of Dr. Hichcock*

Freda's film also stars Barbara Steele, this time in a more sympathetic role as the awful doctor's unsuspecting wife and would-be victim. *Doc-*

or Hichcock was a moderate nternational success, so he und Barbara Steele returned 1 year later in *Lo spettro* (*The Ghost*).

Although his work has never been as highly re-garded as Bava's, Antonio Margheriti was responsi-ble for a handful of decent Gothic thrillers in the early 1960s. The first and best, *La vergine di Norimberga* (aka: *The Virgin of Nuremberg, Hor-or Castle*), was released in 1963 and starred Hammer's most identifiable figure, Christopher Lee. The oth-er two featured—surprise, surprise—Barbara Steele.

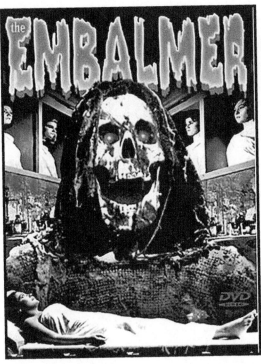

All three productions were reasonably successful and have since been recognized as worthy, if not quite first-rate, horror films.

Unsurprisingly, not everything released in this golden age of Italian horror could aspire to the standards of Bava or Freda, or even Margheriti. Half-hearted, derivative efforts like *Il mostro di Venezia* (aka: *The Embalmer, The Monster of Venice*, 1966) surfaced briefly in U.S. drive-ins before fading into oblivion, while others, such as Massimo Pupillo's *Night of Bloody Horror* (1965) enjoyed cult status for all the wrong reasons—in the case of *Night of Bloody Horror* because of former muscleman Mickey Hargitay. The sight of Jayne Mansfield's ex-husband waxing lyrical about his perfect body before heading off to torture some scantily clad beauty—all the time dressed in tights and covered in body oil—turned *Night of Bloody Horror* into an instant and campy S/M favorite, which it remains to this day. It's something of a shame because Pupillo's previous film, *5 tombe per un medium* (*Five Graves for a Medium*, 1965), was a fairly respectable effort that starred... Barbara Steele. After *Night of Bloody Horror*, Pupillo's career fizzled out, except for a minor *Django* clone with Luigi Montefiore.

In the early 1960s a new strain of horror film appeared: the *giallo*.

Named after its primary inspiration, the yellow-covered pulp thriller novels that were popular at the time, the *giallo* was a crossbreed of German crime mysteries (*krimi*), the films of Alfred Hitchcock and traditional horror movie material. Characterized by an unlikely killer, a complex plot and a series of distractions and red herrings, the *giallo* was the first uniquely Italian style of horror film. Elements of the *giallo* can be found in Mario Bava's 1963 film *La ragazza che sapeva troppo* (*The Evil Eye*), but it wasn't until the release of *Sei donne per l'assassino* (*Blood and Black Lace*) in 1964 that the style truly took shape. The English title summarizes the film and the style so much better than the Italian one, implying violent, stylish (and possibly sexual) entertainment, the cornerstone of the *giallo* for years to come. With *Blood and Black Lace*, Bava confirmed his status as the most important figure in Italian horror.

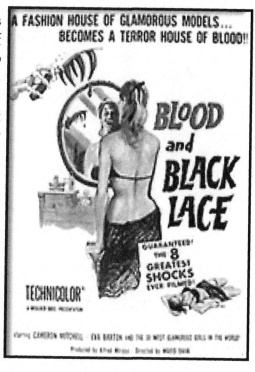

Unfortunately for Bava and his compatriots, the wave of interest in Italian horror films started to fade. Westerns, James Bond-style spy thrillers and sci-fi flicks began to take over, threatening to marginalize anyone who wasn't willing to move with the changing trends. Mario Bava responded with *Terrore nello spazio* (*Planet of the Vampires*, 1965), a respectable effort that has been retrospectively viewed as a major influence on Ridley Scott's *Alien* (1979). Less interesting were Antonio Margheriti's contributions; he accepted a deal to make four sci-fi movies for U.S. television, sporting titles such as *The Devil Men from Space* and *The Deadly Diapanoids*. All four were to be shot in 12 weeks, using the same sets and casts (including a young Franco Nero) and working with a tiny budget. Needless to say, the results were not earth shattering.

Bava did manage to release another horror film, the well-received *Operazione paura* (*Kill, Baby...Kill!*, 1966), but for the rest of the decade he was relegated to directing distinctly second-rate non-horror efforts. *Spie vengono dal semifreddo* (1966), otherwise known as *Dr. Goldfoot and the Girl Bombs*, was a poor sequel to a film that was hardly a work of genius in the first place, while *I coltelli del vendicatore* (*Knives of the Avenger*, 1966) returned to the Viking soap operas Bava had produced in the early years of his career. *Il rosso segno della follia* (*Hatchet for the*

Honeymoon, 1968) saw Bava return to the *giallo*, but the film went unreleased for two years before finally emerging to mixed reviews.

A new talent emerged in 1969, one that would redefine the horror genre and reverse the failing fortunes of the Italian horror film industry. Throughout the 1960s Dario Argento was best known as a film critic and scriptwriter-for-hire, earning himself a story credit on Sergio Leone's *Once Upon a Time in the West* (1968), as well as contributing to B-movie efforts from directors such as Armando Crispino and Umberto Lenzi. In 1969 he released his debut film, a *giallo* called *L'uccello dalle piume di cristallo* (*The Bird with the Crystal Plumage*). Despite a few positive reviews, the film was initially ignored. Eventually rumors began to circulate about this violent and stylish thriller from an unknown director, and soon it was to be hailed as an important and characteristically Italian horror film. While such assertions are essentially true, Argento's visually arresting style was deeply influenced by the films of Mario Bava, particularly *Blood and Black Lace*, not to mention a handful of plot elements taken from Frederic Brown's 1949 novel *The Screaming Mimi* (filmed in 1958 as *Screaming Mimi*).

The success of *The Bird with the Crystal Plumage* encouraged Argento to begin work on a second *giallo*, *Il gatto a nove code* (*The Cat O'Nine Tails*, 1971). Although successful, the film did not earn the same critical acclaim as Argento's debut, and the director himself considers it his worst film. A third *giallo*, *4 mosche di velluto grigio* (*Four Flies on Grey Velvet*) followed in 1972, confirming Argento's status as the primary exponent of the style. Frustrated with the limitations of the *giallo*, Argento turned to historical drama next, releasing *Le cinque giornate* (*The Five Days of Milan*, 1973). This Leone-inspired film failed with audiences and critics alike.

Meanwhile the *giallo* was becoming a staple of popular cinema. A wave of thrillers began to appear in cinemas, sporting convoluted plots, cumbersome titles and international actors in leading roles. One of the main purveyors of such films was Sergio Martino, director of (amongst others) *La coda dello scorpione* (*The Case of the Scorpion's Tail*, 1971) and *Il tuo vizio è una stanza chiusae solo io ne ho la chiave* (*Eye of the Black Cat*, 1972). Like many of the new *gialli*, Martino's films

added a dose of sexuality into the mix; other films, such as Andrea Bianchi's *Nude per l'assassino* (*Strip Nude for Your Killer*, 1975) capitalized heavily on this approach, replacing characterization and plot with sleaze and graphic sex.

Not all directors chose to emulate Argento or dumb down for the sensationalist audiences. Aldo Lado's debut film, the enigmatically titled *Corta notte delle bambole di vetro* (*Short Night of the Glass Dolls*, 1971), mixed political commentary and a Poe-influenced storyline to great effect, making it one of the hidden gems of Italian horror. Lado returned to more traditional *giallo* territory with *Chi l'ha vista morire?* (*Who Saw Her Die?*, 1972) before releasing *L'ultimo treno della notte* (*Late Night Trains*, 1975), a variation on *The Last House on the Left* (1972) that manages to rival Craven's film for nastiness.

Despite his influence on the film, Mario Bava found it difficult to flourish in the wake of *The Bird with the Crystal Plumage*. The Agatha Christie-inspired *Cinque bambole per la luna d'agosto* (*Five Dolls for an August Moon*, 1970) performed poorly at the box office, as did *Hatchet for the Honeymoon*. Compared with the youthful energy of Argento's films, Bava's recent efforts seemed lackluster and uninspired. History has been kinder to his next film, the blackly humorous *Reazione a catena* (*Bay of Blood*, 1971). Although originally criticized for its flimsy story and gleefully gory approach, later commentators have pointed out that it pre-empted a number of slasher movie conventions several years before *Halloween* (1978) and *Friday the 13th* (1980) found favor. Most obvious of these conventions is the presence of a group of luckless (and brainless) teenagers, out for a wild time in the woods. Needless

Reqia di Mario Bava

to say, they're all dispatched in bloody fashion. Unlike a number of Bava's later films, *Bay of Blood* received a U.S. release; unfortunately it was later re-titled as a sequel to *The Last House on the Left*, a film with which it has nothing in common.

In the early 1970s the Italian film industry, no doubt partially influenced by the success of Argento and his followers, began to take a renewed interest in the horror film. The interest was purely commercial; big-budget U.S. horror films like *The Exorcist* (1973) were proving massive box office draws, while lesser exploitation flicks were able to secure substantial profits thanks to their low budgets and a seemingly endless audience for sensationalist trash.

William Friedkin's Satanic classic inspired imitators across the globe, and Italy was no exception. The majority of these films attempted to outdo the original in terms of blasphemy and shocking material; Alberto De Martino's *L'anticristo* (*The Tempter*, 1974) threw bestiality, sex with the devil and even more gross special effects into the mix, making it arguably more entertaining than the original. It helps that *The Tempter* is a technically proficient film, boasting some excellent cinematography from Aristide Massacessi and decent performances from a cast that includes Mel Ferrer, Arthur Kennedy and Alida Valli. Less successful but more amusing is *Chi sei?* (*Beyond the Door*, 1975). Directed by notorious exploitation producer Ovidio G. Assonitis (the man behind *Piranha II: The Spawning*, 1981), *Beyond the Door* tries to string together elements from both Friedkin's film and *Rosemary's Baby* (1968). It doesn't work particularly well, but it is probably the only time you will see Juliet Mills (sister of Hayley) spewing pea soup. She even manages to outshine Richard Johnson (*Zombie*, 1979) and

Juliet Mills stars in *Beyond the Door*, which rips off *The Exorcist* and *Rosemary's Baby*.

Gabriel Lavia (*Deep Red*, 1975; *Inferno*, 1980). Perhaps unsurprisingly, *Beyond the Door* was a box office hit, coming in second only to *Jaws* (1975) in its first week of release.

Ironically, the man who suffered the most at the hand of these diabolical imitators was Mario Bava. His *Lisa e diavolo* (*Lisa and the Devil*, 1972), an atmospheric and stately Gothic horror starring Elke Sommers, Telly Savalas and Alida Valli, was hacked up by the producers, who felt the subject matter wasn't commercial enough. In an effort to rework the film for the mainstream market, several new scenes were shot and inserted into the print. The new material now made Sommers the victim of demonic possession, and featured Robert Alda (father of Alan) as the ubiqui-tous priest. A new title was added, just in case anyone missed the intended con-nection: *La casa del'esorcismo* (*House of Exorcism*). *Lisa and the Devil* isn't Bava's greatest film and would never have been a box office success, but it deserved better. To make matters worse, Ovidio G. Assonitis later released

Daria Nocolodi (mother of Asia Argento) slits her throat in *Shock*, retitled *Beyond the Door 2*.

Bava's *Schock* (*Shock*, 1977), a respectable psycho-thriller starring Daria Nicolodi, as a spurious sequel to *Beyond the Door*.

The Exorcist wasn't the only demonic success story of the decade, but Richard Donner's *The Omen* (1976) inspired few clones. The only one of note is Alberto De Martino's *Holocaust 2000* (1977), a big-budget effort starring Kirk Douglas, Simon Ward, Agostina Belli and Anthony Quayle. Douglas plays an executive in charge of plans to build a highly controversial nuclear plant in the Middle East (we're not told where, but the clues point strongly to Israel). As if that wasn't a stressful enough job, he's also discovered that he's going to father the Antichrist. This is bad, because the devil child could use the nuclear plant to set off a chain of nuclear explosions across the globe, thus effectively destroying humanity. Obviously the story is flawed beyond belief, but the whole film's hysterically overblown attitude (witness the biblical slaughter of the innocents toward the end) makes compulsive viewing. Douglas and the cast give it their best, but *Holocaust 2000* is entertaining for all the wrong reasons.

Foreign poster for *Il paeso del sesso selvaggio*

Probably the most notorious of the Italian horror cycles of the 1970s was the cannibal flick. One part *mondo* documentary, one part jungle adventure and one part splatter film, the cannibal flick was a pure exploitation form, built around graphic violence (often sexual and often featuring real animal slaughter), clichéd tension between civilized and primitive groups and archaic-verging-on-racist presentations of the natives. Accounts differ as to who had the honor of starting off this particular style. Umberto Lenzi claims his 1972 film *Il paeso del sesso selvaggio* (*Deep River Savages*) was the first, while Ruggero Deodato believes that his own *Ultimo mondo cannibale* (*Last Cannibal World*, 1976) was the progenitor. If Lenzi's story is to be believed, he was approached to direct a sequel to *Deep River Savages*. He passed on the proposal, and the producers hired Deodato, who turned the idea into *Last Cannibal World*. Whatever the truth may be, it seems Lenzi gets the prize by dint of chronology alone.

Although the cannibal flick didn't hit its peak until 1980 with Deodato's grimly realistic *Cannibal Holocaust* (see the review in the main section of the book), some activity existed in the area earlier. With his characteristic talent for spotting emerging trends, Aristide Massacessi produced two such movies. The first was one of his multitudinous *Emmanuelle* clones, *Emanuelle and the Last Cannibals* (1977), a title undoubtedly inspired by *Last Cannibal World*. Typically for a Massacessi film, it focuses heavily on near-hardcore porno material, usually featuring his "Black Emanuelle," Laura Gemser. It's poorly made and pretty dull, but it's probably the best sex-and-cannibalism film out there, for what that's worth. Even less entertaining is

Massacessi's *Papaya dei Caraibi* (*Papaya of the Caribbean*, 1978), despite attempts to provide some tension.

Having left the *giallo* behind (temporarily at least), Sergio Martino turned to the cannibal film, directing *La montagna del dio cannibale* (*Mountain of the Cannibal God*, 1978). Unlike most of the other cannibal flicks, *Mountain of the Cannibal God* is relatively well made and boasts a decent cast, including Ursula Andress, Stacy Keach and Claudia Cassinelli. Obviously inspired by *Green Hell*-style jungle adventures, it's probably the most entertaining film of its kind. Sadly, even a competent director like Martino feels the need to include real animal slaughter and the stereotypical bloodthirsty primitives attitude. It was the first of three wilderness adventures for Martino, all of which starred Claudia Cassinelli and were co-written by the director and Cesare Frugoni. The other two are *L'isola degli uomini pesce* (*Island of the Fishmen*, 1979) and *Il fiume del grande caimano* (*The Great Alligator*, 1979). Both are reviewed later in this book.

Pushing the boundaries of good taste well past the breaking point was the mercifully short-lived craze for films based around the sadistic excesses of the Nazis. The horrific practices carried out by the SS and the German army gave exploitation filmmakers plenty of material, which they gleefully adapted for the big screen. Surprisingly, the catalyst for these absurd efforts seems to have been the dubious art-house flick *Il portiere di notte* (*The Night Porter*, 1974), a U.S.-Italian co-production about a concentration camp guard and a prisoner who meet after the war and begin a sadomasochistic relationship. This stylish, well-mounted film stars Dirk Bogarde and Charlotte Rampling and is often described in favorable terms as a haunting and disturbing study of violence and victimization. Maybe so, but it's also sleazy, pretentious and sensationalist. In a similar vein is Tinto Brass' *Salon Kitty* (1976), which explores much of the same territory but at least manages to look like a glossy *Playboy* production (Brass directed the infamous *Playboy* film *Caligula*, 1979). Lee Frost's *Love Camp 7* (1968) is slightly more honest, being openly promoted as an adults-only flick. An-

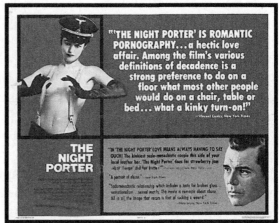

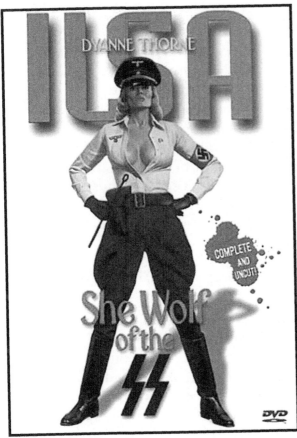

other obvious influence is Don Edmonds' infamous Nazi torture-and-sleaze fest, *Ilsa, She Wolf of the SS* (1974). Purportedly based around the real exploits of a female camp doctor, *Ilsa* (and the slew of sequels that followed, both official and unofficial) featured plenty of sex and pain, including castration, boiling and some bizarre sex-related death scenes.

The worst of the Italian Nazi films is Cesare Canevari's *L'ultima orgia del III Reich* (*The Gestapo's Last Orgy*, 1976), although they're all mean-spirited and offensive. Canevari's film is the most hysterical, presenting a succession of acts of torture and brutality, including prisoners being savaged by dogs, burned to death, raped and sexually abused, and that's before audiences get to the cannibalism. All of these films occupy much the same territory—plenty of graphic brutality toward female prisoners, sadistic and kinky SS officers, very little hardcore material and the occasional attempt at making a political or sociological comment. Bruno Mattei's *KZ9-Lager di Sterminio* (*S.S. Extermination Love Camp*, 1977) incorporated some real footage of concentration camp victims into the film, as did Mario Caiano, in a vain attempt to spice up his dull effort *La svastica nel ventre* (*Nazi Love Camp 27*, 1977), but for the most part there's little to choose between the different films.

Unsurprisingly, most of the Nazi exploitation flicks were directed by hacks jumping on whatever bandwagon happened to be trendy. Mario Caiano churned out a few respectable horror films during the first wave of Italian horror, including *Gli amanti d'oltretomba* (*The Faceless Monster*, 1965), starring Barbara Steele. His co-writer, Fabio

De Agostino, ended up in the same place, directing *Le lunghe notte della Gestapo* (*The Red Nights of the Gestapo*, 1977). Cesare Canevari had worked on *gialli*, Westerns, spy spoofs and *Emmanuelle* clones before dropping out of the industry in the early 1980s. Most prolific of all was Bruno Mattei; aside from his two Nazi flicks, he's directed films in just about every exploitation style there is, always with an emphasis on minuscule budgets.

In 1975 Dario Argento returned to the *giallo* in style, with the acclaimed *Profondo rosso* (*Deep Red*). Co-written by Bernardino Zapponi, one of Federico Fellini's regular scriptwriters, *Deep Red* is Argento's best *giallo* and probably the finest example of the style. While it has certain things in common with *The Bird with the Crystal Plumage*—in particular the central concept, an artist witnessing a murder and struggling to find out exactly what he's seen—*Deep Red* saw the emergence of Argento the stylist. His films have always been visually interesting, but now the aesthetic appeal was just as important as the plot. *Deep Red* is therefore visually stunning—the lighting is excellent, the sets are decorated in garish colors and occasionally splashed with violent slashes of crimson, while Argento's characteristic eye for the macabre provides some truly bizarre sights. Needless to say, *Deep Red* is exceptionally violent. The murders on display include a man's face being smashed against a marble mantelpiece and a woman having her head repeatedly thrust into hot water—some of Argento's most violent scenes. Unsurprisingly, *Deep Red* was heavily censored in many countries, including the United States (where the film was clumsily retitled *The Hatchet Murders*) and Great Britain. More surprisingly, the film was not an international success, despite performing well in Italy.

Deep Red was Argento's finest film so far, but his next effort would surpass that achieve-

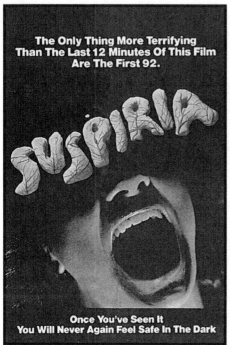

The Only Thing More Terrifying Than The Last 12 Minutes Of This Film Are The First 92.

SUSPIRIA

Once You've Seen It You Will Never Again Feel Safe In The Dark

ment. Moving away from the *giallo*, his next film was a supernatural thriller, co-written by Argento's new partner Daria Nicolodi, who played the female lead in *Deep Red*. Based partially on the writings of Thomas De Quincey (*Confessions of an English Opium-Eater*), *Suspiria* (Latin for "sighs") is a fantastic tale of witchcraft and black magic at an academy of dance in Germany. An international cast shines, including Jessica Harper, an American actress with dance experience (she was in the Broadway production of *Hair*), veteran actress Joan Bennett in one of her last roles and Udo Kier, the German actor most famous for starring in Andy Warhol's *Flesh for Frankenstein* (1973) and *Blood for Dracula* (1974). On a trivia note, Antonio Margheriti oversaw both of the Andy Warhol horror films.

If *Deep Red* placed aesthetic appeal on the same footing as plot and storyline, *Suspiria* went even further. Although initially used to introduce the central characters, the plot is pushed aside relatively quickly in favor of a series of bizarre and often brutal vignettes. Argento occasionally returns to the story to keep the film on track, but on the whole the plot is secondary to the director's wild imaginings. And he is certainly on form here; the whole film looks like a fairytale crossed with a dream. The academy is a strange Gothic building, full of long corridors and huge doors, while other locations seem like an art deco nightmare. The whole film swims in vivid primary colors, with lighting to match, imbuing the scenes—even the film's few traditional moments—with sinister overtones. The murders are some of Argento's finest, particularly the extended opening sequence—a bloody and inventive scene that results in the death of two young women and lets audiences know exactly what they're dealing with.

Upon its release in 1977, *Suspiria* was both a critical and commercial success. Some critics berated the lack of plot and characterization—accusations that persist today—but for the most part Argento was hailed as the new leading light of Italian horror. *Suspiria* continues to be regarded as a genuine horror classic, on a par with the best of Mario Bava's films, and it is often called the best Italian horror movie of the 1970s. Perhaps more importantly, it made Argento an important figure in the world of horror.

Thanks to his newfound status, Argento was able to offer his services to American director George A. Romero, who was looking to prepare a sequel to his 1968 classic, *Night of the Living Dead*. In return for the right to prepare a European cut of the finished film, Argento would provide Romero with the support and financial backing he needed to shoot his movie. The resulting film—*Dawn of the Dead* (1978)—combined graphic gore (courtesy of Tom Savini) with the director's unique brand of social commentary, and the film proved a hit across the globe.

The success of *Dawn of the Dead* provided the necessary impetus to kick-start another wave of Italian horror films. Leading the charge was Lucio Fulci, a talented director with a long and checkered history. Having started his career in the 1950s, making comedies with some of Italy's most popular comedians, Fulci drifted from genre to genre, churning out spaghetti Westerns (*I Quattro dell'apocalisse/The Four of the Apocalypse*, 1975), *gialli* (*Una lucertola/con la pelle di donna/A Lizard in a Woman's Skin*, 1971), historical dramas (*Beatrice Cenci/The Conspiracy of Torture*, 1969) and the occasional horror comedy (*Young Dracula*, 1975).

Fulci had enjoyed moderate success before, but his real breakthrough came in 1979 with the release of *Zombi 2/Zombie* (see review). The box office returns garnered by *Zombie* proved that an Italian product could successfully compete with its American counterparts, giving rise to a slew of zombie-themed horror films. It did not stop at the living dead, however. Having finally found his true calling, Fulci began to develop his Lovecraftian and Poesque

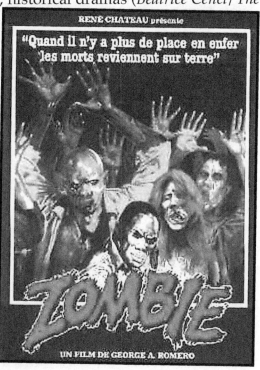

RENÉ CHATEAU présente

"Quand il n'y a plus de place en enfer les morts reviennent sur terre"

ZOMBIE

UN FILM DE GEORGE A. ROMERO

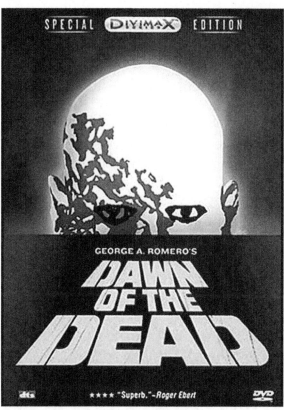

influences into a uniquely Italian format, while journeyman director Antonio Margheriti combined the urban setting of *Dawn of the Dead* with the established cannibal movie. Even an old hand like Riccardo Freda was tempted out of retirement, producing the worthless *L'ossessione che uccide* (*Fear*, 1980).

Unknown to the fans and filmmakers celebrating the newfound popularity, this silver age would be the last stand of Italian horror. By the time the 1980s turned into the 1990s, the domestic horror film faded almost completely, replaced for a brief while by flaccid television horrors before disappearing entirely. Fewer horror films were produced in the 1990s than in any other period since 1957. Directors such as Pupi Avati and Alessandro Capone would occasionally produce a genre movie, but with little impact. Michele Soavi's *Dellamorte dellamore* (1994) was both successful and critically acclaimed, but it represents a last twitch of the corpse—a twitch of the death nerve, if you will—rather than a genuine sign of life.

So what did happen to the Italian horror film? One of the main factors in the decline of the horror film was the steady expansion of Italian television. Until 1976 Italian television was dominated by a single network, mostly controlled by the government; in July of that year state legislation allowed for the creation of private networks, companies broadcasting at a regional level and not under the control of the government (although still regulated by Parliament). A year later, color television was introduced.

The new private networks began searching for material to fill their schedules. Many of them were able to purchase American movies for relatively small fees, often for much less than it would cost to secure domestic films. With audiences now able to see a wide choice of films in the comfort of their own home, box office takings began to decline. In response, theaters started giving precedence to foreign movies and those domestic releases that were likely to perform well at the box office. Considered a marginal genre, horror was almost entirely ignored. Only Dario Argento—a major director, despite his allegiance to horror—had enough status and popularity to guarantee a theatrical release for his films.

Cristina Marsillach is a captive audience in Argento's *Opera*.

Television slowly became the most powerful medium in the land. Television companies were also able to exert an influence over the movie industry; the Cecchi Gori Group, the company responsible for financing and producing Argento's *Opera* (1987), as well as Michele Soavi's *La chiesa* (*The Church*, 1989) and *La setta* (*The Sect*, 1991), started out as a private network. Unsurprisingly, more and more filmmakers gravitated toward television as the way of the future. For the horror genre, this was an unfortunate move. As with American television, the Italian networks weren't interested in graphic gore or sleazy sexuality, two of the key aspects of Italian horror. The resulting made-for-TV horror films were toothless in the extreme, replacing ghoulish vitality with lame humor and pumping pop/rock soundtracks. A director such as Lamberto Bava, the man responsible for violent and energetic films like *La casa con la scala nel buio* (*A Blade in the Dark*, 1983) and *Demoni* (*Demons*, 1985), was reduced to releasing tedious rubbish (*Una notte al cimitero/Graveyard Disturbance*, 1987) before deserting horror entirely for family-oriented fantasy films.

In direct competition, Italy's domestic product stood little chance against its American counterpart. The advertising allowance of many U.S. horror productions was bigger than the entire budget of certain Italian films. Thanks to major studio backing, the most mindless American film could command the kind of budget that even the most high-profile Italian horror directors could only dream of; for example, the budget of *Friday the 13th Part 3* (1982) was 4,000,000 dollars, while Dario Argento's *Inferno* (1980) was made for less than three.

By the early 1980s, the booming U.S. horror industry was beginning to squeeze out the foreign competition. Despite the international success of *Suspiria*, 20th Century Fox didn't release either *Inferno* or *Tenebrae* (1982) to theaters. These films eventually saw a video release, but often with different titles—such as *Unsane* instead of *Tenebrae* or *Creepers* instead of *Phenomena* (1985)—and always with the goriest segments removed. Lucio Fulci's magnum opus *The Beyond* (1981) was stripped of all blood and gore and released as *The Seven Doors of Death*; after the disappointing *Manhattan Baby* (1983), none of Fulci's films received an American theatrical release.

With the Italian horror film sidelined in the domestic market, ignored in the major foreign markets and losing ground to television with every passing year, it's hardly surprising that few directors saw the point in remaining loyal to the genre. By 1994, only Argento was still making horror movies. In the decade following, Italy would lose some of its most prolific and highly regarded exploitation directors—Lucio Fulci, Riccardo Freda, Antonio Margheriti, Aristide Massacessi. Umberto Lenzi had retired, while Michele Soavi and Lamberto Bava worked solely in television. With the old masters either departed or working elsewhere and no fresh talent in development, it seems unlikely that the ghost of Italian horror will rise again.

ITALIAN HORROR A-Z Guide

Absurd (1981)
Aka: Rosso Sangue, Anthropophagus II, The Grim Reaper 2,
Monster Hunter, Zombie 6: Monster Hunter

Director: Peter Newton [Aristide Massacessi]; Story/Screenplay: John
Cart [Luigi Montefiore]; Producer: Aristide Massacessi, Donatella
Donati; Music: Carlo Maria Cordio
Starring: George Eastman [Luigi Montefiore] (Mikos Stenopolis),
Annie Belle (Emily), Charles Borromel (Sergeant Engelman), Katya
Berger, Kasimir Berger, Hanja Kochansky, Ian Danby, Ted Russoff,
Edmund Purdom, Michele Soavi [uncredited]

*A man is taken to the hospital after impaling himself on an iron railing.
His wounds are serious and it's assumed that he will soon die. Before reaching
the point of death, however, the man begins to recover, at a miraculous
speed. He sets off on a
killing spree, terrorizing two
young children and their
babysitters.*

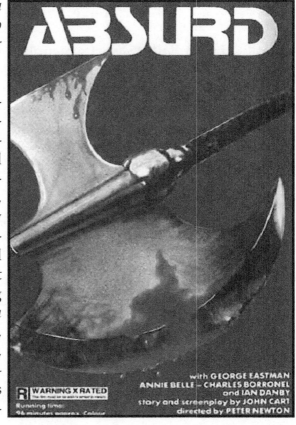

After the decent com-
mercial success of *Anthropophagus* (1980), Massacessi and company decided
to release another over-
the-top splatter movie,
once again written by
and starring Luigi Mon-
tefiore. This time round
a more international cast
was recruited, including
Annie Belle (*The House on
the Edge of the Park*, 1980),
Katya and Kasimir Berger,
the children of genre veteran William Berger, as
well as British exploita-

with GEORGE EASTMAN
ANNIE BELLE – CHARLES BORROMEL
and IAN DANBY
story and screenplay by JOHN CART
directed by PETER NEWTON

tion favorite Edmund Purdom. The presence of Montefiore playing another lumbering maniac lead many countries to publicize the movie as a sequel to *Anthropophagus*, but the two films are unrelated.

Opinions are sharply divided as to which is the better film, *Anthropophagus* or *Absurd*. *Absurd*, yet *another* slasher movie, drew many of its ideas from *Halloween* (1978), and this generally worked against the film. However, the later film boasts a more interesting plot and thankfully does not contain over an hour of dull holiday footage. This time the murders are spaced more evenly throughout the film, making it less of a chore to sit through. It's not quite as graphic as the earlier film, but there's plenty here to please most splatter fans.

Sadly, that's about all there is. The film is ineptly made, lacking all tension and suspense. The acting is pretty poor throughout, which is to be expected for a hastily shot low-budget film. Massacessi's production values have never been particularly high, but if one can stomach his style, *Absurd* is relatively painless viewing. His best effort remains *Beyond the Darkness* (1979), but audiences could do worse than this.

Aenigma (1987)

Director: Lucio Fulci; Story/Screenplay: Giorgio Mariuzzo, Lucio Fulci; Producer: Ettore Spagnuolo, Boro Banjack; Makeup: Giuseppe Ferranti; Music: Carlo Maria Cordio
Starring: Jared Martin (Dr. Robert Anderson), Lara Naszinski (Eva Gordon), Ulli Reinthaler (Jennifer Clark), Sophie D'Aulan (Kim), Jennifer Naud (Grace), Riccardo Acerbi (Fred Vernon), Kathi Wise (Virginia)

A schoolgirl is left in a coma after a prank played by her classmates goes disastrously wrong. Soon afterward a new student enrolls at the same girls' school, and the pranksters begin to die off, one by one.

Although *Aenigma* isn't the worst of Lucio Fulci's latter-period movies, it does highlight how unfocused he had become. Despite the presence of a few worthwhile scenes, too much of the film is made up of derivative ideas, poorly written dialogue and illogical plot developments.

The objection most frequently raised is that Fulci steals openly from Dario Argento's *Phenomena* (1985), which he does: The plot deals with a series of murders at a girls' school and we're also treated to an *army of insects* scene—well, almost, since the creatures in question are snails. Unfortunately, the episode is handled in much the same way as Fulci's other animal-based scenes, which is to say, pitifully (i.e., the spider scene from *The Beyond*, 1981; the bat scene from *the House by the Cemetery*, 1981). Nothing suggests that the creatures are actually hurting the victim, but the girl is assumed to be dead afterward anyway. Stealing from Dario Argento is a com-

mon activity in Italian cinema, but to appropriate elements from one of his least successful films makes little sense. More understandable but equally unwise are the elements drawn from *Patrick* (1978) and Brian De Palma's *Carrie* (1976). *Patrick* wasn't a great success, but De Palma's film had been reworked many times by 1987, contributing to the second-hand feel of *Aenigma*. Fulci's characteristically violent special effects are absent too; perhaps an indication that the director was aware of changing trends within the horror genre. Then again, his willingness to appropriate elements from *Phenomena* suggests he had misjudged the impact of Argento's film.

All this suggests that Fulci was attempting to craft a contemporary horror film that could be shown in America. Unfortunately, in attempting to do so he removed many of the individual elements that made his most successful films so unique—graphic violence, fractured storylines and a strong visual sense. *Aenigma* is not necessarily a bad film, just a bland one. The director makes a brief appearance as a cop.

After Death (1988)
Aka: Oltre la Morte-Zombi 4, Zombie 4, Zombie Flesh Eaters 3

Director: Clyde Anderson [Claudio Fragrasso]; Story/Screenplay: Rossella Drudi; Producer: Franco Gaudenzi; Special Effects: Rodolfo Torrente; Makeup: Franco Di Girolami; Music: Al Festa
Starring: Chuck Peyton [Aka: Jeff Stryker] (Chuck), Candace Daly (Jenny), Alex McBride [Massimo Vanni] (David), Don Wilson (Tommy), Jim Gaines (Dan), Adrianne Joseph (Louise), Jim Moss (Mad), Nick Nicholson (Rod), Fausto Lombardi (scientist), Richard Raymond [Ottavio Dell'Acqua] (scientist)

A group of scientists and their mercenary bodyguards find themselves trapped on a Caribbean island and under attack from a horde of decaying zombies.

After Death is an unashamed effort on the part of Franco Gaudenzi's Flora Films to recoup some of the money lost on Lucio Fulci's ill-fated

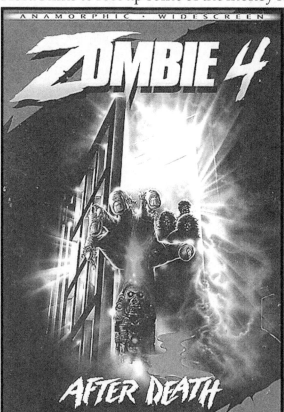

Zombie (1979) follow-up, *Zombie 3* (1988). Using much of the same cast and crew and a lower budget (!), *After Death* is actually the more successful film, if only because it isn't trying to follow a classic such as *Zombie*.

Predictably, *After Death* bears little relation to any of the *Zombie* films. Instead Fragrasso chooses to focus on fast-paced, sharply edited action scenes that rely heavily on excessive gore. This is a wise choice, because the story is patently absurd (a voodoo curse sends an army of zombies after a group of tourists), and the cast, with one or two exceptions, isn't up to much more than firing guns and running around. Overworked stuntman Massimo Vanni seems to be having fun playing a mustachioed mercenary, while Flora Film regulars Ottaviano Dell'Acqua and Fausto Lombardo also appear.

Lacking a decent budget, Fragrasso aims to make the film as gory as possible, and he succeeds fairly well in that respect. Franco Di Girolami's makeup is amateurish but enthusiastically applied, offering up a rainbow of colored body fluids. Despite the director's claims that the last third of the film was heavily cut, it's still gruesome enough to please gorehounds. Given the film's genesis and the reputation of its creators, it's surprising that anything here is worth watching at all. That, at least, is a success of sorts. Composer Al Festa went on to direct *Fatal Frames* (1996).

Alien from the Deep (1989)
Aka: Alien degli abissi

Director: Anthony M Dawson [Antonio Margheriti]; Story/Screenplay: Tito Carpi; Producer: Gianfranco Couyoumdjian, Franco Gaudenzi; Makeup: Giacinto Bretti; Music: Andrea Ridolfi
Starring: Daniel Bosch (Bob), Julia McKay [Marina Giulia Cavalli] (Jane), Charles Napier (Colonel Kovacs), Alan Collins [Luciano Pigozzi] (Dr Geoffrey), Robert Marius (Lee)

Jane, an environmental journalist, is investigating a power plant on a remote tropical island. The tyrannical head of security, Colonel Kovacs, does his best to make life difficult for Jane and her photographer. She discovers that scientists at the plant have been dumping toxic waste into an active volcano, causing dangerous gases to pollute the island. The waste has also attracted the attention of an alien being, who heads toward earth.

Franco Gaudenzi's Flora Films specialized in cheap knock-off versions of hit U.S. films from the previous decade, and *Alien from the Deep* is no different. Antonio Margheriti is a better director than Bruno Mattei, Gaudenzi's usual choice, but by 1989 his career had declined along with the Italian film industry, leaving him to toil on projects such as this.

Despite the differences in plot, Ridley Scott's *Alien* (1979) and James Cameron's follow-up *Aliens* (1986) inspired *Alien from the Deep*. The alien is *very* similar to Scott's creature, while the climax takes place

in an underground tunnel complex that bears more than a passing resemblance to the alien spaceship from the first film, and the deserted colony in the second.

Beyond the derivative elements, any actual substance is tough to find. Scriptwriter Tito Carpi is well-known in exploitation circles, having worked extensively with Antonio Margheriti and Enzo G. Castellari, but his work here is clichéd and trite. His passionate, environmentally minded journalist and his brutal military man are almost stock characters; even the best of actors would have a hard time bringing them to life.

In spite of the limited budget the film becomes a special effects-driven extravaganza. Unsurprisingly, the effects themselves are average at best. Margheriti's handling of the miniature sets and vehicles is characteristically good, but there's no escaping from the fact that such techniques had become obsolete for some time. With poor special effects, hackneyed characters and a monster taken from someone else's movie, the best *Alien from the Deep* can hope for is a place in the so-bad-it's-good file. After this, Margheriti entered semi-retirement, working only sporadically in the years following. He died in 2002, at the age of 72.

Amazonia (1986)

Aka: Schiave bianche: violenza in Amazzonia,
Amazonia: The Catherine Miles Story, Cannibal Holocaust 2,
Forest Slave, White Slave

Director: Roy Garrett [Mario Gariazzo]; Story/Screenplay: Franco Prosperi; Special Effects: Aldo Gasparri; Makeup: Franco Di Girolami; Music: Franco Campanino

Starring: Elvire Audray (Catherine Miles Armstrong), Alvaro Gonzales (Umukai), Dick Marshall, Andrew Louis Coppola, Dick Campbell, Alma Vernon, Grace Williams, Sara Fleszer, Mark Cannon, James Boyle, Peter Robyns, Jessica Bridges, Stephanie Walters, Neal Berger, Deborah Savage, Kim Arnold

Catherine Miles relates the story of her life to a British journalist. On the way to visit her parents' rubber plantation in South America, a cannibal tribe captures Catherine, the same one that also killed her parents. She learns the language and customs of the tribe, waiting for the opportunity to take revenge for the death of her mother and father.

Ironically enough, Franco Prosperi wrote this belated entry into the cannibal subgenre, the same individual who worked on the first *mondo* movies, which in turn influenced the Italian cannibal subgenre. Predictably, it's a shabby, half-hearted affair, made with a cast of amateurs and a budget of dollars. Allegedly based around the experiences of a white woman captured by a cannibal tribe, it's really just an excuse to indulge in the usual cannibal movie tricks: violent death, torture, rape and animal abuse. Plenty of blood and gore abound, but the grue is badly done and completely unrealistic. Throw in a smattering of documentary footage showing animals preying on each other to pad out the running time, and filmmakers have a can-

nibal movie, even though there isn't really that much cannibalism on display. It's probably the least-incompetently made of the lot, which isn't saying much. If viewers watched all the Lenzi and Deodato movies and are still hankering for more Italian cannibal action, then try to get ahold of *Amazonia*. Most viewers however will find the disc more suited to propping up a table leg.

Anthropophagous (1980)

Aka: Anthropophagus, The Anthropophagous Beast, The Grim
Reaper, The Man Beast, The Savage Island

Director: Joe D'Amato [Aristide Massacessi]; Story: Luigi Montefiore,
Aristide Massacessi; Screenplay: Luigi Montefiore; Makeup: Pietro
Tenoglio; Music: Marcello Giombini
Starring: Tisa Farrow (Julie), Saverio Vallone (Alan), Vanessa Steiger
[Serena Grandi] (Maggie), Margaret Donnelly (Henriette), Mark Bodin
(Daniel), Bob Larsen (Arnold), Rubina Rey (Ariette), Simone Baker,
Mark Logan, George Eastman [Luigi Montefiore] (Klaus), Zora Kerova
[Zora Keslerova] (Carol)

*A group of friends take a holiday on a Greek island where a cannibalistic
brute attacks them.*

Thanks to a suitably hysterical media campaign, *Anthropophagous*
became one of the most notorious of the celebrated "video nasties."
Stripped of all gore in some countries and banned outright in others,
uncut copies pass from collector to collector on a regular basis. Unfortunately for all its rumor-fueled reputation, *Anthropophagous* is an
exceptionally dull film.

The film's main failing is its boring middle stretch. After a decent
opening scene that introduces us
to Klaus the cannibal, *Anthropophagous* then procrastinates for over an
hour. Seemingly endless scenes of
pleasant Greek countryside take
place, all accompanied by inane
chatter from the wooden cast
and Marcello Giombini's deeply
irritating score. Anyone expecting scenes of stomach-churning
gore and gratuitous violence will
probably be wondering whether
they've got the right film by this
point.

After an hour or so, the film
eventually moves into splatter

movie territory. Now we see the infamous scenes that caused *Anthropophagous* to be labeled a snuff movie by certain sensationalist authorities. For all of its flaws, Aristide Massacessi's film is hard to forget. The sight of Luigi Montefiore tearing the unborn baby from Serena Grandi's womb has few parallels in splatter movie history, and the image of Montefiore taking a last nibble on his own intestines must be seen to be believed. It's not very realistic—the baby is a skinned rabbit wrapped in bacon—but the sequence is very enthusiastically done. Ultimately, these moments are the only reason to see the film. If the viewer is not interested in extreme gore, *Anthropophagous* is largely a waste of time. Although Massacessi has shown himself to be a capable filmmaker on a few occasions, there's nothing here to suggest the competency of a professional filmmaker. It's a classic case of a film's reputation far exceeding the truth.

The Beyond (1981)
Aka: L'aldilà, E tu vivrai nel terrore—L'aldilà,
The Seven Doors of Death

Director: Lucio Fulci; Story: Dardano Sacchetti; Screenplay: Lucio Fulci, Dardano Sacchetti, Giorgio Mariuzzo; Producer: Fabrizio De Angelis; Special Effects: Giannetto De Rossi, Germano Natali; Makeup: Maurizio Trani, Giannetto De Rossi; Music: Fabio Frizzi
Starring: Katherine MacColl [Catriona MacColl] (Liza Merrill), David Warbeck (Dr. John McCabe), Sarah Keller [Cinzia Monreale] (Emily), Antoine Saint John [Antoine Saint Jean] (Schweik, the painter), Veronica Lazar (Martha), Anthony Flees (Larry), Giovanni De Nava (Joe), Al Cliver [Pier Luigi Conti] (Harris), Michele Mirabella (Martin Avery), Gianpaolo Saccarola (Arthur), Maria Pia Marsala (Jill), Laura De Marchi (Mary-Ann)

After inheriting a ramshackle old hotel from a distant relative, Liza sets out to make it a profitable venture once again. It isn't long before strange things start happening: bloody accidents, visions of death and staff members who disappear mysteriously. As the living dead start to rise and move through the town, Liza and a local doctor make a desperate attempt to escape the rising tide of evil.

Whatever debates and arguments may rage about the merits and flaws of Lucio Fulci's extensive catalogue of films, most critics

agree on one thing: *The Beyond* is the man's finest hour. *Zombie* (1979) might be more influential, and *New York Ripper* (1982) is certainly more notorious and grim, but *The Beyond* represents the most mature and complex realization of Fulci's favorite themes and techniques.

From the very start of the film, the audience is drawn into a strange world overshadowed by portents of doom and menace. The sepia-toned introduction is a throwback to the Universal horror films of half a century before: A mob of stone-faced, resolute locals bearing torches and make-shift weapons march into a New Orleans hotel to confront a man they believe to be a warlock. As punishment for trying to open one of the seven gates of hell, the warlock is nailed to a wall in the cellar and splashed with quicklime and acid. This undeniably gruesome scene helps to introduce the film's storyline, but it also serves as a warning to the squeamish viewer that this vision of hell won't be skimping on the blood and guts. Thanks to the fine efforts of Giannetto De Rossi and Germano Natali, the special effects-driven scenes are some of the finest in Italian splatter history.

Any synopsis would seem to imbue *The Beyond* with a cohesive narrative that is not in fact present in the film. The plot is advanced by a series of vignettes that are often only loosely connected and whose only purpose is to reinforce the atmosphere of dread and horror initiated by the opening sequence. Liza and John move from one bizarre encounter to another, increasingly bewildered and threatened by the supernatural events that are taking over their lives. Lesser characters are treated to elaborate death scenes (and sometimes resurrection scenes, too). Little rationale to the proceedings can be found, as if all earthly considerations were subverted by the alien logic of *The Beyond*.

Despite the crew's best intentions, the film's low-budget origins sometimes show through. The most damaging episode is the library death scene, where a handful of fake spiders dragged along on strings join two real ones to vainly suggest that all of them are real. The mystical nature of the location might explain why a house in New Orleans has a cellar—something that is unlikely due to the region's high water table—but it's not enough to explain away the hospital sign that reads: "Do Not Entry." Neither does the plot tell why John continues to shoot zombies in the chest when he knows the only way to stop them is to shoot them in the head. However, these flaws are not enough to substantially diminish the achievement.

Much has been made of the lack of pace, plot and characterization in *The Beyond*, as well as in Fulci's other Gothic horrors. However, Italian horror has always placed a film's aesthetic appeal above other considerations, and it's fair to say that *Suspiria* (1977) has not attracted quite as much criticism, despite a similar lack of plot and characterization. Lucio Fulci might not have the status of Dario Argento, and *The Beyond* is not as visionary or perfectly realized as *Suspiria*, but to pick holes in one and not the other reveals a double standard. *The Beyond* does pick up the pace in its final act anyway, as the living dead begin to spill forth into the real world, making way for a memorable climax.

Fulci's career was inconsistent and varied to say the least, and several of his films hint at the level of talent that was waiting to be fully realized. In *The Beyond*, more than any other of his films, it is possible to

In *The Beyond*, the painter Schweik is punished for dabbling in forbidden arts.

see just how much talent the man possessed. It is a classic horror film in every way. Look out for Fulci's cameo as a librarian.

Beyond Darkness (1990)
Aka: La casa 5

Director: Clyde Anderson [Claudio Fragrasso]; Story/Screenplay: Clyde Anderson [Claudio Fragrasso], Sarah Asproon [Rossella Drudi]; Special Effects/Makeup: James Ryder; Makeup: Elle Holshouser; Music: Carlo Maria Cordio
Starring: Gene Le Brock (Peter), David Brandon (Father George), Barbara Bingham (Annie), Michael Stephenson (Martin), Theresa F. Walker (Carole), Stephen Brown (Reverend Jonathon)

Peter and his family move into a new house in Louisiana. Soon the vengeful spirit of a convicted child murderer seeks to sacrifice their children. With the help of tormented Jesuit priest Father George, Peter must save his family and exorcise the evil ghost.

Beyond Darkness is one of the best films to emerge from Aristide Massacessi and Donatella Donati's production company Filmirage. This isn't much of a compliment, given that their output also includes such monstrosities as Crawlers and Troll II (both 1990). However, this Amityville Horror knock-off is fairly entertaining and well made. Claudio Fragrasso makes the best of a trite and clichéd script, and he actually tries to inject some originality into the piece. The supernatural scenes are presented like hallucinations, all handheld, slow-motion camera shots and misty sets drenched in dry ice and lace curtains. David Brandon delivers a memorable performance as the alcoholic Father George, although the rest of the cast members fail to distinguish themselves.

Even with a charismatic lead performance and some interesting visual touches, Beyond Darkness is still stuck firmly in low-budget, derivative territory. It never manages to break free from its origins, and the final shot is perhaps one of the most tiresome clichés in the horror canon. The film is not a total failure, however, and it's certainly more interesting than many of Filmirage's other releases.

Trivia notes: *Beyond Darkness* was originally to be directed by Edoardo Margheriti, son of Antonio Margheriti. The Italian title—*La casa 5*—has nothing to do with the American *House* series. Instead it marks the film out as one of a fake series of unrelated movies. Sam Raimi's first two *Evil Dead* films were titled *La casa* and *La casa 2* in Italy, while Umberto Lenzi's *Ghosthouse* (1988) was titled *La casa 3*. *La casa 4* is Fabrizio Laurenti's *Witchcraft* (1988).

Beyond the Darkness (1979)
Aka: Buio omega, Buried Alive, Blue Holocaust

Director: Joe D'Amato [Aristide Massacessi]; Story: Giacomo Guerrini; Screenplay: Ottavio Fabbri; Producer: Oscar Santaniello; Music: Goblin
Starring: Kieran Canter [Wilhelm Kantz] (Francesco Weiler), Cinzia Monreale (Anna/Teodara/Eleanor), Franca Stoppi (Iris), Sam Modesto (Cossuto), Anna Cardini (Jan, the hitchhiker), Lucia D'Elia (jogger)

Left distraught after the death of his fiancée, Francesco decides to steal her corpse and embalm it. With the help of his housekeeper Iris, he's forced to take drastic measures to cover up his peculiar tastes, which soon drive him to procure fresh corpses to share his bed.

The Southern Gothic melodramas of William Faulkner, sometimes flavored with the fevered imaginations of H.P. Lovecraft or Edgar Allan Poe, inspired the best Italian horror films. Lucio Fulci acknowledges the presence of these themes in his most significant work, something that is reflected in the Louisiana loca-

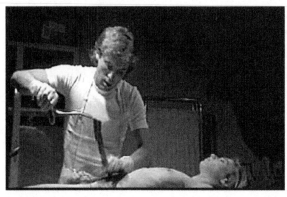
Young Francesco (Kieran Canter) explores his unsavory urges in the disturbing *Beyond the Darkness*.

tion of *The Beyond* and the New England setting for *The House by the Cemetery*, while *City of the Living Dead* openly steals the town of Dunwich from Lovecraft. Most films update these ideas slightly, transposing them into modern times and replacing the silk and crushed velour with pastel shades and bell-bottoms. However, these productions retain the essential air of corruption and decay and the fantastic plot developments that are the main themes of Gothic literature. One of the finest of these films—not to mention one of the most controversial—is *Beyond the Darkness*, the first Gothic horror film from notorious exploitation director Aristide Massacessi. Built around a young man's growing taste for necrophilia, it's not a film for the morally conservative or easily offended.

It will come as no surprise to viewers familiar with Massacessi's work that *Beyond the Darkness* relies heavily upon gore for much of its shock value. Some fairly convincing efforts in the special effects area led early critics to mistakenly assert that real corpses were used for the taxidermy and mutilation scenes. Needless to say, no human body parts were used; any realism in those particular scenes almost certainly stems from the presence of animal offal and surplus material purchased from a local butcher. It's unclear whether the heart that Francesco takes a bite out of had once belonged to an animal, although it's entirely possible. The accusations that the film contains actual snuff footage undoubtedly made the director very happy, since a number of his previous movies—in particular *Emanuelle[1] in America* (1977)—had tried hard to convince the audience that they were watching videotaped murder.

Despite his appreciation for gore and general perversion, Massacessi was not responsible for the story behind *Beyond the Darkness*. The main concept (and several of the smaller details) was taken from *Il terzo occhio*, a 1966 Franco Nero thriller written and directed by Mino Guerrini. In the modern version Guerrini's son Giacomo is given the story credit, while Ottavio Fabbri wrote the revised script.

Naturally D'Amato's film concentrates heavily on gore, downplaying the thriller aspects of the story in favor of visual horror and excess. Reports of audience members fleeing in horror and throwing up can be found, and even notoriously hard-to-shock 42nd Street audiences left in disgust, according to Michael Weldon.[2]

Excessive or not, *Beyond the Darkness* is not your average exploitation fare. For starters it boasts a masterful score from Goblin[3] that manages to create an atmosphere of tension and unease that overrides the somewhat leisurely pace, a frequent problem with Massacessi's films. The script is minimalist at best, and dialogue conveys very little of the story. Very few direct references to murder, necrophilia or cannibalism occur, although the viewer has no doubt about what is going on. The dinner scene highlights Massacessi's approach, coming as it does immediately after the dismemberment of a luckless hitchhiker. Clever editing and gruesome close-ups are combined to hint at the similarity between the scraps of human flesh that Iris collects from the bathroom floor and the foul-looking stew she serves for dinner. There's nothing more offensive than some messy eating on display, but the viewer (and Francesco) quickly realize that the housekeeper's tastes include more than sexual perversions. It's actually the film's most unpleasant scene. All this information is conveyed with barely a word from either character.

One of Massacessi's finest films, *Beyond the Darkness* has its share of flaws. It is too slow in places, and occasionally the film tries too hard to be sinister, instead coming across as arch and camp. But the film is a bona fide exploitation classic, and deservedly so. Perhaps it's not as cerebral as the films of Dario Argento; then again, it doesn't aspire to be. It's just a fine slab of ghoulish entertainment. Naturally the critics disagreed, but the film managed to play across the world in a relatively uncut form and achieved a reasonable degree of commercial success. Massacessi considers it to be his best horror film—a statement which is difficult to disagree.

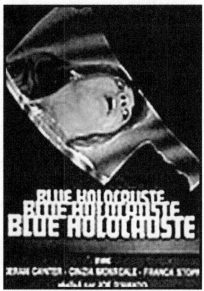

Black Angel (1989)
Aka: Arabella l'angelo nero

Director: Max Steel [Stelvio Massi]; Story/Screenplay: R. Filipucci; Producer: Francesco Vitulano; Makeup: Marisa Marconi; Music: Serfran
Starring: Tini Cansino, Valentina Visconti, Francesco Casale, Carlo Mucari, Renato D'Amore, Giose Davi, David D'Ingeo, Rena Niehaus, Evelyn Stewart [Ida Galli]

The young wife of a disabled writer spends her nights prowling the city in search of sexual experiences that her husband can use as material for his new novel. Meanwhile, someone else is stalking the city and brutally murdering her casual sex partners.

This cheap little shocker continues the time-honored tradition of using the *giallo* format as an excuse for presenting an extremely sleazy film. Although the director and scriptwriter appropriated elements from many different exploitation movies, *Giallo a Venezia* (1979) and *The New York Ripper* (1982) seem to be the prime inspiration for the film's more lurid and disgusting moments. Despite his background as a cinematographer on some worthwhile films, Stelvio Massi appears to have directed *Black Angel* in his sleep. His cast delivers uninspired performances, and the supposedly erotic sequences are hilariously ineffective. Viewers watching this film for reasons of cheap titillation might—stressing the word *might*—get something out of this, but there are many more pleasurable ways to spend 90 minutes of your life.

The Black Cat (1981)
Aka: Il gatto nero

Director: Lucio Fulci; Story: Biagio Proietti, Edgar Allan Poe; Screenplay: Biagio Proietti, Lucio Fulci; Producer: Giulio Sbarigia; Special

Effects: Paolo Ricci; Makeup: Franco Di Girolami, Rosario Prestopino; Music: Pino Donaggio

Starring: Patrick Magee (Professor Robert Miles), Mimsy Farmer (Jill Travers), David Warbeck (Inspector Gorley), Al Cliver [Pier Luigi Conti] (Sergeant Wilson), Dagmar Lassander (Lillian Grayson), Bruno Corazzari (Ferguson), Geoffrey Copleston (Inspector Flynn), Daniela Dorio [Daniela Doria] (Maureen Grayson)

A quiet English town falls prey to a series of gruesome murders. A police inspector, aided by a visiting photographer, investigates. As the bodies start to pile up, suspicion falls on a reclusive old man who claims to have the power to communicate with the dead. But what part does the old man's elusive black cat play?

Coming between *The City of the Living Dead* (1980) and *The Beyond* (1981), *The Black Cat* has often been considered a minor Lucio Fulci effort, interesting in places and well-made, but a definite step backward from *Zombie* (1979) and his Gothic horror films. While this is essentially true, the film is not without merit, and it does boast a great performance from Patrick Magee, as well as some interesting camerawork and a solid supporting cast.

Viewers expecting Fulci's characteristically gory approach with heavy Gothic overtones will probably be disappointed, but *The Black Cat* is entertaining enough for the open-minded fan. It certainly has more in common with the director's earlier thrillers than with the splatter films with which he is most identified. The plot depends more on tension than violence, which (for Fulci) means many close-ups of eyes. If audiences find this

favorite technique of Fulci's infuriating, be warned that he uses it more in this film than in any of his others. However, the attempts at creating an air of Englishness are pretty much on the mark, particularly Pino Donaggio's folk-inflected score. The film often comes across as a BBC detective drama rather than a horror film (not necessarily a bad thing), but manages to keep the specter of the supernatural present much of the time. The dubbing is better than usual, hiding the Italian origin of the supporting cast.

Although not as exciting as Fulci's more visceral horrors, *The Black Cat* is still worth tracking down. It is solid proof (as if any were really necessary) that Fulci was a genuinely talented director who had more to offer than blood and guts.

The Black Cat (1989)
Aka: Il gatto nero, De profondis,
Demons 6: De profondis

Director: Luigi Cozzi; Story/Screenplay: Luigi Cozzi; Producer: Luigi Cozzi, Antonio Lucidi; Special Effects: Antonio Corridori, Armano Valcaudo; Makeup: Franco Casagni, Rosario Prestopino; Music: Vince Tempera

Starring: Urbano Barberini, Brett Halsey, Michele Soavi, Florence Guerin, Caroline Munro, Luisa Maneri, Karina Huff, Alessandra Acciai, Giada Cozzi, Michele Marsina, Jasmine Main, Antonio Marsina

Despite several warnings, a film crew plans to make the third film in the "Three Mothers" series. Unfortunately they attract the attention of Levanna, the real Third Mother, who tries to use the film as a gateway into the real world. Anne, the actress cast as Levanna, must try to stop her.

Despite the title, this film has nothing whatsoever to do with Edgar Allan Poe. Halfway through shooting, the American backers decided the film would be more successful if released as part of a collection of Poe-inspired stories. The proposed series never materialized, but Cozzi's film was stuck with the inappropriate title. It was even recycled as part of the *Demons* series.

In reality, *The Black Cat* is an occult horror film tinged with the director's characteristic science fiction touches. Cozzi uses Dario Argento's work as a launching point, building his film around an attempt to shoot the final episode in Argento's *Three Mothers* trilogy, the sequel to *Suspiria* (1977) and *Inferno* (1980). Unsurprisingly, cast and crew members begin to die off in suspicious circumstances. It's a classic *giallo*-style plot. Sadly, Cozzi chooses to emulate Argento extensively, something that serves only to highlight the fact that he is nowhere near as capable as his mentor. In lesser hands Argento's trademarks seem clichéd and hysterical, especially when they are so slavishly copied. To make matters worse, many of the film's key scenes rely upon poor special effects, reminiscent of the director's infamous turkeys, *Hercules* (1982) and *Hercules II* (1985).

Ultimately Cozzi's talents and the budget at his disposal are not enough to meet the demands of this ambitious film. Respected stars such as Urbano Barberini and Brett Halsey help to generate interest, but for the most part they're working with inferior material. If viewers do manage to sit through the entire movie, they will be rewarded with another of the infamous science fiction scenes that earned the director the nickname "Cosmic Cozzi," but it's not necessarily worth it.

Black Demons (1991)
Aka: Demoni 3, Black Zombies

Director: Umberto Lenzi; Story: Umberto Lenzi; Screenplay: Olga Pehar; Producer: Giuseppe Gargiulo; Special Effects/Makeup: Franco Casagni; Music: Franco Micalizzi
Starring: Keith Van Hoven, Joe Balogh, Sonia Curtis, Philip Murray, Juliana Texeira, Maria Alves

A group of friends are on holiday in Brazil. One of them is eager to see a macumba ceremony, so he heads off to find one. After taping the ritual, he returns to the group and the hotel they're staying in. Unfortunately he then decides to play the tape back in a local cemetery, causing the buried slaves to rise from the dead.

Ten years after his major zombie opus *Nightmare City* (1980), director Umberto Lenzi returned to living dead territory with *Black Demons*, a voodoo-themed fright flick. Unfortunately, the world no longer was interested in Italian zombies (unsurprising after misfires like *Zombie 3*, 1987) and the film was marketed as a sequel to Lamberto Bava's *Demons*. Whereas Bava's film is fast-paced, over-the-top and highly entertaining, *Black Demons* is slow, plodding and almost entirely boring.

Saddled with a cast that included a handful of seasoned actors and many beginners, it's hardly surprising that Lenzi wasn't able to churn out a good film. Mind you, the script is consistently awful and would have challenged even the greatest of actors, let alone those with a background in unpredictable Latin American soap operas. While *Nightmare City* wisely favored pace and energy over plot and characterization, *Black Demons* crawls along at a snail's pace. There's no *army of the dead* here, just six zombies, the resurrected corpses of murdered slaves. Our heroes—a luckless and unsympathetic bunch of tourists—manage to howl and scream in the right places, but any attempt at creating interest in their fates falls hopelessly flat. To give Franco Casagni his due credit, the makeup on the zombies is pretty good, but it's not enough to keep the audience happy.

Umberto Lenzi's best films are usually either genuinely entertaining efforts like *Nightmare City* or laughably wretched, like *The House of Lost Souls* (1988), but *Black Demons* is neither. It's only for those who felt that Bruno Mattei's *Hell of the Living Dead* (1981) showed real promise.

A Blade in the Dark (1983)
Aka: La casa con la scala nel buio

Director: Lamberto Bava; Story/Screenplay: Dardano Sacchetti, Elisa Briganti; Producer: Mino Loy, Luciano Martino; Special Effects: Giovanni Corridori; Music: Guido De Angelis, Maurizio De Angelis Starring: Andrea Occhipinti (Bruno), Anny Papa (Sandra), Fabiola Toledo (Angela), Michele Soavi (Tony), Stanko Molnar (Giovanni), Valeria Cavalli (Katya), Lara Naszinski (Giulia), Giovanni Frezza, Marco Vivio

Bruno, a young composer, rents a villa in order to complete his latest work. Although he initially believes himself to be alone, it isn't long before Bruno realizes that there may be something strange going on in the villa and he sets about assembling the clues.

Although well received by critics, Lamberto Bava's debut *Macabre* (1980) was not a commercial success. Fearing that the film's emphasis on tension and atmosphere—rather than violence—had driven audiences away, Bava resolved to make his next film more in line with public tastes. His opportunity came when he was asked to direct a television miniseries in a *giallo* style. Working at breakneck speed, Bava managed to complete all four 25-minute episodes in three weeks. Ironically, his use of violence and graphic gore horrified the producers, who claimed it was too extreme for television. The film was re-cut and released to theaters, where it proved a moderate success. It also cemented Bava's reputa-

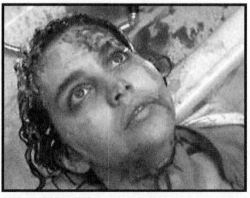

Angela (Fabiola Toledo) has her throat slit in *A Blade in the Dark*, one of Bava's best films.

tion as a skilled purveyor of the horrific and morbid.

A Blade in the Dark is certainly a violent film, and it's hardly surprising that it wasn't suitable for television. The notorious bathroom scene rivals anything Argento created and is guaranteed to stick in the viewer's mind. The other murders are less graphic but equally cruel, and Bava's camera lingers on the victim's death throes until the very end. The film's television background means that each murder is equally spaced throughout the movie, allowing astute viewers to predict when the next killing will be.

With only a small budget, Bava was forced to rely upon a single location—actually a house belonging to the producer—for most of the film. However, the house in question is an excellent setting for a *giallo* since it features a sparse color scheme that relies primarily on pastel shades. This simplistic feel enhances the equally minimalist score. The central character's metronome echoes the slow tempo of the music, which in turn mimics the sound of the killer's footsteps and the clicking of the knife used to dispatch the victims.

Despite its humble beginnings, *A Blade in the Dark* is one of Bava's best films. It's also a classic later-period *giallo*. It's not as plot-heavy as *Tenebrae* (1982), but that's not necessarily a criticism. There's enough style and brutality on display here to please most fans of Italian horror, and many others besides. The director's career might have gone off the rails somewhat in later years, but here he's at the top of his form. Trivia: The director appears briefly in the editing suite. Andrea Occhipinti later became a respected producer, and worked on Alejandro Amenábar's *Abre los ojos* (1997).

Blood Delirium (1988)
Aka: Delirio di sangue

Director: Sergio Bergonzelli; Story: Sergio Bergonzelli; Screenplay Sergio Bergonzelli, Fabio D'Agostini; Special Effects: Raffaele Mertes, Delio Catini, The Corridori Brothers [Giovanni & Antonio Corridori]; Makeup: Guerrino Todero; Music: Nello Ciangherotti
Starring: John Phillip Law, Gordon Mitchell, Brigitte Christensen

After the death of his wife, a painter finds it increasingly difficult to procure suitable subjects for his art. However, the discovery of his butler's morbid habits brings with it a new source of inspiration, and the pair soon turn to grave-robbing and murder.

Allegedly based on the life of Vincent Van Gogh, *Blood Delirium* is an obscure piece of trash that has rightly been forgotten. It's one of the few films that manages to combine necrophilia, murder, maggot-ridden corpses, insane painters, metaphysical ravings and still fail to hold the viewer's interest. Fans of former strongman Gordon Mitchell might be interested to see the muscle-bound actor in one of his strangest roles (he's the murderous necrophiliac butler), but beyond that, *Blood Delirium* is a tedious waste of time.

Blood Link (1982)
Aka: Extrasensorial

Director: Albert De Martino [Alberto De Martino]; Story: Max De Rita [Massimo De Rita], Albert De Martino [Alberto De Martino]; Screenplay: Theodore Apstein; Producer: Robert Palaggi; Makeup: Giulio Natalucci; Music: Ennio Morricone
Starring: Michael Moriarty (Craig Manning/Keith Manning/Thomason), Penelope Milford (Julie), Cameron Mitchell (Bud Waldo), Sarah Langenfeld (Christine), Martha Smith (Hedwig), Virginia McKenna (woman in ballroom), Reinhold K. Olszewski (Inspector Hessinger), Geraldine Fitzgerald (Mrs. Thomason)

An American doctor begins to see visions of brutal murders. Suspecting that his psychotic twin brother is responsible, he travels to Germany to try to stop the killing spree. As the two get closer and closer, the differences between them start to blur.

ENNIO MORRICONE'S ORIGINAL SOUNDTRACKS

ORIGINAL SOUNDTRACK MUSIC FROM THE FILMS:

UN ESERCITO DI 5 UOMINI

EXTRASENSORIAL (The Link)

This grim thriller is a cut above the average for later period *gialli* and is certainly worth tracking down. The director is the man responsible for the awful *Formula for a Murder* (1985), but here he displays reasonable talent. The plot relies heavily on the clichéd *twins with a psychic link* concept, but the theme is put to good use here. The film's main asset is Larry Cohen's favorite actor Michael Moriarty, who delivers excellent performances as the twins. He successfully manages to blur the distinction between the two brothers and provides *Blood Link*'s most effective moments. His standout scene shows him beating Cameron Mitchell's aged boxer to death, all the time grinning playfully and making jokes.

The rest of the cast is competent, especially Penelope Milford and veteran Cameron Mitchell, an icon of the exploitation scene. He starred in Mario Bava's groundbreaking *giallo, Blood and Black Lace* (1964), as well as less worthy projects such as *The Toolbox Murders* (1978). The ever-creepy Alex Diakun also makes a brief appearance. Ennio Morricone provided the score, but it's not one of his best and doesn't significantly affect the film.

Blood Link is an entertaining and intelligent film that should interest fans of Italian thrillers. It does rely heavily on nudity, but that's to be expected with this kind of exploitation film. Even if the plot is not particularly appealing, the movie is worth watching for Michael Moriarty's performance alone. He always seems shifty and devious, but here he manages to come across as genuinely evil.

Bloody Psycho (1989)
Aka: Nel nido del serpente, Bloody Psycho, Lo specchio,
The Snake House

Director: Henry L. Ackerman [Leandro Lucchetti]; Story/Screenplay:
Leandro Lucchetti, Giovanni Simonelli; Producer: Luigi Nannerini,
Antonio Lucidi; Makeup: Giuseppe Ferranti; Music: Lanfranco
Perini
Starring: Peter Hintz, Loes Kamma
[Louise Kamsteeg], Brigitte Christensen,
Sacha Darwin [Sacha Maria Darwin],
Nubia Martini, Annie Cerreto, Marco
Di Stefano, Alessandra Massari, Marco
Massari, Vassili Karis

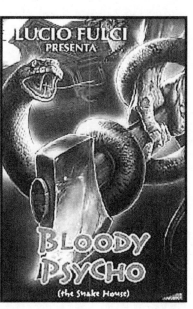

*During a stay at a medieval castle be-
longing to one of his clients, a psychiatrist
is tormented by visions and supernatural
phenomena.*

[Notes: Bears the credit: *"Supervised by
Lucio Fulci."* Clips from this film were
used in Lucio Fulci's *Nightmare Concert*
(1990). Synopsis taken from *Spaghetti
Nightmares* (see bibliography).]

Body Puzzle (1992)
Aka: Misteria

Director: Larry Louis [Lamberto Bava]; Story: Teodoro Agrimi, Do-
menico Paolella; Screenplay: Lamberto Bava, Teodoro Agrimi, Bruce
Martin; Producer: Pietro & Mario Bregni; Makeup:/Special Effects:
Franco Casagni; Music: Carlo Maria Cordio
Starring: Joanna Pacula (Tracy), Tomas Arana (Detective Michele/Mike
Livett), François Montagut (The Killer), Gianni Garko (Police Chief),
Erika Blanc [Erika Bianchi Colombatto] (Dr. Corti), Matteo Gazzolo
(Gigli), Susanna Javicoli (Signora/Mrs. Consorti), Bruno Corazzari
(Professor Brusco), Ursula von Baechler (Katia/Kate Lelli), Sebastiano
Lo Monaco (Mortician), Giovanni Lombardo Radice (Morangi)

The widow of a famous concert pianist becomes the target of a twisted serial killer who leaves parts of his victims at her house. The detective investigating the case—who soon becomes the widow's lover—desperately tries to piece together the clues while the trophies mount up.

Despite winning acclaim for his excellent *A Blade in the Dark* (1983), Bava has never been entirely happy making *gialli*, and his impatience with the format is easy to spot in his later attempts, particularly *Delerium* (1987) and *Body Puzzle*, his last theatrical release to date. For much of the film, Bava's direction is dull and pedestrian, only coming alive during the violent murder scenes, which recall the vibrant and stylized work that characterized his early films. Unfortunately many U.S. versions are savagely edited, removing much of the gore and stripping the murder scenes of any tension. Noted cinematographer Luigi Kuveiller helps to keep the film visually interesting.

PIETRO e MARIO BREGNI
presentano

JOANNA PACULA   TOMAS ARANA

BODY PUZZLE
BODY PUZZLE

FRANÇOIS MONTAGUT
GIANNI GARKO • ERIKA BLANC • MATTEO GAZZOLO
USANNA JAVICOLI • BRUNO CORAZZARI • URSULA VON BAECHLER
SEBASTIANO LO MONACO • GIOVANNI LOMBARDO RADICE
fotografia LUIGI KUVEILLER scenografia DAVID BASSAN
montaggio PIETRO BOZZA musiche originali di CARLO MARIA CORDIO
una produzione P.A.C. Produzioni Atlas Consorziate
regia di LAMBERTO BAVA

Unfortunately, the best efforts of the cast and crew cannot overcome the inherent weakness of the script. Policemen amble about, missing every obvious clue and connection, while the heroine behaves as if there's nothing wrong, despite the preponderance of body parts being dumped in her house. The plot itself stretches logic to the breaking point and unwisely invites comparisons with Juan Piquer Simón's awful *Pieces* (1983) and Eric Red's superior *Body Parts* (1991).

One of the film's greatest flaws is the over-reliance on a single piece of classical music that plays every time the killer starts to stalk a victim. Most foreign versions use Carl Orff's otherwise excellent *Carmina Burana*, but copyright issues forced U.S. distributors to use Mussorgsky's *Night on Bare Mountain* instead. While it starts out as an interesting idea, the piece is used several times throughout the film and quickly wears out its welcome. Carlo Maria Cordio's score is better, but it's sadly underused.

It's a shame that Lamberto Bava's last movie before moving into made-for-TV fantasy films wasn't more of a success. While the uncut version holds some interest for the well-orchestrated murder scenes, the edited film is largely pointless. Interested parties are advised to check out Bava's early films, which better indicate the man's undeniable talent.

Bodycount (1986)
Aka: Camping del Terrore

Director: Ruggero Deodato; Story: Alex Capone [Alessandro Capone]; Screenplay: Alex Capone [Alessandro Capone], David Parker, Jr. [Dardano Sacchetti], Sheila Goldberg, Luca D'Alisera; Producer: Alessandro Fracassi; Special Effects: Roberto Pace; Makeup: Mario Di Salvio; Music: Claudio Simonetti
Starring: Bruce Penhall (Dave Calloway), Mimsy Farmer (Julia Ritchie), David Hess (Robert Ritchie), Luisa Maneri (Carol), Nicola Farron (Ben Ritchie), Andrew Lederer (Sidney), Stefano Madia (Tony), John Steiner (Dr. Olsen), Nancy Brilli (Tracy), Cynthia Thompson (Cissy), Valentina Forte (Pamela Hicks), Ivan Rassimov (Deputy Sheriff Ted), Eleni Pompei (Sharon), Charles Napier (Charlie, the sheriff)

A pair of teenagers are slain in the woods near a campsite, and a small boy witnesses the whole event. Fifteen years later, two truckloads of youngsters turn up for some wilderness fun, and the killings start again. A local legend tells of a demon summoned to protect Native American burial grounds from trespassers, but who is really responsible for the carnage?

Bodycount has attracted a fair amount of criticism over the years, mostly because it's seen as another dumb slasher movie. Which is pretty accurate—the film makes no attempt to be original, settling for the well-established slasher movie clichés. It's also fairly redundant, since the initial slasher boom was long over by 1986. But *Bodycount* does have a few things going for it. For a start, there's that excellent cast. We have veterans of the European exploitation scene like Mimsy

Farmer, Deodato favorites such as John Steiner, Valentina Forte and Ivan Rassimov, and newer faces like the lovely Nancy Brilli (*Demons 2*, 1986). Throw in another great angst-ridden performance from the iconic David Hess, and the movie features a damn fine group of actors. The material might not be wonderful, but viewers can still get a lot of enjoyment from seeing so many familiar faces. Claudio Simonetti turns in a decent score, and the northern Italy locations double for the mid-west United States quite nicely.

Beyond that, viewers are into standard slasher movie territory. The script is pretty poor, and the dialogue contains some terrible attempts at recreating youthful banter. The characters themselves are two-dimensional; it's hard to care when they get killed off. As a Deodato film *Bodycount* is a disappointment, being neither as stylish as *Phantom of Death* (1987) nor as energetic as *Cut and Run* (1985). There's a fair amount of gore on display, but nothing to compare with *Cannibal Holocaust* (1979). If viewers are feeling in the mood for a mock-American slasher, then *Bodycount* might be appropriate, but viewers looking for something characteristically Italian will be ultimately disappointed. Check out Soavi's *Stagefright* (1987) instead.

Trivia: Dardano Sacchetti claims he had nothing to do with the script, but the producer wanted to add his name to the credits to generate foreign interest (as with *Specters*, 1987). Alessandro Capone also wrote and directed *Witch Story*: (1989), another American-style Italian horror film.

Burial Ground (1981)
Aka: Le notti del terrore, Zombi 3: Le notti del terrore, The Nights of Terror, The Zombie Dead, Zombie 3

Director: Andrea Bianchi; Story / Screenplay: Piero Regnoli; Producer: Gabriele Crisanti; Special Effects / Makeup: Giannetto De Rossi, Rosario Prestopino; Music: Elsio Mancuso, Bert Rexon [Berto Pisano]

Starring: Karin Well (Janet), Gian Luigi Chirizzi (Mark), Simone Mattioli (James), Antonella Antinori (Leslie), Roberto Caporali (George), Peter Bark (Michael), Claudio Zucchetto (Nicholas), Anna Valente (Kathleen), Renato Barbieri (Professor Ayres), Maria Angela Giordano (Evelyn)

An archaeologist excavating a tomb somewhere in the Italian countryside manages to awaken a troop of ancient zombies, who tear the scholar apart. Meanwhile, a group of his friends gather at his villa, unaware that the zombies are moving closer.

1980-81 proved to be a prolific time for the Italian zombie movie. For that brief period, the concept was popular enough to attract the attention of several of Italy's leading exploitation filmmakers. One of these was Gabriele Crisanti, a second-rate producer with an eye for sensationalist material. He was the driving force behind the brutal thriller *Giallo a Venezia* (1979) and the pointless but bloody *Patrick Still Lives* (1980), both directed by Mario Landi. For his next project, Crisanti hired Andrea Bianchi, the man responsible for *Malabimba* (1979), a minor *Exorcist* clone that fully explored the pornographic possibilities suggested by demonic possession. Piero Regnoli, a veteran of the spaghetti Western scene and longstanding associate of Crisanti, provided the script. Unsurprisingly, Giannetto de Rossi and Rosario Prestopino were hired to do the special effects and makeup.

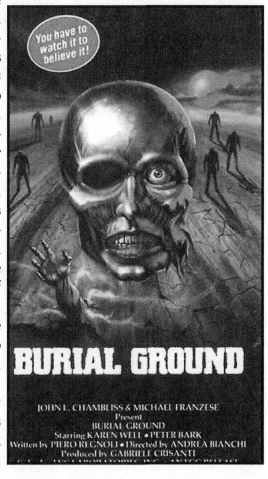

Burial Ground has many flaws, not the least of which is the director's noticeable lack of ability and the useless cast.

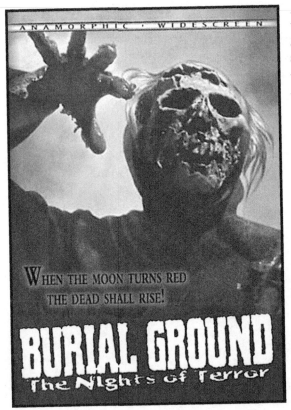

When the moon turns red the dead shall rise!

BURIAL GROUND
The Nights of Terror

Mercifully Bianchi has the good sense to resort to static set-ups, allowing the action to simply unfold in front of the camera. This simplistic technique suits the one-note story quite well, since its appeal is purely visual. The cast, however, is not so lucky; there's nothing that can deflect attention from the fact the actors are generally inept. When they're running around and screaming they're not quite as bad, but the few attempts at characterization are almost painful to watch.

Perhaps the oddest aspect of *Burial Ground* is the bizarre incest subplot between Michael and his mother Evelyn. At one point Michael attempts to caress his mother's breasts and thighs, exclaiming, "I loved your breast so much, mama!" Not surprisingly he gets a swift slap from Evelyn, but she feels guilty about rebuking her son and ends up letting him bite chunks out of her after he's become a zombie. Given that Michael is supposed to be about seven years old, the scenes between him and his mother should be repulsive, but the actor was really in his late 20s sporting a disastrous wig. The sight of a short—but clearly adult—actor in an obvious wig, trying to caress a seductive young Italian actress while pretending he's her son, is simply laughable. The actress—Maria Angela Giordano—later stated that she found it hard to avoid laughing out loud while filming the scene. At the time she was married to producer Crisanti, and she admits that she probably wouldn't have done the scene if it were not for him. Still, such a ridiculous scene doesn't compare to being stabbed in the crotch in *Patrick Still Lives*.

The unrelentingly grim atmosphere that surrounds *Burial Ground* is partially provided by the score, which combines Tangerine Dream-esque synths with haunting string sounds and occasional ill-advised forays into easy-listening jazz. The electronic sounds came courtesy of Elsio Mancuso. An earlier score by Berto Pisano (billed as "Bert Rexon") is the source of the eerie orchestra sounds. Pisano was a long-time associate of Crisanti's, who probably thought it was cheaper to edit new and old material together than come up with an entirely new score.

Since its release *Burial Ground* has become known as something of a golden turkey, a truly bad film that warrants viewing on a purely humorous level. This isn't entirely fair; Prestopino's makeup is excellent, turning these zombies into desiccated husks that collapse when hit rather than the festering ghouls of *Zombie* (1979). Sadly, not all of the work is quite so effective, and some of the actors are clearly wearing half-finished masks rather than professionally applied makeup. However, De Rossi does lay the blood on thick and copiously, appropriately since that's the film's sole selling point. *Burial Ground* remains worthwhile only for the casual gorehound or the dedicated follower of Italian horror films.

Cannibal Apocalypse (1980)
Aka: Apocalypse domani, Cannibals in the Streets,
Invasion of the Flesh Eaters, Virus

Director: Anthony M. Dawson [Antonio Margheriti]; Story: Jimmy Gould [Dardano Sacchetti]; Screenplay: Jimmy Gould [Dardano Sacchetti], Anthony M. Dawson [Antonio Margheriti]; Producer: Maurizio Amati, Sandro Amati; Special Effects/Makeup: Giannetto De Rossi; Music: Alexander Blonksteiner
Starring: John Saxon (Norman Hooper), Elizabeth Turner (Jane Hooper), John Morghen [Giovanni Lombardo Radice] (Charles Bukowski), Cindy Hamilton [Cinzia De Carolis] (Mary), Tony King (Tommy Thompson), Wallace Wilkinson [Venantino Venantini] (Lieutenant Hill), Ray Williams [Ramiro Oliveros] (Dr. Phil Menday-ers), John Geroson, May Heatherly (Mary), Ronnie Sanders, Vic Perkins, Jere Beery, Joan Riordan

The North Vietnamese take two U.S. soldiers prisoner. When they are recaptured, the soldiers are found eating human body parts and are eventually placed in a mental asylum. Years later, one of them is released, but he quickly begins to spread the virus that turned him into a cannibal, sparking off a wave of flesh-eating attacks.

Cannibal Apocalypse is unique among Italian cannibal movies. The action doesn't take place in the jungle (except for the opening sequence, the film is entirely set in Atlanta), there's no dubious civilized man vs. savages subtext, and mercifully, no graphic animal slaughter. Perhaps most importantly, the cannibals here are white. Instead of the usual "Green Hell" adventures as seen in Umberto Lenzi's and Ruggero Deodato's cannibal films, *Apocalypse* is equal parts Vietnam adventure and cop thriller, all mixed in with the characteristic Italian penchant for extreme splatter and morbidly horrific themes.

Like many Italian horror films, the central premise of *Cannibal Apocalypse* is rather shaky. The idea that cannibalism can be passed on like a disease is patently ridiculous, but Margheriti doesn't dwell on the specifics for too long, preferring to get the action underway.

Japanese program for *Cannibal Apocalypse*

Before long there's a trio of 'Nam vet cannibals rampaging across Atlanta killing, eating and/or infecting the people they come across. It's safe to say few movies have explored similar territory.

Margheriti has always been a skilled director, and he shows his abilities here. The flea market scene and the final flight through the sewers are excellently staged and impressively tense. Above all else, *Cannibal Apocalypse* is a horror film, so the action is accompanied by a healthy dose of blood and gore, including the film's standout scene: A shotgun blast rips into Bukowski's chest, allowing viewers to see daylight through the bloody hole. It's not particularly convincing, but it is *very* eye-catching.

At the time, veteran actor John Saxon was less than impressed with having to appear in such a gratuitously exploitative piece, but his taciturn performance is central to the film and fits in perfectly. Giovanni Lombardo Radice delivers a characteristically reliable turn as the unstable Bukowski (*Charles* Bukowski, no less), and the rest of the cast members are fine in their parts. This is still low-budget exploitation territory, so one can't expect Marlon Brando here, but for the most part the performances are competent.

As I mentioned earlier, the plot isn't particularly well thought out, and the special effects, while clearly intended to mimic those in *Dawn of the Dead* (1979), are not quite as good. Even so, *Cannibal Apocalypse* is a solid action-horror film that deserves to be regarded as an exploitation classic. *Cannibal ferox* (1981) might be better known and more notorious, but in my opinion Margheriti's film is easily the more entertaining.

Cannibal ferox (1981)
Aka: Make Them Die Slowly, Woman From Deep River

Director: Umberto Lenzi; Story/Screenplay: Umberto Lenzi; Producer: Mino Loy, Luciano Martino; Special Effects: Giannetto De Rossi; Makeup: Giuseppe Ferranti; Music: Budy Maglione [Maria Fiamma Maglione], Carlo Maria Cordio
Starring: John Morghen [Giovanni Lombardo Radice] (Mike Logan), Lorraine De Selle (Gloria Davis), Bryan Redford [Danilo Mattei] (Rudy Davis), Zora Kerova [Zora Keslerova] (Pat), Walter Lloyd [Walter Lucchini] (Jo Castellani), Meg Fleming [Maria Fiamma Magliona] (Myrna Stanton), Robert Kerman (Lieutenant Rizzo), John Bartha [Janos Bartha] (henchman), Venantino Venantini (Sergeant Ross), 'El Indio' Rincon (Suarez)

A group of anthropologists head off into the Amazon jungle to study cannibalism among the native tribes. They meet up with a pair of drug dealers who are busy exploiting the tribesmen and their land. Eventually the drug dealers go too far and spark a revolt that quickly turns into a bloodbath.

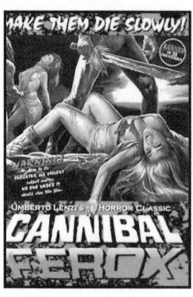

Not many films can seriously claim to be even nastier than *Cannibal Holocaust* (1979), but Umberto Lenzi's *Cannibal ferox* pulls it off. Thankfully no store bought morality's on display here; Lenzi wants nothing more than to present a cavalcade of atrocities, one after the other. It doesn't make the gratuitous animal slaughter any more acceptable, but at least he's not being a hypocrite like Deodato.

The plots are reasonably similar. A group of anthropologists heads into the South American jungle determined to debunk the myth of cannibalism. Unsurprisingly they get into trouble with the natives—who are of course cannibals—and then the film descends into an orgy of killing and torture as the simple jungle folk take their revenge. Lenzi throws a parallel plot about New York drug barons and emerald smugglers into the pot, resulting in one complicated mess of a film. However, it's abundantly clear that the director has no interest in providing a coherent and cohesive plot, since it only serves as a means to introduce the many special effects-driven scenes.

Predictably, Lenzi's not interested in coaxing decent performances from his cast, because they're only there to squirm and scream and die horribly. Giovanni Lombardo Radice appears to be having great fun, clearly aware that the film is going to be worthless. Character players like hardcore porn star Robert Kerman (also in Lenzi's *Eaten Alive!* 1980) and Venantino Venantini do the best they can with their badly written roles, but this isn't Shakespeare; credible performances would be entirely wasted here.

For a film that exists to show simulated brutality at its most extreme, fans would think the special effects would be great. Giannetto De Rossi is a talented craftsman, but for whatever reason, his work here is pretty poor. The scenes of actual animal slaughter highlight just how unrealistic the special effects are. This isn't going to bother fans of the film much, but viewers expecting to see De Rossi's usually excellent handiwork are likely to be disappointed.

Cannibal ferox has secured its place as Umberto Lenzi's most graphic and bloodthirsty film, and becomes one of the most reprehensible works in the Italian horror genre. *Cannibal Holocaust* has at least its (relatively) high production values and innovative structure in its favor, but Lenzi's film is low-budget, low-ability trash with no redeeming features whatsoever.

Cannibal Holocaust (1980)

Director: Ruggero Deodato; Story/Screenplay: Gianfranco Clerici; Producer: Franco Palaggi, Franco Di Nunzio; Makeup: Massimo Giustini; Music: Riz Ortolani

Starring: Robert Kerman (Professor Monroe), Francesca Ciardi (Faye Daniels), Perry Pirkanen (Jack Anders), Luca Barbareschi (Mark Tomaso), Salvatore Basile, Ricardo Fuentes (Chaco), Gabriel York (Alan Yates)

A documentary team disappears in the Amazon rainforest. A second team, sent in to look for them, manages to recover their footage and piece together what happened, revealing the orgy of violence and brutality that resulted in the death of the film crew.

Cannibal Holocaust is undoubtedly the most notorious film in this book. Both reviled for the scenes of animal slaughter and praised for

เรื่องจริง! ของคนนุ่งผ้าเตี่ยว
กินทุกอย่าง เถื่อนทุกแบบ
เพราะชีวิตมีค่าแค่เพนนีเดียว...

CANNIBAL HALLOCAUST II

Turkish poster for *Cannibal Holocaust*

the extreme realism of the pseudo-documentary footage, the film's influence continues to this day, kept alive by *The Blair Witch Project* and reality TV. Every time a film like *Natural Born Killers* tries to satirize the media's love affair with violent and repellent images, a new link is created in a chain that began with *Cannibal Holocaust*.

Despite its flaws, Deodato's film is not just another bloody exploitation flick. For one thing, the director's obvious talent lifts his movie above pure trash like Lenzi's *Cannibal ferox* (1981). While such films exist purely to shock and/or titillate, *Cannibal Holocaust* has greater aspirations. Although the natives abuse each other in ritualistic fashion and end up tearing the Western filmmakers apart, our sympathies must lie with the natives. The film crew has exploited their subjects in order to get the most sensational footage possible, even if that means raping and killing. Deodato forces his audience to acknowledge that the natives, acting out of self-defense and ignorance, retain the moral high ground compared to the supposedly civilized people, whose actions have no moral justification whatsoever.

Unfortunately, Deodato's moralizing backfires. In interviews, he claims that his actions (the slaughter of animals) were justified by the lifestyle of the natives around him—they killed and ate such creatures, so no harm was done, especially since the natives always took the remains for food. "Perhaps we overdid it a bit with the turtle," he says, "however, that also was eaten."[4] This is a patently false assertion, along the same lines as the film crew's belief that the existence of war between tribes gives them the right to kill natives. When Deodato encourages his actors to tear apart—and consume—a living turtle, not a single native can be found in the shot. Deodato stages the death of several animals to titillate or disgust his audience, and his justification is just as sordid as the one he ascribes to his fictional film crew.

Cannibal Holocaust is an exceptionally well-constructed film, moral arguments aside. The documentary footage recovered by the second team is the most realistic I have ever seen, complete with grain, print damage, overexposure, natural lighting and variable sound quality. It is this film-within-a-film frame that secures Deodato's film a level of notoriety, containing as it does murder, rape, mutilation, animal slaughter, misogynistic brutality and extremely graphic violence. Even without the violence, cut versions retain the same unrelentingly grim atmosphere that makes the film so difficult to watch.

As a landmark of Italian cinema, *Cannibal Holocaust* is an important film that deserves to be considered in any serious study of the genre. In an era when footage of Bosnian war atrocities is readily available to the public, Deodato's film has lost little of its impact or relevance.

Cannibals (1981)
Aka: Mondo Cannibale, Barbarian Goddess,
Cannibal Girl, White Cannibal Queen

Director: Jésus Franco; Story/Screenplay: A.L. Mariaus [Marius Lesoeur], Jeff Manner [Jésus Franco]; Special Effects: Michael Nizza; Music: Robert Pregadio
Starring: Al Cliver [Pier Luigi Conti] (Jerry Taylor), Sabrina Siana (Lena), Candy Coster [Lina Romay] (Ana), Robert Foster [Antonio Mayans] (Yakake), Barbara Shelton (Shirley Night)

An American anthropologist sees his wife eaten and his daughter kidnapped by a cannibal tribe. Years later he mounts an expedition to the area to find out what happened to her. The same tribe eventually attacks this expedition, and the tribe now worships the anthropologist's daughter as its great queen.

This is one of a handful of Spanish-Italian co-productions directed by Jésus Franco, possibly the most famous of the European exploitation directors. Although the best of Franco's work displays a surprising level of ability and a flair for hazy, dream-like imagery, most of his films are lazy exercises in nudity and gore, shot on minuscule budgets that make use of whatever locations happened to be nearby. Unsurprisingly, *Cannibals* falls into the latter category.

Viewed as an example of terrible filmmaking, it's most definitely an entertaining effort. The cannibal attack scenes are handled in slow motion, presumably to pad out the running time, and they are punctuated with various crunching and slurping noises from the soundtrack. Franco didn't want or couldn't afford a decent special effects technician, so even the flesh-eating scenes are rather tame and bloodless. Instead of using documentary footage to show wild animals, we're presented with a plastic crocodile. Add to this the sight of Pier Luigi Conti struggling to make it appear that he has only one arm (the other was cut off by the cannibals, apparently) and we have a film that's considerably more fun to watch than it should be.

La casa del buon ritorno (1986)

Director: Beppe Cino; Story/Screenplay: Beppe Cino; Producer: Beppe Cino; Music: Carlo Siliotto

Starring: Amanda Sandrelli, Stefano Gabrini, Francesco Costa, Fiammetta Carina, Lola Ledda, Stanis Ledda, Fabrizio Capuani, Eloisa Cino, Eleonora Salvadori, Elvira Castellano

The ghosts of his past torment a young man, who returns to his parents' home.

[Synopsis taken from *Spaghetti Nightmares* (see bibliography).]

The Church (1989)
Aka: La chiesa, Demons 3

Director: Michele Soavi; Story: Dario Argento, Franco Ferrini, Lamberto Bava [uncredited]; Screenplay: Dario Argento, Franco Ferrini, Michele Soavi; Producer: Mario & Vittorio Cecchi Gori, Dario Argento; Special Effects: Renato Agostini, Sergio Stivaletti; Makeup: Rosario Prestopino; Music: Keith Emerson, The Goblins [Goblin], Philip Glass, Simon Boswell
Starring: Hugh Quarshie (Gus), Tomas Arana (Evan), Feodor Chaliapin (The Bishop), Barbara Cupisti (Lisa), Antonella Vitale (Model), Giovanni Lombardo Radice (Reverend), Asia Argento (Lotte)

A group of devil worshippers are buried beneath a great cathedral. Centuries later the seal is accidentally broken and the long-dormant evil begins to escape, infecting the worshippers and visitors. One priest discovers what is happening and tries to find the secret mechanism that will cause the cathedral to collapse, trapping the evil once again.

Michele Soavi's second film is a stately Gothic horror firmly rooted in the style of *Suspiria* (1977) and *Inferno* (1980). It would be lazy to characterize *The Church* as a mere Argento knock-off, however, since it is an arguably more enjoyable and coherent film than both *Phenomena* (1985) and *Opera* (1987).

From the outset it is obvious that *The Church* is not going to be a quiet or subtle horror film. A lengthy medieval prologue introduces us to the basic theme—demons trapped beneath a massive Gothic cathedral—and presents two of the film's main aspects, a loud and appropriately grandiose soundtrack and an eye-catching visual style. Plot and characterization are kept to a minimum and are largely dispensed with after the first hour in favor of a series of elaborate and disturbing set pieces. As with Argento's Gothic horrors, nightmare logic quickly takes over, although the film resolves itself in a decent climax.

Not surprisingly for a film that was originally to have been part of the *Demons* series, *The Church* features a number of gory episodes, courtesy of Rosario Prestopino. Sergio Stivaletti provides one of his finest effects—a writhing mass of body parts in the shape of a demon's head—as well as a handful of other marvels. Everything is done professionally, avoiding the low-budget feel that cursed many late 1980s Italian productions.

Arriving at a time when Italian horror was becoming increasingly dominated by tepid made-for-TV efforts, *The Church* stood out as a return to the values of the past. Unfortunately it did not herald a renaissance, and Soavi's next film, *The Sect* (1991), represented a holding pattern. However, *The Church* remains one of the best Italian horror films of the decade and a worthy successor to the works of Dario Argento and Lucio Fulci.

The City of the Living Dead (1980)
Aka: Paura nella città dei morti viventi, The Gates of Hell

Director: Lucio Fulci; Story/Screenplay: Lucio Fulci, Dardano Sacchetti; Producer: Giovanni Masini; Special Effects: Giannetto De Rossi; Makeup: Franco Rufini, Rosario Prestopino; Music: Fabio Frizzi
Starring: Christopher George (Peter Bell), Katriona MacColl [Catriona MacColl] (Mary Woodhouse), Carlo De Mejo (Gerry), Antonella Interlenghi (Emily Robbins), Giovanni Lombardo Radice (Bob), Daniela

 Doria (Rosie Kelvin), Fabrizio Jovine (Father Thomas), Luca Paisner [Luca Venantini] (John Robbins), Michelle Soavi (Tommy Fisher), Venantino Venantini (Mr. Ross), Enzo D'Ausilio (Deputy), Adelaide Aste (Madame Teresa), Luciano Rossi, Robert Sampson (detective), Janet Agren (Sandra)

A New York reporter and a young psychic travel to an isolated New England town in an effort to prevent the gates of hell from opening and releasing the resurrected dead upon the world. As the time grows near, the separation between the world of the living and the world of the dead begins to disappear.

After the great commercial success of *Zombie* (1979), Lucio Fulci once again turned to the living dead. This time we're firmly in Gothic horror territory, inspired by Dario Argento's *Inferno* and the works of H.P. Lovecraft (the town of Dunwich crops up frequently in Lovecraft's stories). Although not as highly regarded as Fulci's masterpiece *The Beyond* (1981), *City of the Living Dead* is a significant film. It's the first time the director begins to experiment with the themes and ideas that appear in his finest works, in particular the de-emphasis of plot in favor of heavily visual episodes punctuated by scenes of extreme gore and graphic violence.

A plot exists here, it is quite obvious that the story takes second place to the bizarre set pieces. Fulci concentrates on the increasingly ghoulish and violent scenes, with very little attention paid to the story. Some of these scenes have become classic Fulci gore moments, most notably Giovanni Lombardo Radice's bloody D.I.Y. lobotomy and Daniela Doria's gut-wrenching demise. In the end, the plot raises more questions than it answers, especially concerning the curious ending.

The film does have its flaws. Madame Teresa's character verges on being a caricature, and her dialogue is clichéd and trite. The investigating policeman is equally bad, throwing his weight around like a low-rent, out-of-place Shaft on the verge of exploding into violence. Central to that particular scene is a mysterious fireball that materializes in the corner of the room. Sadly, the special effects aren't quite up to the task, and the final effect is amateurish and silly. Fulci's annoying habit of using close-up shots of the eyes to express tension is in full flow here, and this technique doesn't work particularly well, either.

Flaws and unresolved plot devices aside, *City of the Living Dead* is a success as a film. *The Beyond* is better, because the director's dream of a purely visual film is almost fully realized, but it's safe to say that without *City of the Living Dead*, *The Beyond* wouldn't have been possible. In its own right, *City* is an entertaining slab of Gothic doom-and-gloom, from the bloody and violent murders to the climactic showdown in the tunnels beneath Dunwich. *City of the Living Dead* is an essential Italian horror film. Fulci appears briefly as the Dunwich coroner, Dr. Thompson.

Contamination (1980)
Aka: Contamination-Alien arriva sulla terra,
Alien Contamination, Toxic Spawn

Director: Lewis Coates [Luigi Cozzi]; Story / Screenplay: Lewis Coates [Luigi Cozzi], Erich Tomek; Producer: Charles Mancini [Claudio Mancini], Ugo Valenti; Special Effects: Giovanni Corridori; Music: Goblin
Starring: Ian McCulloch (Commander Ian Hubbard), Louise Marleau (Colonel Stella Holmes), Marino Mase (Lieutenant Tony Aris), Siegfried Rauch (Hamilton), Gisela Hahn (Perla de la Cruz), Carlo De Mejo (Agent Young), Carlo Monni (Dr. Turner)

A deserted ship drifts into New York harbor. The harbor authorities board the ship and discover a number of large, pulsating green eggs, as well as the bloody remains of the crew. One of the investigators manages to find out the significance of the giant eggs: They explode, showering anyone close by with green slime. Anyone hit by the green slime will explode too. Managing to avoid a messy death, Colonel Stella Holmes attempts to track the source of the ship and the eggs it carries. Hubbard, a former astronaut and the only man to have previously encountered the mysterious eggs, joins her. Together they head to South America and a plantation that may hold the secrets behind the plague of pulsating eggs.

Luigi Cozzi's *Contamination* was one of the earliest of a series of *Alien*-inspired movies that emerged after the release of Ridley Scott's chest-bursting hit. Although the film remains earthbound throughout, the pulsating green eggs and the graphic splatter scenes are derivative of *Alien*. Beyond that, Fulci's *Zombie* (1979) is a clear influence, particularly in the casting of Ian McCulloch and the New York harbor scenes. Not surprisingly, one of *Contamination*'s main selling points is the considerable amount of green slime mixed with blood and gore. It must

be said however that the seemingly endless scenes of people exploding in a shower of blood and slime get boring very quickly.

To his credit, Ian McCulloch tries hard to make the script come alive, but by his own admission his heart wasn't in the project and it's not hard to see why. The direction is basic for the most part, while the special effects are enthusiastic but poorly done. The poor lighting could be attributed to the film's low-budget origins, until audiences discover that the lighting was kept deliberately low by the director so as not to reveal the poor quality of the special effects.

Given the derivative nature of the material and the low production values, it's unlikely many viewers will hail this as a piece of classic Italian science fiction. Splatter fans might find it more enjoyable, but even they might find the repetitive explosion scenes somewhat dull. *Contamination* isn't Luigi Cozzi's worst effort and it's definitely not as bad as some other films from the period. However, the film is *boring*, something decent exploitation films should never be.

The Curse (1987)
Aka: The Farm

Director: David Keith; Story/Screenplay: David Chaskin, H.P. Lovecraft [uncredited]; Producer: Ovidio G. Assonitis; Special Effects: Ron Petruccione, Louis Fulci [Lucio Fulci]; Makeup: Frank Russell [Franco Ruffini]; Music: Franco Micalizzi
Starring: Wil Wheaton (Zachary Hayes), Claude Akins (Nathan Hayes), Malcolm Danare (Cyrus), Cooper Huckabee (Dr. Alan Forbes), John Schneider (Carl Willis), Amy Wheaton (Alice Hayes)

A strange meteorite lands in Tennessee, causing toxic slime to dissolve into the ground and contaminate the land and the crops growing there. The townspeople begin to turn into drooling mutants while a local farm boy tries to convince the authorities that there's something desperately wrong.

The Curse, an Italian-U.S. co-production, would probably have disappeared by now were it not for some interesting cast and crew choices. The main character is played by Wil Wheaton, one of the stars of *Stand by Me* (1986) and later one of the regular cast on *Star Trek: The Next Generation*. Wheaton's real-life sister Amy plays sister Alice Hayes. Most curious, however, is the presence of Lucio Fulci, credited as associate producer and special optical effects designer.

Even with Fulci handling some of the special effects (it's not clear which ones), *The Curse* is a terrible film. The special effects themselves are pretty bad, consisting mostly of lots of slime coupled with poorly applied makeup. Actor David Keith makes his directorial debut here, but he's working with a second-rate script (writer David Chaskin was also responsible for the atrocious *A Nightmare on Elm Street Part 2: Freddy's Revenge*) and simply isn't skilled enough to construct something worthwhile. A decent cast might have been able to bring the film up a little, but Wil Wheaton and Claude Akins are pretty much on their own here.

As a footnote to Fulci's varied and extensive career, *The Curse* is of minor interest. Yet it's still one of the many cheap and forgettable horror movies produced during the 1980s.

Curse II: The Bite (1988)
Aka: The Bite

Director: Fred Goodwin [Federico Prosperi]; Story/Screenplay: Fred Goodwin [Federico Prosperi], Susan Zelouf; Producer: Ovidio G. Assonitis, Kenichi Tominaga; Special Effects/Makeup: Screaming Mad George; Music: Carlo Maria Cordio
Starring: Jill Schoelen, J. Eddie Peck, Jamie Farr, Savina Gersak, Marianne Muellerleile, Al Fann, Sidney Lassick

A radioactive snake bites a young man, and his arm begins to mutate into a deadly snake head that drives him to attack people.

Curse II: The Bite (a joint Italian/Japanese/American production) is largely unrelated to the original *Curse*. Producer Assonitis owned the rights to both movies and marketed *The Bite* as a sequel. Without the presence of Jill Schoelen, the attractive heroine of *The Stepfather* (1988) and *Cutting Class* (1989), and Jamie Farr from *M*A*S*H*, the film would most likely be a total loss. Surprisingly, Screaming Mad George's usually reliable effects are very poor here, resembling a sock puppet rather than a specially made prosthesis.

While decent special effects would be an asset, they wouldn't be able to cover up the fact that

The Bite consists of one small idea stretched out to fill 98 minutes. Too much time is spent either traveling from one deserted location to the next or watching J. Eddie Peck writhing in agony and clutching his arm. The ending is limp and somewhat predictable, making *The Bite* only worth tracking down for serious fans of Schoelen or Farr.

A third film, *Curse III: Blood Sacrifice* (1991), appeared. Originally called *Panga*, this film has no connection to either *The Curse* or *Curse II: The Bite*. *Catacombs*, an Italian/U.S. co-production filmed in 1988, saw release in 1993 as *Curse IV*. Featuring a score by Pino Donaggio and decent cinematography from Sergio Salvati, it's the best installment in the series.

Cut and Run (1985)
Aka: Inferno in diretta, Amazonia-la jungle blanche

Director: Ruggero Deodato; Story/Screenplay: Cesare Frugoni, Dardano Sacchetti; Producer: Alessandro Fracassi; Makeup: Maurizio Trani, Alberto Blasi; Music: Claudio Simonetti
Starring Lisa Blount (Frances Hudson), Leonard Mann [Leonardo Manzella] (Mark Ludman), Willie Aames (Tommy Allo), Richard Lynch (Colonel Horne), Richard Bright (Bob Allo), Michael Berryman (Quecho), Eriq La Salle (Fargas), Gabriele Tinti (Manuel), Valentina Forte (Ana), John Steiner (Vlado), Karen Black (Karin)

A journalist and her cameraman head into the South American jungle to track down a colonel who was believed to have died in Guyana during the Jonestown massacre. They step into the middle of a bloody war between drug dealers and native tribesmen.

Following the reviled but commercially successful *Cannibal Holocaust* (1979)—and to a lesser extent, *The House on the Edge of the Park* (1980)—Ruggero Deodato's career stalled heavily. In the five years between *House* and *Cut and Run* he directed only one film, a flimsy *Road Warrior* cash-in called *The Atlantis Interceptors* (1983). However, *Cut and Run* managed to convince the Italian film industry that Deodato could create successful films without resorting to animal slaughter or gross misogyny.

In a conscious move, *Cut and Run* repeats the Amazonian setting of *Holocaust* and recycles the concept of a film crew headed deep into the jungle. Equally deliberately, no animal slaughter occurs and no prolonged scenes of rape and sexual abuse. The story is connected to Jim Jones, though—perhaps a nod to Umberto Lenzi and *Eaten Alive!* (1980)? There's no shortage of violence, but it's curiously simplistic. Plenty of people are skewered, dismembered or shot, but the majority of victims are white drug dealers or the natives that serve them. No ambiguous moral arguments appear here: Good guys survive and bad guys die.

The film's greatest asset is the excellent cast. It includes several American B-movie/television regulars—Lisa Blount (later in John Carpenter's *Prince of Darkness*, 1987), Richard Bright, Willie Aames, Richard Lynch, Karen Black—and a number of Italian exploitation stars like Gabriele Tinti, John Steiner and Luca Barbareschi, many of whom had worked with Deodato before. Appearing in his debut role is Eriq La Salle, later famous as Dr. Benton on TV's *ER*. Thanks to this competent and experienced cast, only a few weak performances appear. Richard Bright's television executive is overplayed and irritating, as is Willie Aames' histrionic turn, but these are minor complaints and don't really affect the film.

Unlike *Cannibal Holocaust*, *Cut and Run* does not linger excessively on the violence and gore. The opening scene is brutal, but it's over relatively quickly, unlike the protracted scenes that make *Holocaust* such a grueling experience. Deodato is firmly in action-adventure territory here, and thankfully, he leaves the extreme material behind. Instead he includes a handful of violent scenes to spice up the story and concentrates more on characters and story. Not everything makes sense, but it's a definite progression from his earlier works.

Trivia: Originally titled *Marimba*. Wes Craven was supposed to direct. Pre-production began in 1980 but stalled shortly afterward. Dirk Benedict—later famous as Templeton Peck, aka "Face" from *The A-Team*—was to be the star.

Dagger Eyes (1983)
Aka: Mystere

Director: Carlo Vanzina; Story: Enrico Vanzina; Screenplay: Enrico Vanzina, Carlo Vanzina; Music: Armando Travojoli
Starring: Carole Bouquet (Mystere), John Steiner (Ivanov), Janet Agren (Pamela), Gabriele Tinti (Mink Visione), Duilio Del Prete (Captain Levi), Philip Coccioletti (Colt), Peter Berling (Reinhardt), Marcia Briscoe (Martha), Jinn Steffen (Puttana)

A call girl finds herself mixed up in political intrigue when her client is murdered.

Another entertaining *giallo* from the writer-director of *Nothing Underneath* (1983). Carlo Vanzina, co-scripting with his brother Enrico, mixes in political intrigue and a spy thriller ethos with the usual erotically tinged material. These elements are pretty clichéd, but they make a refreshing—if rather silly—change from the norm.

The main cast, with the exception of Philip Coccioletti, all are exploitation regulars. John Steiner appears to be having fun in his turn as a Russian assassin, but Janet Agren delivers a typically wide-eyed and clueless performance. The rest of the cast is mostly wooden, but that's probably to be expected from a low-budget *giallo*. More than one critic suggested Vanzina should return to comedy, where he and his father (the famous Steno, aka Stefano Vanzina) achieved great success, but *Dagger Eyes* is perfectly watchable. Ironically enough, Carole Bouquet was also in *For Your Eyes Only* (1981).

Dangerous Obsession (1986)
Aka: Il miele del diavolo, The Devil's Honey

Director: Lucio Fulci; Story/Screenplay: Ludovica Marineo, Vincenzo Salviani, Jésus Balcazar, Lucio Fulci; Producer: Vincenzo Salviani; Special Effects: Alvaro Gremigna, Fernando Caso; Music: Claudio Natili
Starring: Brett Halsey (Dr. Wendell Simpson), Corrinne Clery (Carol Simpson), Blanca Marsillach (Jessica), Stefano Madia (Johnny), Paola Marina (Paola), Bernard Seray (Nicky)

After her abusive boyfriend is killed in a motorcycle crash, a young woman directs her anger at the doctor who was unable to save his life. She kidnaps him and subjects him to a regime of sex and torture.

Few people watching *The Beyond* (1981) would guess that the director would end up making a movie influenced by *9 1/2 Weeks* (1986), but *Dangerous Obsession* is such a film. Although frequently darker in tone, *Dangerous Obsession* owes a tip of the hat to erotic successes like *9 1/2 Weeks* and *Last Tango in Paris* (1972).

As would be expected from a Lucio Fulci film—even one that's intended to be an erotic thriller—the story revolves around pain and death. Unsurprisingly there are many sex scenes, including a sodomy scene reminiscent of *Last Tango* and a great deal of S/M material. Interestingly, Fulci directs these scenes competently, sometimes managing to evoke the required air of eroticism. His direction isn't always successful, but perhaps more so than one would expect.

Story-wise *Dangerous Obsession* isn't much, and the conclusion doesn't exactly go anywhere. But it's a well-made film, arguably more entertaining than the director's later genre efforts. Not what you'd expect from Fulci, but it's worth seeing if you find it.

Dawn of the Mummy (1981)

Director: Frank Agrama; Story: Ronald Dobrin, Daria Price; Screenplay: Frank Agrama, Ronald Dobrin, Daria Price; Producer: Frank Agrama; Special Effects / Makeup: Maurizio Trani; Special Effects: Luigi Batistelli, Farid Abdoul Hai, Tony Didio, Jr.; Music: Shuki Levy Starring: Brenda King, Barry Sattels, George Peck, John Salvo, Ibrahim Khan, Joan Levy, Ellen Faison, Dianne Beatty

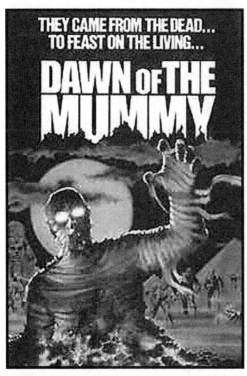

A group of American models decide that an ancient Egyptian tomb would be the ideal location for their photo shoot. Unfortunately they manage to bring the Pharaoh buried within back to life, as well as his army of undead followers.

We can thank DVD for resurrecting this low-key entry in the roster of Italian zombie films, but this is no cult classic waiting to be discovered. The film's one of the more amateurish films from the period, which entirely is what audiences would expect from the director of *Queen Kong* (1976). The cast is uniformly terrible and seems to have appeared in very little else besides *Dawn of the Mummy*. However, this is a zombie splatter film, so only the zombies and the gore are relevant. With Maurizio Trani's name in the credits, audiences might expect something good in that respect. After all, Trani worked on some of Fulci's best (and goriest) films: *Zombie* (1979), *The Beyond* (1981) and *New York Ripper* (1982). Sadly this is not the case. Trani's makeup is pretty basic (certainly not as impressive as his work on Fulci's zombies) and the gore becomes liberally applied butcher's offal. There aren't enough extras so the zombies are filmed from different angles to give the impression of increased numbers. In short, this is a film with little plot, bad makeup and cheap gore. Stick with Fulci instead.

Dead Waters (1994)
Aka: Dark Waters

Director: Mariano Baino; Story/Screenplay: Mariano Baino, Andrew M. Bark; Producer: Victor Zuev; Special Effects/Makeup: Richard Field, David Mundin; Music: Igor Clark

Starring: Louise Salter (Elizabeth), Venera Simmons (Sarah), Maria Kapnist (Mother Superior), Valeriy Bassel (fisherman), Sergey Rugens, Alvina Skarga (old blind woman), Georgiy Drozd, Anna Rose Phipps (Theresa), Lubov Snegur (Mother Superior's assistant), Pavel Sokolov (boat owner), Tanya Dobrovolskaya (Elizabeth as a child), Valeriy Kopaev (priest), Ludmila Marufova (nun), Kristina Spivak (Sarah as a child)

A young woman travels to an isolated convent near her birthplace to discover why her late father made payments to the order. When she arrives it appears the nuns are hiding some dark secrets, possibly about her birth.

Although hailed in some quarters as a return to the golden era of Italian horrors, *Dead Waters* is only partially successful. It's certainly superior to the majority of *nunsploitation* films (such as Bruno Mattei's *The Other Hell*, 1980); however, too many nods to Argento and Bava are evident and therre are not enough original ideas.

The main flaw is the derivative plot. Baino is pretty adept at creating an atmosphere of tension and menace, but the underlying themes are well worn and will hold few surprises for the experienced viewer. His attempts to recreate the stylized imagery of his predecessors are just as flawed. Much of the film is bathed in a yellow light that would have been effective if used sparingly, but Baino relies upon it too heavily here, giving the film a washed-out, bleached appearance.

While *Dead Waters* is an interesting film that certainly indicates a respectable degree of talent on the director's part, it also suffers from a lack of new ideas and a little too much respect for past masters. Italian horror needed new blood and fresh ideas, things that *Dead Waters* does not have. Nonetheless, it remains an interesting film for fans of the genre.

Delirium (1987)
Aka: Le foto de Gioia, Photos of Joy

Director: Lamberto Bava; Story: Luciano Martino; Screenplay: Gianfranco Clerici, Daniele Stroppa; Makeup: Rosario Prestopino, Maurizio Silvi, Gilberto Provenghi; Music: Simon Boswell
Starring: Serena Grandi (Gioia/Gloria), Daria Nicolodi (Evelyn), Vanni Corbellini (Tony), David Brandon (Roberto), George Eastman [Luigi Montefiore] (Alex), Katrine Michelsen (Kim), Karl Zinny (Mark), Lino Salemme (Inspector Corsi), Sabrina Salerno (Sabrina), Capucine (Flora)

The friends and employees of a magazine editor and former model are being killed off one by one.

Although often derided as a worthless erotic thriller, *Delirium* isn't as bad as it's made out to be. It doesn't match the best of Lamberto Bava's work, but it's considerably better than his made-for-television efforts and remains an undiscovered classic of 1980s trash cinema.

Predictably, the film's main selling point is sex. The cast features the voluptuous Serena Grandi, who actually seems to be a competent actress, even though she is still required to disrobe several times throughout the film. At least she's not getting slaughtered like an animal this time (cf. *Anthropophagous*, 1980). Former Miss Denmark Katrine Michelsen (also in *Specters*, 1987) and sex-symbol-turned-pop star Sabrina Salerno play two of the victims, also spending most of their screen time naked. Despite the emphasis on eroticism, Bava assembled a first class cast of Italian exploitation regulars, including Daria Nicolodi, David Brandon and Luigi Montefiore. They're working with substandard material, but it's good to see familiar and respected faces. Several lesser cast members are Bava regulars too—Lino Salemme was in both *Demons* films as well as two later-period Fulci movies, while Karl Zinny was also in *Demons* (1985) and *Graveyard Disturbance* (1987).

Simon Boswell's score is decent enough if audiences don't mind 1980s-style pop rock, but the makeup and special effects are pretty bad. Bava wanted to portray the killer's visions, presenting the victims as he saw them, but the sight of a supermodel with a single giant eyeball is neither gruesome nor disturbing. Even so, the cinematography and editing are both competent (if unimaginative) and overall all professionally made. Those expecting a *giallo* masterpiece will be disappointed, but if the viewer can switch off quality control for 90 minutes, *Delirium* is an entertaining diversion.

Dellamorte dellamore (1994)
Aka: Cemetery Man, Demons '95, Of Death and Love

Director: Michele Soavi; Story: Tiziano Sclavi; Screenplay: Gianni Romoli; Producer: Tilde Corsi, Gianni Romoli, Michele Soavi; Special Effects/Makeup: Sergio Stivaletti; Music: Manuel De Sica
Starring: Rupert Everett (Francesco Dellamorte), François Hadji-Lazaro (Gnaghi), Anna Falchi (She), Mickey Knox (Marshall Straniero), Fabiana Formica (Valentina), Clive Riche (Dr. Verseci), Katja Anton (thin girl), Barbara Cupisti (Magda), Anton Alexander (Franco), Pietro Genuardi (new Mayor Civardi), Patrizio Punzo (Claudia's mother), Stefano Masciarelli (Mayor Scanarotti)

Francesco Dellamorte is the custodian of Buffalora cemetery, an unusual place where the dead rise from their graves seven days after burial (sometimes less, sometimes more) and must be killed once again and re-buried. While coping with the peculiarities of his job, Francesco struggles to understand the world around him and make human conections.

Dellamorte dellamore is one of the best horror films made in the past 20 years and perhaps the most original film in this book. Although it is firmly rooted in the horror genre—the

central character is the custodian of a cemetery where the dead rise seven days after burial—the film also addresses existential concerns and maintains a healthy streak of black humor throughout.

The reluctant hero is Francesco Dellamorte, a man devoted to avoiding the harsh realities of life. He doesn't report the "returners" (as he calls them), because then the cemetery will be shut down and he'll have to find another job. Francesco's only friend is his assistant Gnaghi, a brutish creature that drools a lot but never manages to talk. They're both outcasts, neither able to interact with the world of the living, so they take refuge in the world of the dead. A bullet to the brain and some spadework and it's done; a stunt that's a lot easier than trying to form and maintain relationships. As Francesco says, "Anything to avoid thinking about life." Unsurprisingly, the custodian's morbid idyll is interrupted by the arrival of a beautiful woman who appears to be as obsessed with death as he is. From here the film takes a turn into some very strange territory, as Francesco begins to explore the nature of the world outside the cemetery.

Central to the success of the film is Rupert Everett's wonderful performance as Francesco. He manages to capture the character's air of boredom and languid discontent perfectly; this trait is unsurprising since Everett was the model for Tiziano Sclavi's original comic book character (Dellamorte is the hero of the long-running *Dylan Dog* series). Anna Falchi, a model of Finnish descent, plays his mysterious female companion. Her character is strongly reminiscent of Kim Novak in *Vertigo* (1958), which is ironic given that Falchi would go on to play the actress in *C'è Kim Novak al telefono* (1994). French rock star François Hadji-Lazaro plays Gnaghi, a demanding role that requires expressiveness but no speech. Hadji-Lazaro is perfect, however, and the combination of guttural noises and gestures is readily comprehensible.

As with most Italian zombie films, *Dellamorte dellamore* contains a certain amount of graphic gore. Although Francesco prefers a single headshot to deal with the returners, occasionally he has to do the job with a spade or graveyard ornament. Sergio Stivaletti provides the necessary blood and gore, keeping everything to earthy tones that match the look of the cemetery.

After a humorous and interesting first half, *Dellamorte dellamore* takes a turn into existential territory and becomes complex and sometimes difficult. It remains interesting as we watch Francesco attempt to divine the exact nature of his environment and its other occupants. The conclusion is heavily philosophical, something that might alienate viewers not interested in existential dilemmas. But it's all part of the film's charm—how many other movies can you name that manage to successfully mix gore, humor and philosophical concerns?

Dellamorte dellamore was Michele Soavi's last theatrical film before family concerns forced him to withdraw from the industry for a while. Since then he has become a highly respected television director, but *Dellamorte* remains his finest achievement and a true landmark in the horror film genre.

Demonia (1990)

Director: Lucio Fulci; Story/Screenplay: Piero Regnoli, Lucio Fulci; Producer: Ettore Spagnuolo; Special Effects/Makeup: Franco Giannini, Giuseppe Ferranti; Music: Giovanni Cristini

Starring: Brett Halsey (Professor Paul Evans), Meg Register (Liza), Lino Salemme (butcher), Christina Engelhardt (Susie), Pascal Druant (Kevin), Grady Thomas Clarkson (Sean), Ettore Comi (John), Carla Cassola, Michael J. Aronin (Lieutenant Andy), Al Cliver [Pier Luigi Conti] (Porter)

Archaeologists in Sicily begin to excavate a crypt, unaware a group of devil-worshipping nuns were executed and buried on the site five centuries before. When these scientists open the crypt, the evil escapes and begins to affect the group.

Although ultimately unsuccessful—artistically and commercially—*Manhattan Baby* (1982), *Murder-Rock Dancing Death* (1984) and *The Devil's Honey* (1986) reflect Lucio Fulci's desire to change and evolve. *Demonia*, however, sees the director cynically attempting to rework his own successes. While not considered the worst film in his extensive filmography, the spectacle of Fulci ripping off his own films has not met with universal approval.

From start to finish, *Demonia* plays like a compendium of references to Fulci's best-known films. The prologue lifts the opening scene from *The Beyond* (1981), while the following scene is cribbed from *City of the Living Dead* (1980). There's Al Cliver, who appears in nine of the director's films, including *Zombie* (1979); the actor warrants a bigger part than he's given here. As in *The Beyond*, the central female character is called Liza. Catriona MacColl was offered a part in the film, a tacit admission from Fulci that his later films would have benefited from a strong heroine played by a first-rate actress. Perhaps aware of the director's failing fortunes, she turned down the offer.

Unfortunately Fulci was in no position to capitalize on his great successes, primarily because he lacked the support of a capable and reliable crew. In place of Dardano Sacchetti we have Piero Regnoli, the mastermind behind sleaze like *Malabimba* (1979) and *Patrick Still Lives* (1980), not to mention the *Zombie* cash-ins *Nightmare City* (1980) and *Burial Ground* (1981). Luigi Ciccarese provides the pedestrian camera work, displaying none of Sergio Salvati's natural talent for framing and shot composition. Salvati worked on *Zombie*, one of Fulci's great triumphs. In contrast, Ciccarese shot the execrable *Zombie 4: After Death* (1988). The irony isn't hard to spot.

In short, *Demonia* is a pitiful attempt at clawing back some small fragment of Fulci's previous reputation. Depressing and mediocre, even dedicated fans will have a hard time finding something to appreciate here.

Demons (1985)
Aka: Dèmoni

Director: Lamberto Bava; Story: Dardano Sacchetti; Screenplay: Dario Argento, Lamberto Bava, Dardano Sacchetti, Franco Ferrini; Producer: Dario Argento; Special Effects/Makeup: Sergio Stivaletti, Rosario Prestopino; Music: Claudio Simonetti

Starring: Urbano Barberini (George), Natasha Hovey (Cheryl), Karl Zinny (Ken), Fiore Argento (Hannah), Paola Cozzo (Cathy), Fabiola Toledo (Carmen), Nicoletta Elmi (Ingrid, the usherette), Stelio Candelli (Frank), Nicole Tessler (Ruth), Giancarlo Geretta (Rosemary), Bobby Rhodes (Tony, the pimp), Guido Baldi (Tommy), Giovanni Frezza (Kurt)

While watching a horror movie in a cinema, some audience members begin to transform into demons. With the doors sealed shut, the rest of the audience must find a way out before the demons kill them all.

Lamberto Bava's *Demons* was one of the most successful Italian horror films of the decade. Arriving just in time to catch the mid-1980s rental video explosion, the film proved a favorite throughout Europe and America, cementing Bava's reputation as a master of gore-soaked horror. And *Demons* is certainly gory. It's also energetic, funny and very entertaining.

The plot is simplistic to say the least—various passers-by are given free

Lamberto Bava's *Demons* shows the perils of accepting free cinema tickets.

tickets to a movie being shown at Berlin's Metropol theater. The film is a horror movie, apparently based on Mario Bava's *Black Sunday* (1960). It's no ordinary dumb horror flick, however, and the events on the screen seem to inspire bizarre occurrences within the audience, most notably one girl's transformation into a gruesome pus-dripping demon. Non-stop action erupts from there on as the creature rampages through the audience, turning its victims into yet more demons. The survivors desperately try to escape, but there's no way out of the theater, and they must fight the growing horde if they wish to survive.

If this sounds like a clichéd plot with absolutely no subtext or deeper meaning, that's because that's all *Demons* is. *Demons* is an unrepentant all-style, no-substance film, clearly inspired by Dario Argento's forays into supernatural territory, *Suspiria* (1977) and *Inferno* (1980). However Bava's film has *pace*, something that is generally lacking from Argento's Gothic horrors. No slow build-up to an atmosphere of grim terror—as soon as the demons emerge, the race is on, and the pressure is kept up until the very end.

Argento's influence can also be seen in the characters, a bizarre bunch to say the least. The cast includes a couple of female students (one of whom is played by Fiore, Dario's daughter), a hilarious white-suited pimp (played by Bobby Rhodes) and two of his whores, a blind man whose guide keeps disappearing to meet up with her boyfriend and the usual group of horny young guys on the prowl for some fun. They're the kind of people that wouldn't be found in the same company, unless of course, they've been offered free tickets by a mysterious leather-clad, steel-masked stranger lurking in the subway. As a further point of interest, Michele Soavi plays the stranger, who also has a role in the film-within-a-film. Oh, and look out for Bava's cameo as a man on the subway.

Unfortunately, one of Argento's favorite devices, a loud heavy metal soundtrack, saddles the production. The soundtrack's not quite as intrusive as the one in *Phenomena* (1985) because there's less ambience to disrupt, but the music is still pretty annoying. "Fast As A Shark," the breakthrough hit from German proto-thrash band Accept, might have been the cutting edge of metal in 1985, but years later it sounds laughably bad. We also have anthemic hits from Billy Idol and Motley Crue, which are a little better but still not perfect. Whoever thought it would be good to include Go West's execrable hit "We Close Our Eyes" should be flogged in the streets.

Complaints aside, *Demons* remains a very entertaining film. The film's kinetic energy is enough to sweep aside the inevitable niggles about continuity, plot and characterization (or the lack thereof). Combined with a large dose of grotesque yet tongue-in-cheek gore, we have what is probably the last great Italian splatter movie (not counting the sequel).

Demons 2 (1986)
Aka: Dèmoni 2, Dèmoni 2…L'incubo ritorna,
Demons 2…The Nightmare Returns

Director: Lamberto Bava; Story/Screenplay: Dario Argento, Lamberto Bava, Franco Ferrini, Dardano Sacchetti; Producer: Dario Argento; Special Effects/Makeup: Sergio Stivaletti, Rosario Prestopino; Music: Simon Boswell
Starring: David Knight (George), Nancy Brilli (Hannah), Coralina Cataldi Tassoni (Sally), Bobby Rhodes (Hank), Asia Argento (Ingrid), Virginia Bryant (Christine)

A demon bursts through the television screen and bites a young woman. She transforms into a demon and attacks her friends. Soon the whole apart-

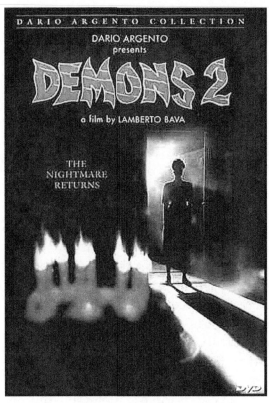

DARIO ARGENTO COLLECTION

DARIO ARGENTO
presents

DEMONS 2

a film by LAMBERTO BAVA

THE
NIGHTMARE
RETURNS

ment building is overrun by demons and the few survivors must find a way out.

Given the commercial success of *Demons* (1985), it's unsurprising that a sequel followed quickly. More surprising is just how good *Demons 2* is; in fact, it's arguably better that the first film. Many similarities exist. Once again we have a disparate group of characters (not quite as bizarre as the earlier group, though) trapped in a single location, this time a hi-tech high-rise apartment block, and the demons emerge through another visual medium—television. Some of the same actors appear in both films, most notably Bobby Rhodes, playing a bodybuilder this time. Lesser actors such as Lino Salemme and Eliana Hoppe are also carried over to the sequel. We even have another Argento daughter; this time it's Asia, making her feature film debut. Lamberto Bava makes his traditional cameo appearance, this time as Ingrid's father.

Rather than banding together to fight the oncoming threat, the building's occupants are all trapped in separate locations doing the best they can. Bobby Rhodes and his bodybuilder friends try to fortify the basement garage and present a unified defense, but the real hero of the film is George, a handsome physics student trying to get home to his pregnant wife Hannah. She's been trapped in her apartment since the power failure. George and Hannah are the only characters that manage to fend off the demons and stay alive. She has to cope with a newborn child-demon—a nice nod to traditional horror film fears à la *Rosemary's Baby*—while George gets to kick a recently demonized prostitute in the head repeatedly while trying to climb up an elevator cable. These are two standout scenes, but many great moments occur throughout.

The music is considerably better the second time around. Simon Boswell's score mimics Claudio Simonetti's work from the first film, but here they turned to mid-1980s Goth music for the hits. We have Peter Murphy, Love and Rockets, the Cult, the Smiths and Fields of the Nephilim—a veritable who's who of bleak British music. One excellent scene has the demons sprawling down a dimly lit corridor in slow motion with the ambient strains of Dead Can Dance playing in the background.

All of the familiar elements are included here: the hyperkinetic pace, the gross-but-funny gore moments, the absence of subtext and the blatant references to other films (here we're given the usual steals from George Romero with aspects of David Cronenberg's *Shivers* thrown in). But the package as a whole is better presented, with noticeably higher production values. The plotting and editing is sharper, and some of the rough edges, particularly concerning the special effects, have been smoothed out. Viewers who enjoyed the first film will find plenty to appreciate here, and maybe *Demons 2* will impress some of those who didn't fall for the charms of the original.

The Devil's Veil (1989)
Aka: La maschera del demonio, Demons 5

Director: Lamberto Bava; Story: Massimo De Rita, Giorgio Stegani, Lamberto Bava; Screenplay: Massimo De Rita, Giorgio Stegani; Producer: Lamberto Bava, Andrea Piazzesi; Special Effects: Sergio Stivaletti; Makeup: Franco Casagni; Music: Simon Boswell
Starring: Giovanni Giodelli, Debora Kinski [Deborah Caprioglio], Stanko Molnar, Mary Sellers, Alessandra Bonarota, Laura Devoti,

Michele Soavi, Stefano Molinari, Ron Williams, Eva Grimaldi (Anibas)

A group of skiers plunge through a crevasse into a strange subterranean world, where they accidentally release the spirit of a long-dead witch.

Given that his career has been overshadowed by the achievements of his renowned father, it seems strange that Lamberto Bava should choose to remake one of Bava senior's most famous films. While he is most definitely a capable director, by the late 1980s the younger Bava was reduced to making television movies that occasionally made decent use of his abilities (i.e., *The Prince of Terror*, 1988). More often than not, these made-for-TV films are embarrassingly bad. Sadly, *The Devil's Veil* is closer to the second category.

In its favor, *The Devil's Veil* seems to have been shot on a reasonable budget, something that's reflected in the quality of the sets. The crypt and the underground locations are all excellent, although the crevasse in the opening sequence doesn't look real. Cinematographer Gianfranco Transunto comes up with some interesting camera angles and tracking shots, but the endless dry ice and beams of white light get boring after a while. The cast, most of whom have appeared in several other films, are better than average, but the script is pretty substandard and makes use of annoyingly obvious word-puzzles. The hero and heroine are dull virginal types that are nowhere near as interesting as their bitchy, demonically inclined friends. Sergio Stivaletti provides a few nice special effects, but there's nothing as exciting or gruesome as his more famous work. The scene in the shed features some great effects and makeup, and it's easily the most interesting moment in the film.

The Devil's Veil runs out of ideas after about 60 minutes, but it hangs around for another 30, recycling the same argument between two characters over and over again. It's so frustrating that even the most open-minded viewer will be tempted to switch the damn thing off. If Mario Bava was given the opportunity to see this film, I don't imagine he'd be very impressed.

Dial: Help (1988)
Aka: Minaccia d'amore, Ragno gelido

Director: Ruggero Deodato; Story: Franco Ferrini; Screenplay: Ruggero Deodato, Joseph Caravan, Mary Caravan; Producer: Galliano Jusi, Giovanni Bertolucci; Special Effects: Germano Natali; Makeup: Rosario Prestopino, Luigi Ciminelli; Music: Claudio Simonetti
Starring: Charlotte Lewis (Jenny Cooper), Marcello Modugno (Ricardo), Mattia Sbragia (Mole), Carola Stagnaro (Carmen), Victor Cavallo, Carlo Monni, William Berger (Professor Irving Klein)

A malicious spirit that inhabits telephones and phone cables torments a beautiful model.

This so-called erotic thriller is perhaps the strangest of Deodato's horror films. The plot defies easy classification and will probably leave most viewers mystified or infuriated. Sadly the film's 1980s rock video sheen probably seemed like a great idea at the time, but, more than 15 years later it looks like a serious misstep.

Characteristic of this MTV-inspired approach is the casting of Charlotte Lewis, the English schoolgirl who managed to attract media attention (and a movie career) thanks to  her catwalk figure and photogenic facial features. She's a competent actress, but it's hard to imagine anyone comfortably portraying a young woman being menaced by a psychotic telephone. Like so many aspects of the film, she's there to provide surface appeal. The rest of the cast are largely undistinguished, with only veteran William Berger standing out from the crowd.

Absurd plot and music video approach aside, *Dial: Help* is still an entertaining movie. The movie is well directed and edited, moving along at a decent pace, and a decent Claudio Simonetti score backs it up quite nicely. Deodato is talented enough to keep things interesting, but the conclusion is confusing and silly. Anyone looking for the kind of gore that characterized his other films will be very disappointed, but the open-minded viewer should enjoy the film.

Bizarrely, Franco Ferrini originally wrote the story for Dario Argento, but Argento chose to make *Phenomena* (1985) instead. *Dial: Help* continues the theme of communications-media-as-dangers-to-mankind that Ferrini touched upon in the two *Demons* movies.

Dinner with a Vampire (1988)
Aka: A cena col vampiro

Director: Lamberto Bava; Story: Luciano Martino; Screenplay: Dardano Sacchetti, Lamberto Bava; Special Effects: Sergio Stivaletti, Paolo Ricci; Makeup: Rosario Prestopino; Music: Simon Boswell, Mario Tagliaferri
Starring: George Hilton, Patrizia Pellegrino, Riccardo Rossi, Valeria Milillo, Yvonne Sciò, Daniele Aldrovandi, Igor Zalewski, Roberto Pedicini, Letizia Ziaco, Stefano Sabelli, Isabel Russinova

A mysterious middle-aged man hires a group of young people and takes them to his sprawling mansion, where they quickly find themselves unable to leave.

Here's another dismal half-hearted television movie from the man once renowned for the brutality of his films. This time we have a group of young actors, singers and dancers hired by Yurik the vampire to see if they can find a way to kill him. He's bored with immortality, and the myths about crosses and garlic don't work. A potentially interesting idea is undermined by sloppy plotting (Why is he hiring actors? What was that rubbish about their "innocence"?) and atrocious dubbing that transforms every sentence into a dramatic exclamation. The cast isn't bad, except for the overacting vampires, but the actors are hardly working with decent material. Worst of all is the third-rate impersonation of Marty

Feldman's performance from *Young Frankenstein* (1974). Simon Boswell recycles the same song that he used in *Graveyard Disturbance* (1987) *The Church* (1988), *Lord of Illusions* (1995) and several other films. On the plus side the locations and sets are well decorated and sumptuous, but it's not enough to redeem this lazy piece of rubbish. George Hilton, star of *The Case of the Bloody Iris* (1971) and *My Dear Killer* (1972), is capable of much, much better.

The Door to Silence (1991)
Aka: Le porte del silenzio

Director: H. Simon Kittay [Lucio Fulci]; Story/Screenplay: Jerry Madison [Lucio Fulci]; Producer: John Gelardi [Aristide Massacessi]; Special Effects: Ross J. La Manta; Makeup: Pietro Tenoglio; Music: Franco Piana
Starring: John Savage (Melvin Devereux), Sandi Schulz (mystery woman), Richard Castleman (hearse driver), Jennifer Loeb (Margie), Elizabeth Chugden (Sylvia Devereux), Joe "Cool" Davis (minister), Bob Shreves (judge), Mary Coulson (Aunt Martha), Fred Lewis (bartender), Maureen Rocquin (juke box girl), Duncan Boyer (Cajun hunter)

While driving home from his father's funeral, a businessman finds himself drawn into a series of encounters with a mysterious hearse.

It's a shame that Lucio Fulci's last film should invite comparisons with the 1980s version of *The Twilight Zone*, but in all seriousness *The Door to Silence* feels like clichéd television material. The storyline, cribbed from Ambrose Bierce and *Carnival of Souls* (1962), will be familiar to most viewers and holds no surprises. It's unfortunate that the film gives away its secrets well before the end and yet expects the viewer to sit through further exposition scenes. Presumably this was Fulci's attempt at building the story slowly and moving inexorably toward an eye-opening climax that never arrives.

John Savage gives a credible performance as the man haunted (ho, ho) by a series of bizarre occurrences, but the rest of the cast come and go without making any real impact. With a secondhand story, a lack of any real tension or suspense, a wooden cast and Aristide Massacessi's usual production standards, *The Door to Silence* is an unremarkable end to a varied and interesting career.

Eaten Alive! (1980)
Aka: Mangiati vivi!, Doomed to Die,
Eaten Alive by the Cannibals, The Emerald Jungle

Director: Umberto Lenzi; Story / Screenplay: Umberto Lenzi; Producer: Luciano Martino, Mino Loy; Special Effects: Paolo Ricci; Makeup: Raul Raneri; Music: Budy Maglione [Maria Fiamma Maglione]
Starring: Robert Kerman (Mark Butler), Janet Agren (Sheila Morris), Ivan Rassimov (Reverend Jonas Melvyn), Paola Senatore (Diana Morris), Me Me Lai (Mowara), Mag Fleming [Maria Fiamma Maglione] (Alma), Franco Fantasia (Brother Reeves), Gianfranco Codati, Alfred Joseph Berry, Michele Schmiegelia, Mel Ferrer (Professor Carter)

A woman heads into the jungle to find her sister, believing a charismatic cult leader kidnapped her. Together the two must escape from the cult and avoid the cannibals who lurk outside the camp.

Eaten Alive! is the second of Lenzi's cannibal-themed efforts, and probably the least interesting. *Man From Deep River* (1972) has some historical significance—it's the first Italian cannibal movie—while *Cannibal ferox* (1981) is possibly the most bloodthirsty of the lot. Sadly *Eaten Alive!* offers only hilariously bad acting and a Jim Jones-based plotline to recommend it.

The cast includes Italian exploitation favorites, such as hardcore porn star Robert Kerman from *Cannibal Holocaust* (1979), cannibal film regulars Ivan Rassimov and Me Me Lai, as well as Mel Ferrer and Janet Agren. Unfortunately Lenzi appears unsure how to get the most from his cast. Rassimov sleepwalks through his role as Jonas Melvyn, the psychotic cult leader, while Me Me Lai's death scene from Deodato's *Last Cannibal World* (1977) is recycled here. Janet Agren is saddled with an awful mock-Southern accent that makes the poor dialogue sound even worse. Only Robert Kerman turns in a half-decent performance, probably because he knows that this isn't Shakespeare and decides to have fun with the role instead. Typically for an Italian cannibal movie, *Eaten Alive!* makes use of some documentary and mondo footage, pre-

sumably to save on the expense of filming in the jungle. The film isn't edited particularly well and such reused footage stands out quite prominently. A fair amount of animal abuse occurs. Unlike *Cannibal Holocaust,* no attempt is made to justify this carnage with some spurious sociological explanation, which makes the film's intent less patronizing and hypocritical, but it's no less disgusting.

Eaten Alive! is a largely unspectacular slice of cannibal mayhem. It's not the goriest of its kind, nor is it the most well produced. The film functions fairly well as a clichéd action-adventure, but the general brutality and violence work against it. With *Nightmare City* (1981) Lenzi showed himself capable of directing enjoyable action movies, but this doesn't stand as one of his worthwhile films.

The Erotic Nights of the Living Dead (1980)
Aka: Le notte erotiche dei morti viventi, The Island of the Dead,
Night of the Zombies, Sexy Nights of the Dead,
Sexy Nights of the Living Dead

Director: Joe D'Amato [Aristide Massacessi]; Story/Screenplay: Tom Salina [Aristide Massacessi]; Producer: Oscar Santaniello, Massimo Alberini; Makeup: Massimo Camilletti, Maria Grazia Mazzolini; Music: Pluto Kennedy [Marcello Giombini]
Starring: Laura Gemser (Luna), George Eastman [Luigi Montefiore] (Larry O'Hara), Dirce Funari [Patrizia Funari] (Fiona), Mark Shannon [Manlio Cersosimo]

A disparate group of travelers find themselves on a Caribbean island populated by an old man, his mysterious daughter and a growing number of zombies.

If that title doesn't send a shiver up your spine, you're not human! Seriously, though, *The Erotic Nights of the Living Dead* does have a few points of interest. It boasts great Caribbean locations (authentic-looking ones, unlike the Italian setting that doubles for the Caribbean in

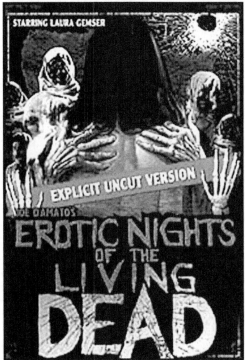

Zombie Holocaust, 1980) that usually provide a nice backdrop to whatever's going on. The final third is effectively paced, as the zombies move in on their victims in search of bloody meat, and the flesh-ripping special effects are pretty entertaining.

On the negative side, *Erotic Nights* suffers from the poor pacing that affects most erotic thrillers. Extended soft-core sex scenes may be interesting if that is what audiences are watching for, but that means that the plot grinds to a halt while the protagonists writhe around for a while. *Erotic Nights* isn't exactly blessed with an exciting plot in the first place, so these scenes are likely to cause most viewers to reach for the fast-forward button. The film heats up when the zombies arrive, but unfortunately they're not great examples of Italian undead. Most of this has to do with the makeup. Obviously modeled on Giannetto De Rossi's work in *Zombie* (1979), the zombie makeup consists of smeared brown faces and the odd maggot here and there.

As a film, *Erotic Nights* is certainly no worse than Massacessi's other horror efforts, *Anthropophagous* (1980) and *Absurd* (1981), so if viewers found those films entertaining *Erotic Nights* might be worth tracking down. The film is an interesting side note in the history of the Italian zombie movie, but it's not really worth a second viewing.

Evil Clutch (1988)
Aka: Il bosco, Presa tenace

Director: Andreas Marfori; Story / Screenplay: Andreas Marfori; Producer: Agnese Fontana; Special Effects: (mechanical) Gianni Albertini; Special Effects / Makeup: Bruno Biagi, Donatella Mondani, Elisa Calcinari, Paolo Forti; Music: Adriano Maria Vitale
Starring: Coralina Cataldi Tassoni (Cindy), Diego Ribon (Tony), Luciano Crovato (Algernon), Elena Cantarone (Arva), Stefano Molinari (Fango)

A vacationing couple find themselves menaced by demons and zombie-like creatures in a strange forest.

Her kiss may be heaven, but her touch is hell.

UNCUT
UNEDITED

Evil Clutch is generally regarded as one of the worst Italian horror films ever made. While this might not be *strictly* true—worse offerings than this exist—the film is certainly very close to the bottom of the pile. Films like this are made when people sit down and devise a series of excellent splatter scenes but forget to work on a story. The result is a collection of energetic, over-the-top special effects tacked on to a non-existent storyline, and such special effects sequences alone must carry the movie. Andreas Marfori lacks the visual inventiveness of Argento or Fulci to make a bare bones scripted movie interesting.

The plot is pretty derivative, so many references to more famous horror films, especially *The Evil Dead* (1981) and Lamberto Bava's *Demons* (1986), occur. Most infuriating is the repeated use of Sam Raimi's trademark knee-level tracking shots. The amateurish special effects, characterized by poorly built prosthetics, are clearly inspired by Sergio Stivaletti's work. The pinnacle of the special effects work is a many-tentacled creature that's just about good enough to compete with any rubber monster from the 1950s.

Screeching her way through the awful script is Coralina Cataldi Tassoni, best known as the foul-tempered Sally from *Demons 2* (1986). Tassoni has since stated that appearing in *Evil Clutch* was a terrible mistake, and it's hard to disagree. Toward the end of the film she spends about seven minutes doing nothing except running along crying her eyes out. It's not hard to see why.

Eyewitness (1990)
Aka: Testimone oculare

Director: Lamberto Bava; Story: Massimo De Rita, Giorgio Stegani, Lamberto Bava; Screenplay: Massimo De Rita, Giorgio Stegano; Producer: Lamberto Bava, Andrea Piazzesi; Makeup: Franco Casagni; Music: Simon Boswell
Starring: Barbara Cupisti, Stefano Davanzati, Alessio Orano, Giuseppe Pianviti, Mary Sellers, Loredano Romito, Francesco Casale, Antonella Angelucci, Santi Bellina, Gianfilippo Conte

Barbara Cupisti stars in *Eyewitness.*

A blind woman is the main witness to a brutal murder.

[Notes: Made for television. Part of the *"Alta tensione"* series. Synopsis taken from Internet sources.]

Fear (1980)
Aka: L'ossessione che uccide, Murder Obsession, Satan's Altar, The Wailing

Director: Robert Hampton [Riccardo Freda]; Story: Antonio Cesare Corti, Fabio Piccioni; Screenplay: Antonio Cesare Corti, Fabio Piccioni, Riccardo Freda; Producer: Enzo Boetani, John Collur [Giuseppe Collura], Simon Mizrahi; Makeup: Lamberto Marini, Sergio Angeloni; Music: Franco Mannino
Starring: Stefano Patrizi (Michael), Martine Brochard (Shirley), Henri Garcin (Hans), Laura Gemser (Beryl), John Richardson (Oliver), Anita Strindberg (Glenda), Silvia Dionisio (Deborah)

Michael, an actor, returns to his family home, followed soon after by some friends from his current film project. A mysterious assailant slays them one by one while Michael's mother and her sinister manservant begin to act very strangely indeed.

Throughout the 1960s Riccardo Freda was one of Italy's premier horror directors. He gave Mario Bava his first breaks in the business and is widely credited with kick-starting the Italian horror boom of the late 1950s. His fortunes faded in the decade following, however,

leading him to direct *Fear*, a miserable attempt to cash in on the recent rebirth of interest in Italian horror. Unfortunately, nothing here could possibly hope to emulate the success of energetic and vital works like *Zombie* (1979) or *Inferno* (1980).

The cast features familiar exploitation faces, including competent players like John Richardson and Anita Strindberg. Sadly, someone decided that Laura Gemser should be cast, presumably to interest the *Black Emanuelle* crowd. She's a terrible actress, but it's obvious from the first 60 seconds (she's naked in her first onscreen appearance) that's she's not there for her acting ability. Any possibility of a decent result is cut short by the script. The two main scriptwriters were (separately) responsible for *Nightmare City* (1980) and *Queen Kong* (1976), hardly the greatest recommendation in the world. On top of all this the film features Franco Mannino's absurd score clattering and banging around like a cartoon soundtrack.

The decent locations and Freda's admirable eye for the atmospheric might have been enough to save *Fear* from ignominy, but just too much is wrong with the film. Needless to say, it did nothing to resurrect the aging director's career, and *Fear* remains his last completed project. Only Freda completists or Gemser fans should bother tracking this down, and even they should be ready for disappointment.

Formula for a Murder (1985)
Aka: Formula per un assassino, 7 Hyden Park: La casa maledetta

Director: Martin Herbert [Alberto De Martino]; Story/Screenplay: Martin Herbert [Alberto De Martino], Frank Walker [Vincenzo Man-

CHRISTINA NAGY   DAVID WARBECK
CARROLL BLUMENBERG

ROSSANO BRAZZI

ESTATEGIA
PARA UN DELITO

dir
MARTIN HERBERT

nino]; Producer: David Colby [Fabrizio De Angelis]; Makeup: Harris
Girol; Music: Francesco De Masi
Starring: Christina Nagy (Joanna), David Warbeck (Craig), Carroll
Blumenberg (Ruth), Rossano Brazi (Dr. Sernich), Andrea Bosic (Father
Peter), Loris Loddi (Father Davis)

*A disabled heiress begins to suspect that her considerate companion is
trying to get his hands on her personal fortune.*

Alberto De Martino showed himself to be a reasonable exploitation
director in the 1960s and 1970s, but his career took a sharp dive in the
next decade. This derivative *giallo* isn't as bad as rubbish like *Puma
Man* (1980) or *Miami Golem* (1985), but it's still pretty poor.

The film features a standard inheritance plot, something that can
work reasonably well in the hands of a talented director. Unfortunately
it's also saddled with a number of incredible plot developments, including the possibility that the heiress might have a fatal heart attack
the next time she has sex. On top of that we have a limp and ambiguous
ending, making *Formula for a Murder* a very irritating film. On the plus
side, Warbeck delivers a strong performance, but it's not enough to
hide the basic script problems. He does a passable Jack Nicholson-style
psycho impression toward the end, but he's mostly wasted here. For
some reason, Francesco De Masi's score recycles sections of his work

on *The New York Ripper* (1982), probably at the instigation of Fabrizio De Angelis, who produced both films.

If one has to see any of Alberto De Martino's later films, go for *Blood Link* (1982), a taut and powerful thriller. *Formula for a Murder* will interest only David Warbeck fans or hardcore *gialli* completists.

Ghosthouse (1987)
Aka: La casa 3

Director: Humphrey Humbert [Umberto Lenzi]; Story: Humphrey Humbert [Umberto Lenzi]; Screenplay: "Cinthia Mc.Gavin" [sic]; Special Effects: Dan Maklansky, Robert Gould, Roland Park; Makeup: Peter Moor [Pietro Tenoglio]; Music: Piero Montanari
Starring: Lara Wendel (Martha), Greg Scott (Paul), Mary Sellers (Susan), Ron Houck (Mark), Martin Jay (Jim), Kate Silver (Tina), Donald O'Brian [Donald O'Brien] (Valkos), Kriten Fougerousse (Henrietta), Willy M. Moon (Pepe), Susan Muller (Henrietta's mother), Alain Smith (Sam Baker), William J. Devany (Lieutenant), Ralph Morse (coroner), Robert Champagne (mortician), "Hernest Mc. Kimnoro"[sic] (cemetery custodian)

A ham radio operator and his girlfriend pick up a series of mysterious broadcasts and track them to an old abandoned house. Meeting up with a group of teenagers, they begin to explore, only to find that the house holds some deadly secrets.

Yet another *Amityville Horror* rip off, this time created by the ever-prolific Umberto Lenzi. It's actually not a bad effort, as far as low-budget, late-1980s Italian horror films go. Meant to appeal to an American audience, many characteristically Italian aspects are eliminated. The cast consists mostly of annoying young Americans who are always arguing and are several brain cells short of a full set. They wander off on their own, despite all the strange events going on around them, and it's no real surprise when they get killed. We have the traditional haunted house phenomena: ghostly, groaning voices, poltergeist activity and visions of a ghostly young girl. A vicious looking clown puppet seems to be behind the killings as well, probably a reference to *Magic* (1978) and Stephen King's *It*.

In terms of plot, *Ghosthouse* has no new tricks up its sleeve, although Lenzi does try to spice it up a little by including a local psycho and some strange accounts of grave robbing. Sadly, all of this is ignored in favor of a basic vengeful ghost story. The film's climax is pretty weak and rips off Argento's *Inferno* (1980), which didn't have a great ending in the first place. When such an ending is done with cheap camera trickery, it looks even worse. On the whole *Ghosthouse* is an entertaining piece of trash, and it offers good evidence that Lenzi isn't the talent-free hack some critics dismiss him as. *Ghosthouse* is certainly better than the later *Amityville Horror* sequels.

The film does, however, boast some of the sloppiest credits I've ever seen. The little girl is referred to three times as Henriett, rather than Henrietta. A period is inserted into the middle of names beginning with "Mc," as in "Mc. Gavin." The police lieutenant is listed only as "Lieu Tenent" and I'm not sure what to make of "Hernest Mc. Kimnoro." In case you're wondering what happened to the first two *La casa* films, that's the title of Sam Raimi's first two *Evil Dead* films in Italy.

The Ghosts of Sodom (1988)
Aka: I fantasmi di Sodoma, Sodoma's Ghost

Director: Lucio Fulci; Story: Lucio Fulci; Screenplay: Lucio Fulci, Carlo Alberto Alfieri; Producer: Luigi Nannerini, Antonio Lucidi; Music: Carlo Maria Cordio
Starring: Claus Aliot (Mark), Mary Salier (Celine), Robert Egon (Willy), Jessica Moore [Luciana Ottaviani], Alan Johnson (Paul) [uncredited], Sebastian Harrison (John) [uncredited], Teresa Razzauti (Anne) [uncredited], Pier Luigi Conti [uncredited]

The ghosts of long-dead Nazis torment a group of teenagers.

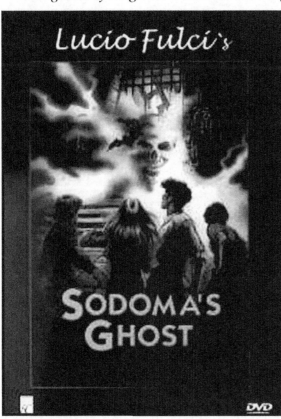

With *The Ghosts of Sodom*, Fulci jumps on the Nazi sex film bandwagon only a decade after it rumbled past. The Nazi theme, merged with the standard 1980s horror film device of teenagers staying in a deserted old house, concludes with the widely acknowledged Worst Ending Ever, making the film one of Fulci's least inspired films.

This barely scripted mess doesn't even contain the seeds of a decent movie. The central idea—sadistic and sex-crazed Nazi ghosts return to haunt the scene of their demise—is poorly expressed and pretty tame; all these terrible Nazis can manage is Russian roulette and a few illusions. The real tortures and psychopathic urges of the Third Reich are barely touched upon. The absurd ending ultimately negates any threat the ghosts might represent.

More depressing than terrifying, *The Ghosts of Sodom* is Fulci at his most disinterested. There's little evidence of any direction, and the script is half-hearted and lazy. It's hardly surprising then that the cast was less than committed. All in all, a drab pointless film.

Giallo a Venezia (1979)
Aka: Gore in Venice, Thrilling in Venice, Mystery in Venice

Director: Mario Landi; Story/Screenplay: Aldo Serio; Producer: Gabriele Crisanti; Music: Berto Pisano
Starring: Leonora Fani [Eleonora Cristofani] (Flavia), Jeff Blynn (Inspector DePaul), Gianni Dei (Fabio), Michele Renzullo, Eolo Capritti, Vassili Karamesinis (Bruno), Giancarlo Del Duca, Maria Angela Giordano (Marzia), Maria Mancini

A double murder marks the start of a wave of brutal killings. The Venetian police begin trawling through the sordid personal lives of the victims in an effort to identify the killer.

This unsavory film has the distinction of being one of the most notorious *gialli* ever made. Thanks to the relative difficulty of acquiring an English-language copy, it's become something of a holy grail to Eurotrash completists. But should fans try to track down this grim piece of trash? In a word (or three), good God, no!

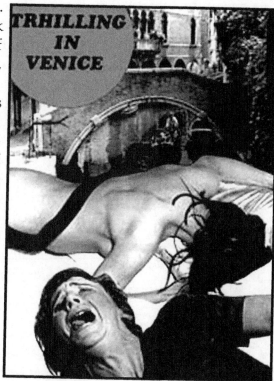

Giallo a Venezia brings new meaning to the word *sleazy*. Much of the film features soft-core scenes of a man subjecting his young wife to a seemingly endless parade of sexual indignities, both with himself and anyone else who happens to be around. Graphic violence usually punctuates these lengthy sex scenes. Certainly the film deserves its reputation as far as blood and gore goes. It is *very*

graphic, culminating in Maria Angela Giordano's leg being messily hacked off. However, the film does lack the sense of style that elevates the better *gialli* above the ordinary. The only indication of any directorial ability is the shot where Giordano's body is reflected in the killer's mirror shades. Beyond that, it's all master shots with the occasional brief tracking shot and shaky close-ups. Berto Pisano's annoying jazz score is actually pretty appropriate for the sex scenes, but elsewhere it's horrendously out of place.

The sex and violence are clearly the film's main selling points, but *Giallo a Venezia* has very little besides to recommend it. Non-existent direction, an atrocious script—from the man who wrote Antonio Bido's respectable *Watch Me When I Kill* (1977)—and a detective that couldn't deduce his way out of a paper sack (and constantly eats eggs, probably an effort to give the character a Kojak-style mannerism) easily make this one of the worst Italian horror films from the period.

Graveyard Disturbance (1986)
Aka: Una notte nel cimitero

Director: Lamberto Bava; Story: Dardano Sacchetti; Screenplay: Dardano Sacchetti, Lamberto Bava; Special Effects: Angelo Mattei; Makeup:

Fabrizio Sforza; Music: Simon Boswell Starring: Gregory Lech Thaddeus (Robin), Lea Martino (Tina), Beatrice Ring (Micky), Gianmarco Tognazzi (Johnny), Karl Zinny (David)

A group of friends find themselves in a mysterious tavern, where they accept a bet: Spend a night in the catacombs and win a mound of treasure. Once they're in the catacombs, however, they soon discover they aren't alone.

Graveyard Disturbance is the first film in the *Brivido Giallo* series, a collection of four movies that Lamberto Bava directed for Reteitalia, an Italian television company. It marked the start of Bava's television career, which would become his focus in later years. After *Graveyard Disturbance*, Bava would direct only two more theatrical features.

Like most made-for-television horror films, it's cheap, childish and devoid of controversial content (nudity, gore, etc.). None of the characters are hurt during their adventure, and even the final conflict—with Death itself (!)—is bloodless and sanitized. The special effects are generally terrible, with an odd over-reliance on flashing red eyes. Fabrizio Sforza produces a passable *Demons* imitation for the maggot-ridden corpses, but then provides the Grim Reaper with a store-bought plastic mask. Needless to say, such sequences are very non-threatening. Sforza went on to work on *Hannibal* (2001), probably not on the strength of his work here.

Bava and Sacchetti turn in an awful script, heavy on cliché, one sadly lacking in any characterization or tension. Clearly modeled on similar American efforts, the movie tries to include ironic references to other horror films, but the filmmakers would have done better to use one or two original ideas. As it is, *Graveyard Disturbance* is not only Lamberto Bava's worst film; it's one of the least-inspired Italian horror efforts of the 1980s. Trivia note: Bava and his son Fabrizio appear as shopkeepers.

The Great Alligator (1979)
Aka: Il fiume del grande caimano, Alligator,
The Great Alligator River

Director: Sergio Martino; Story: Cesare Frugoni, Sergio Martino, Ernesto Gastaldi; Screenplay: Ernesto Gastaldi, Luigi Montefiore, Maria Chianetta, Sergio Martino; Producer: Luciano Martino; Special Effects: Paolo Ricci; Makeup: Stefano Trani; Music: Stelvio Cipriani
Starring: Barbara Bach (Alli Brandt), Claudio Cassinelli (Daniel), Mel Ferrer (Mr. Joshua), Romano Puppo (Peter), Fabrizia Castagnoli (Minou), Enzo Fisichella, Lory Del Santo, Anny Papa, Bobby Rhodes,

Clara Colosimo, Peter Boom, Giulia D'angelo, Marco Mastantuono, Piero Jossa, Marco Giannoni, Geneve Hutton (Sheena), Silvia Collatina, Richard Johnson (Father Jonathan)

An unscrupulous businessman builds a holiday resort on an African river. Before long a giant alligator, considered to be a god by the natives, begins devouring the locals, most of whom work in the resort. While the owner tries to keep the whole affair quiet, a journalist and an anthropologist try to convince authorities of the danger.

Japanese poster for *The Great Alligator*

Despite the difference in animal, *The Great Alligator* is Sergio Martino's contribution to the spate of European *Jaws*-inspired movies that emerged in the late 1970s and early 1980s. Many of the cast and crew, including stars Barbara Bach and Claudio Cassinelli, appeared in his earlier film *The Island of the Fishmen* (1979). Coincidentally, Mel Ferrer appeared in the extra footage shot for *Screamers*, the U.S. release of *The Island of the Fishmen*.

The similarities to Steven Spielberg's film are readily evident. An unscrupulous businessman (Mel Ferrer, for once given some decent screen time) builds a resort on an African river. Before long a giant alligator appears and begins devouring the locals, most of whom seem to work at the resort. Unsurprisingly only plucky journalist Cassinelli and sexy anthropologist Bach realize the danger, while Ferrer wants to keep the problem quiet so it doesn't affect his business. The first half of the movie is interesting but painfully slow, especially since the viewer will almost certainly know what's coming next. Thankfully, the film's final acts are well paced and exciting. The natives are characteristically one-dimensional, as they are in most Italian jungle adventures, acting primitive and superstitious. The cast is better than average, although it's a shame Richard Johnson (*Zombie*, 1979) wasn't given a bigger role; he's wasted as an eccentric hermit. Stelvio Cipriani's excellent score, which ranks as one of his best, certainly helps the film.

The alligator itself is well executed, and Martino is a skilled enough director to keep the model obscured by murky water and dazzling sunshine until the film's climax. It's not as effective as Spielberg's monster, but it is considerably better than the creature from Lamberto Bava's *Monster Shark* (1984). There's enough here to lift *The Giant Alligator* above most exploitation efforts of the period, and it still stands up well today. Watch this before any of the other Italian *Jaws* rip-offs.

Hansel e Gretel (1989)
Aka: Non si serviziana e bambini

Director: Giovanni Simonelli; Story/Screenplay: Giovanni Simonelli; Producer: Antonio Lucidi, Luigi Nannerini; Makeup: Giuseppe Ferranti; Music: Lanfranco Perini Starring: Elisabete Pimente Boaretto, Lucia Prato, Ronald Russo, Giorgio Cerioni, Mario Sandro De Luca, Renzo Robertazzi, Silvia Cipollone, Massimiliano Cipollone, Paul Muller, Maurice Poli

The director of a hospital resorts to drastic measures to secure fresh organs.

[Notes: Part of the *"Lucio Fulci presents..."* collection. Clips from this film were used in Lucio Fulci's *Nightmare Concert* (1990). Synopsis taken from *Spaghetti Nightmares* (see bibliography).]

Hell of the Living Dead (1981)
Aka: Inferno dei morti viventi, Hell of the Living Death,
Night of the Zombies, Virus, Zombie Creeping Flesh

Director: Vincent Dawn [Bruno Mattei]; Story/Screenplay: Claudio Fragasso, J.M. Cunilles; Makeup: Giuseppe Ferranti; Music: Goblin
Starring: Margit Evelyn Newton [Margit Gansbacher] (Lia Rousseaux), Frank Garfield [Franco Garofalo] (Santoro), Selan Karay [Selamattin Karadag] (Vincent), Robert O'Neil [José Gras] (Lt. Mike London), Gaby Renom (Peter), Luis Fonoll (Osbourne)

An accident at a chemical plant in Papua, New Guinea, releases toxins into the environment and starts to bring the dead back to life. A commando team is sent in to deal with the problem, but they quickly find themselves fighting for their lives.

This absurd Spanish-Italian co-production is one of the worst zombie movies ever made. It's been called the worst horror movie ever made *period*. Based around a ludicrous plot about Third World revolt, the only vaguely interesting feature of the film is the concept of jungle-based zombies—but even that has already been seen in Marino Girolami's *Zombie Holocaust* (1980), a movie that looks like a work of art compared to *Hell of the Living Dead*.

Given the low budget, it's not surprising that Mattei utilized a fair amount of material from other places. Extensive nature footage is mixed in, along with several scenes culled from mondo films. None of this material is edited particularly well, and several different ethnic groups (from at least two different continents) are depicted. The worst instances see Margit Newton walking up a forest path. She looks to her left (cue nature footage) and then to her right (cue even more footage), with none of it visible when the camera returns to Ms. Newton. Not even the score is original; it's spliced together from sections of Goblin's work on *Dawn of the Dead* (1978), Aristide Massacessi's *Beyond the Darkness* (1979) and Luigi Cozzi's *Contamination* (1980). Writer and assistant director Claudio Fragasso claims to have directed a chunk of the original footage, so it's hardly surprising the end result is one jumbled mess. Despite Giuseppe Ferranti's general abilities, the special effects are abysmal. The zombies are mostly African types, and it's obvious the producer couldn't afford to give them all makeup, as a number of unadorned faces run past the camera.

Basically, there's no reason to watch *Hell of the Living Dead* unless audiences are looking for mistakes and a good beer-drinkin' movie. Even then, I can think of a few films that would be more entertaining.

Hell's Gates (1990)
Aka: Le porte dell'inferno

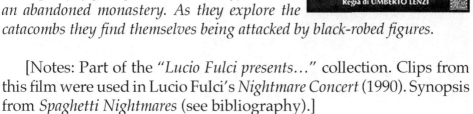

Director: Umberto Lenzi; Story/Screenplay: Umberto Lenzi, Olga Pehar; Producer: Luigi Nannerini, Antonio Lucidi; Special Effects: Antonio Corridori; Makeup: Gabrielle Trani; Music: Piero Montanari
Starring: Giacomo Rossi Stuart. Barbara Cupisti, Peter Genuardi, Lorenzo Majnoni, Paul Muller, Gaetano Russo, Andrea Damiano, Mario Luzzi

A group of geologists discover a crypt beneath an abandoned monastery. As they explore the catacombs they find themselves being attacked by black-robed figures.

[Notes: Part of the *"Lucio Fulci presents…"* collection. Clips from this film were used in Lucio Fulci's *Nightmare Concert* (1990). Synopsis from *Spaghetti Nightmares* (see bibliography).]

Hitcher in the Dark (1989)
Aka: Paura nel buio

Director: Humphrey Humbert [Umberto Lenzi]; Story: Humphrey Humbert [Umberto Lenzi]; Screenplay: Olga Pehar; Producer: Aristide Massacessi [uncredited]; Music: Carlo Maria Cordio
Starring: Josie Bissett (Daniela), Joe Balogh (Mark), Jason Saucier (Kevin), Robin Fox (Mark's father), Thomas Mitchell (Big Man Store

[sic]), Fay W. Edwards (secretary), Tom Schulteis (policeman), Mel Davis (man), Sandra Parker (Toyota's woman), Gary Wade Morton (2nd policeman), Dan Smith (Pontiac man), Michael Lewis (TV reporter)

A young girl finds herself being stalked by a mother-fixated psychopath in a Winnebago.

Thanks to the casting of Josie Bissett, later a star of TV soap *Melrose Place,* this sleazy slice of pure exploitation received an extended shelf

life. Prior to moving into the mainstream, she did a couple of low-budget Italian movies, *Hitcher in the Dark* and *Desire*, a cheap erotic thriller directed by Bruno Mattei.

Although the film's often described as a *giallo*, *Hitcher in the Dark* is closer to the American psycho killer flicks from the 1970s and 1980s. Joe Balogh (also in Lenzi's *Black Demons*, 1991) stars as a handsome young man who travels the countryside, taking attractive young women back to his camper van, where he kills them. Prior to slaughtering them, he tries to get them to dress up as his mother. References to *Psycho* (1960) abound, not surprisingly. Lenzi tries to create a psychological thriller based around the battle of wills between Joe Balogh and his main victim, in much the same vein as Terence Stamp and Sammatha Eggar in *The Collector* (1965), but he fails miserably. The killer has very little in the way of depth or realism. Apparently, Lenzi's idea of psychological insight is to have a grown man giggle while watching children's cartoons.

Although the last half-hour has a decent pace and manages to be reasonably interesting, most of the film is hampered by Joe Balogh's wooden performance and Lenzi's simplistic direction. Against the director's wishes, an extra final scene was added, harming the film even further. *Hitcher in the Dark* wouldn't have been a masterpiece without that scene, but it would have been a little more palatable.

The House by the Cemetery (1981)
Aka: Quella villa accanto al cimitero

Director: Lucio Fulci; Story: Elisa Livia Briganti; Screenplay: Dardano Sacchetti, Giorgio Mariuzzo, Lucio Fulci; Producer: Fabrizio De Angelis; Special Effects/Makeup: Giannetto De Rossi, Maurizio Trani; Music: Walter Rizzati
Starring: Katherine MacColl [Catriona MacColl] (Lucy Boyle), Paolo Malco (Dr. Norman Boyle), Aria Pieroni (Anne, the babysitter), Giovanni Frezza (Bob Boyle), Silvia Collatina (Mae Freudstein), Dagmar Lassander (Laura Gittleson), Giovanni De Nava (Dr. Freudstein), Daniela Doria (1st female victim), Gianpaolo Saccarola (Daniel Douglas), Carlo De Mejo (Mr. Wheatley), John Olson, Elmer Johnson, Ranieri Ferrara, Teresa Rossi Pasante (Mary Freudstein)

A family moves into an old house, unaware of its gruesome past. Unfortunately, one of the former residents still lurks there, and he has some unpleasant plans for the Boyle family.

Although not greeted with the same rabid enthusiasm as *The Beyond* (1981), *The House by the Cemetery* is still one of Lucio Fulci's better efforts. Grounded in the same warped logic as its predecessor, it's not quite as gory, but there's still enough bloodshed to please the most jaded of splatterhounds. In keeping with the Lovecraftian influence

upon the director's work, this time the setting is New England.

Many Fulci trademarks are in place here. Once again we have new occupants moving into an isolated house. This time it's a couple—Paolo Malco and Catriona MacColl—with their young son, but as before the house is the scene of violent murders. The son, played by Giovanni Frezza, becomes involved with the ghostly apparition of a young girl, once again displaying the supernatural associations that Fulci often ascribes to small children. Some of the locals behave very strangely, particularly when they meet the Boyles. A wealth of premonitions, ghostly sightings, animals going crazy and portents of doom appear, all to be expected in one of Fulci's Gothic horror films. To round it all off, we have the lovely Daniela Doria once again meeting an unpleasant end, as she does in *City of the Living Dead* (1980), *The Black Cat* (1981) and *The New York Ripper* (1982).

Perhaps more so than *The Beyond*, *The House by the Cemetery* is a purely visual film. Although a plot appears, it's hampered by endless red herrings. Plenty of scenes add dramatic effect, but they don't gel with the storyline and are not resolved. For example, why does everyone in the town insist that Dr. Boyle has been there before? If the house has been empty for nearly a century, how did Dr. Freudstein get the required body parts to survive? Other parts of the film see characters acting completely at odds with typical human reactions. Lucy Boyle, for instance, doesn't question why her babysitter is mopping up blood from the kitchen floor, something that would surely have attracted her attention. Trying to balance all the red herrings and non-sequiturs is an infuriating and pointless task. Fulci has moved even further along the road toward image-based, structure-free films that work on a purely audio-visual level. The film's not a total success, since so many of the elements hint at a structure that isn't there. This unwise reliance upon red herrings and faux-plot devices is what stops the film from reaching the same heights as its predecessor. Nonetheless, *The House by the Cemetery* is one of Fulci's better films, a worthy companion piece to *Zombie* (1979), *The Beyond* and *City of the Living Dead*. It's a shame he chose not to explore the style any further, but these four films rank as his finest works. The director appears briefly as Dr. Boyle's New York publisher.

The House of Clocks (1989)
Aka: La casa del tempo

Director: Lucio Fulci; Story: Lucio Fulci; Screenplay: Gianfranco Clerici, Daniele Stroppa; Special Effects/Makeup: Giuseppe Ferranti; Music: Vince Tempera
Starring: Keith Van Hoven (Tony), Karina Huff (Diana), Paolo Paoloni (Uncle Victor), Bettine Milne (Aunt Sarah), Peter Hintz (Paul), Al Cliver [Pier Luigi Conti] (Peter), Carla Cassola (Maria), Paolo Bernardi (the nephew), Francesca De Rose (the niece), Massimo Sarchielli (store-keeper)

A gang of criminals forces its way into a country house and kills the inhabitants, an elderly couple. The couple's guard dogs trap the gang members inside the house. While the gang tries to find a way out, the clocks in the house start to run backward, and the corpses come back to life.

The House of Clocks was Lucio Fulci's second entry in the *Houses of Doom* series. Its partner, *The Sweet House of Horrors* (1989), is one of the director's best later-period films. Sadly, the same half-hearted execution and sloppy plotting that affects many of Fulci's later films hampers *The House of Clocks*. While the central premise has definite potential, the concept's internal logic is violated repeatedly. This leads to a chain of plot holes that does nothing except harm the film.

Hardly any likable characters appear in the film and this doesn't help. Even the supposed victims

are murderers themselves, while their opponents are just as bad. No attempts at characterization occur beyond the early revelation that the elderly couple are pretty unpleasant, and such a revelation would

The three burglars soon to be trapped in a temporal nightmare, in *The House of Clocks*.

have been better left until later on. On the whole there's nothing here that isn't simply an excuse for the splatter scenes, which are in keeping with Fulci's earlier standards. The whole thing ends in poor fashion, with a twist that probably looked much better on paper than on film. A waste of a decent idea and a talented cast, *The House of Clocks* is a disappointment.

The House of Lost Souls (1989)
Aka: La casa del anime erranti

Director: Umberto Lenzi; Story/Screenplay: Umberto Lenzi; Special Effects/Makeup: Giuseppe Ferranti; Music: Claude King
Starring: Joseph Alan Johnson, Stefania Orsala Garello, Matteo Gazzolo, Laurentina Guidotti, Gianlugi Fogacci, Yamaouchi Haruhiko, Licia Colò, Constantino Meloni, Charles Borromel

A group of geologists take shelter in an isolated motel that was the scene of several horrific murders in years gone by. Before long sinister things start to happen and the group members are killed off, one by one.

The House of Lost Souls is one of a pair of films that Umberto Lenzi prepared for a television miniseries called *Le case del terrore* (*Houses of Doom*). Lucio Fulci directed the other two, and they're generally superior to Lenzi's efforts. This one is a standard vengeful ghost story.

Armed with a terrible script and a group of amateur actors (with the exception of veteran Charles Borromel), Lenzi relies upon gore and special effects to hold the audience's interest. Some of the makeup is effective, particularly the corpse paint, but the disappearing ghost head is terrible. Plenty of blood's on display, but the sight of a small boy being decapitated by a washing machine (!) is unintentionally funny. So is the ghostly Buddhist monk in a wheelchair, and one man's attempts to find hidden corpses with the aid of a metal detector. Somehow, he manages to locate them.

Lenzi is not a particularly great director—he's more prolific than talented—but he's turned out a handful of decent films. Unfortunately, *The House of Lost Souls* only works on a so-bad-it's-good level and is pretty unsatisfying as a horror film. Lucio Fulci's contributions to the series—*The Sweet House of Horrors* and *The House of Clocks*, both 1989—are much better. Joseph Alan Johnson had a brief spell as a slasher movie regular, appearing in *Slumber Party Massacre* (1982), *Berserker* (1987) and *Iced* (1988).

The House of the Yellow Carpet (1982)
Aka: La casa del tappeto giallo

Director: Carlo Lizzani; Story: Aldo Seleri (as stage play); Screenplay: Lucio Battistrada, Filiberto Bandini; Producer: Filiberto Bandini; Music: Stelvio Cipriani
Starring: Erland Josephson (Achille Cimatti/the professor), Beatrice Romand (Franca), Vittorio Mezzogiorno (Antonio), Milena Vukotic (the psychiatrist)

A young couple puts a rug up for sale and a man comes to view the item when the wife is alone. He appears normal enough at first but it quickly becomes apparent that he isn't going to leave. He

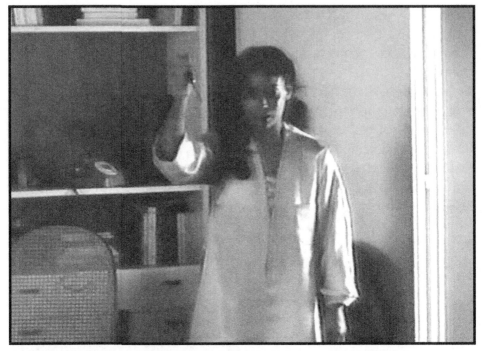

A housewife deals with a terrifying visitor in *The House with the Yellow Carpet*.

tells the woman that he once owned the carpet, and murdered his wife on it—thus beginning a campaign of psychological terror.

This curious little thriller is an interesting change from the usual *giallo* material. Stage plays don't always transfer well to film, but here it's a definite bonus. The use of one primary location—a small apartment—results in a genuine sense of claustrophobia, and the presence of a larger cast might have eroded the incredible tension between the two central characters.

Although there's little overt violence, *The House of the Yellow Carpet* possesses an almost tangible atmosphere of dread. Director Carlo Lizzani builds up the tension while a few choice moments—particularly the self-injection scene—are inserted to rattle the audience. The final revelations hark back to the original *Twilight Zone* and *Alfred Hitchcock Presents…* rather than the kind of sordid secrets that lie beneath most *gialli*, but that's not a problem.

The House of the Yellow Carpet is an old-fashioned and thoroughly entertaining little mystery that doesn't really deserve to be relegated to the ranks of forgotten Italian horror films. Viewers with a fear of hypodermic needles should perhaps stay away, however.

The House of Witchcraft (1989)
Aka: La casa del sortilegio

Director: Umberto Lenzi; Story: Gianfranco Clerici, Daniele Stroppa; Screenplay: Umberto Lenzi; Special Effects: Giuseppe Ferranti, Ditta Ricci, Aldo Mafera; Music: Claude King
Starring: Andy J. Forest, Sonia Petrovna, Susanna Martinkova, Marina Giulia Cavalli, Maria Stella Musy, Paul Muller, Alberto Frasca, Maria Clementina, Maria Cumani Quasimodo

After being plagued by a recurring nightmare, a young man arranges a vacation at a villa in the countryside. When he arrives there, he finds that it's the same villa he's been seeing in his dreams.

Umberto Lenzi's second contribution to the *Houses of Doom* series is a fairly typical witch story featuring black cats, shape changing, cauldrons, old crones and seductive young females. This sounds more enjoyable than it is, mostly because Lenzi lays off the sex and gore, elements that often fuel low-budget Italian horror films, in favor of clichéd plot devices and ham-fisted attempts at suspense.

After introducing a gaggle of thin and stereotypical characters, Lenzi throws as many ominous signs and omens into the mix as possible, ultimately rendering the plot nonsensical. It doesn't help that he repeats the same footage—with minor differences, admittedly—no less than *three times*, presumably to highlight the fact that this was a significant episode in the hero's life. It's also unfortunate that the scene in question revolves around a particularly fake-looking plastic

head. Giuseppe Ferranti's work here is well below average, and the murders are anemic and bloodless. The English-language version is cursed by truly atrocious dubbing that serves only to accentuate the poor script and lackluster acting.

Although Lenzi is capable of producing energetic and enjoyable horror films, *The House of Witchcraft* is not one of them. Quickly shot on a clearly limited budget, the only point of interest is the main location, a 16th-century house that Daria Nicolodi's uncle owned. Both this film and *The House of Lost Souls* (1989) were shelved soon after completion, and rightly so.

The House on the Edge of the Park (1980)
Aka: La casa sperduta nel parco, The Ripper on the Edge,
The House at the Edge of the Park

Director: Ruggero Deodato; Story/Screenplay: Gianfranco Clerici, Vincenzo Mannino; Producer: Franco Palaggi, Franco Di Nunzio; Makeup: Raoul Ranieri; Music: Riz Ortolani
Starring: David Hess (Alex), Annie Belle [Anne Brilland] (Lisa), Christian Borromeo (Tom), Giovanni Lombardo Radice (Ricky), Marie Claude Joseph (Glenda), Gabriele Di Giulio (Howard), Brigitte Petronio (Cindy), Karoline Mardeck, Lorraine De Selle (Gloria)

A psychopathic rapist and his simple-minded companion brutalize a group of wealthy young people

Even in a notorious subgenre like the rape-revenge movie, Ruggero Deodato's *The House on the Edge of the Park* has acquired a reputation for brutality and sleaze. Obviously influenced by Wes Craven's *The Last House on the Left* (1972)—even to the point of casting David Hess as yet another psychopathic killer—the plot is so flimsy that Deodato can't even lay claim to the dubious morality that Craven's film possessed. Random episodes of torture and brutality are strung together by a plot so paper-thin it doesn't stand up to even the slightest examination.

Central to this atrocity exhibition is David Hess' characteristically over-the-top performance as Alex. Scriptwriter Gianfranco Clerici gives him some lines that refer to a class struggle, perhaps trying to provide a motivation for his behavior. Ultimately, such attempts are wasted, since it's abundantly clear that Alex simply enjoys hurting people. However, Hess does provide a grimly enjoyable performance, allowing Alex's violent mood swings and occasional moments of rationality to give the character depth. Giovanni Lombardo Radice's performance as Ricky is less successful,

primarily because his character becomes less and less logical as the film continues. Ultimately he's just there to provide Alex with another misguided stab at genuine human emotion, something he's clearly not capable of experiencing.

By far the most troublesome aspect of *The House on the Edge of the Park* is the film's apparent attitude toward rape and sexual abuse. Italian exploitation cinema has always been harsh in its treatment of women, but Deodato's film goes too far. Presenting a rape scene that begins with violence and force but ends up being consensual because *the victim starts to enjoy the experience* is beyond the boundaries of acceptability. In a similarly twisted moment, one of the captives freely offers herself to Ricky, apparently sensing the general decency of his character, which allows her to forget that Ricky and Alex have been brutalizing the group of friends for over an hour by that point. When the film eventually returns to the plot, we are expected to believe that Alex's victims were willing to be brutalized, raped and tortured *because they were waiting for the moment to strike.* Such objectionable ideas are a frequent component of Gianfranco Clerici's work, which includes both Deodato's cannibal films, where we see rape victims punished with murder or responding favorably to their abusers. Clerici's other works include *Nazi Love Camp 27* (1977) and Lucio Fulci's notoriously misogynistic *New York Ripper* (1982).

The House on the Edge of the Park has little to recommend it. It's a professionally made film that supports Deodato's status as a talented director. However, to highlight such aspects is to ignore the film's overtly misogynistic and loathsome subject matter and Clerici's woefully inadequate script. At least Aldo Lado's equally immoral *Late Night Trains* (1975) had the sense to stick to Wes Craven's Bergman-inspired plot. Ultimately the movie is only likely to appeal to fans of rape-revenge movies—all others should probably steer clear.

Inferno (1980)

Director: Dario Argento; Story/Screenplay: Dario Argento; Producer: Claudio Argento; Special Effects: Germano Natali; Music: Keith Emerson
Starring: Eleonora Giorgi (Sara), Gabriele Lavia (Carlo), Veronica Lazar (nurse), Leopoldo Mastelloni (butler), Irene Miracle (Rose), Daria Nicolodi (Elise), Sacha Piteoff (Kazanian), Alida Valli (Carol), Leigh McCloskey (Mark)

Rose, a poetess living in New York, finds a book that tells of three powerful witches. She believes one of them to be living in her building, and sends a letter to her brother Mark in Rome describing her discovery. Narrowly avoiding an attempt on his own life, Mark flies to New York only to find that his sister is missing.

As the sequel to one of the most highly regarded Italian horror films ever made, *Inferno* has invariably attracted a fair degree of criticism. It seems churlish, however, to criticize the film for not being as groundbreaking and exciting as *Suspiria* (1977); while it may not live up to the standards of its predecessor, *Inferno* is still a worthy film with much to recommend it.

The events in *Suspiria* are organized around a simple storyline: an American student discovers strange goings-on at a German dance  academy. *Inferno* dispenses with a central plot, further eroding the film's links to mainstream cinema. Here Argento has almost entirely entered dream territory, eschewing even the tenuous logical constraints that were used in *Suspiria*. Very little in *Inferno* makes any sense; conversations are circular and bizarre, characters behave in strange and illogical fashions. Who would dive into a pit of dark water in an unfamiliar cellar, even if their house keys were at the bottom? How many women would invite a total stranger back to their apartment to make them feel safer? The dream-like feel of the film is enhanced by Argento's skillful use of color and light, making simple things and familiar locations seem sinister and ominous.

Any attempt to follow the story or connect one event logically to another will be ultimately unsuccessful. *Inferno* is only entertaining when viewed as a series of hallucinatory images—such as might appear in dreams or nightmares—that approach the viewer on a purely sensory level. Of course, this makes the film highly irritating to the viewer expecting conventional cinematic technique. While *Suspiria* treads a perfect line between reality and what might be called "dream-logic," with each aspect present in exactly the right quantity, *Inferno* makes no concessions to reality. Unfortunately this makes the film more of a cinematic experiment than a genuine piece of entertainment, something that is sure to alienate many viewers.

It doesn't help that *Inferno* has a few notable flaws. Compared with the excellent music produced by Goblin for *Suspiria*, Keith Emerson's work is bombastic and intrusive. It lacks all subtlety and rarely manages to enhance the atmosphere of the key scenes, something Goblin achieved admirably. Emerson's preferred mix of classical themes and progressive rock stylings is a definite step backward from *Suspiria's* unique score.

The film's climax is irrevocably damaged by the revelation that Mater Tenebrarum, the second of the three evil witches, is nothing more than a cheap plastic skeleton, and a poorly animated one at that. With a decent budget and a talented crew behind him, I'm sure Argento could have come up with something more effective. It's very hard to make skeletons look real on film, and here the attempt fails miserably.

What we're left with is a film that will probably test the patience of all but the most ardent Argento followers. *Inferno* is by no means a bad movie, and it's a wonderful cinematic experiment, but the film's inherently confusing nature makes it less approachable than the director's other works. His next film, 1982's *Tenebrae*, saw Argento return to safer, more coherent territory.

The Island of the Fishmen (1979)
Aka: L'isola degli uomini pesce, The Fishmen,
Island of Mutations, Screamers, Something Waits in the Dark

Director: Sergio Martino; Story: Cesare Frugoni, Luciano Martino; Screenplay: Sergio Donati, Cesare Frugoni, Sergio Martino; Producer: Luciano Martino; Special Effects: Paolo Ricci, Cataldo Galiano; Make-up: Nilo Lacoponi, Manlio Rocchetti, Stefano Trani; Music: Luciano Michelini

Starring: Barbara Bach [Barbara Venturini] (Amanda Marvin), Claudio Cassinelli (Lieutenant Claude de Ross), Richard Johnson (Edmund Rackham), Franco Javarone (José), Roberto Posse (Peter), Giuseppe Castellano (Skip), Francesco Mazzieri (Francois), Beryl Cunningham (Shakira), Joseph Cotten (Professor Marvin)

After a prison ship is wrecked in a storm, the ship's doctor and a handful of prisoners wash up on a desolate island. The island's wealthy occupant gives them shelter, but the doctor begins to suspect that all is not well. Sure enough, a scientist and his beautiful daughter are held hostage, but why?

The Island of the Fishmen is an entertaining romp through mad-scientist/mutant-creature territory firmly in the H.G. Wells vein. All the familiar elements are there—a smooth but utterly nasty type (here played by Richard Johnson), a well-meaning but weak-willed scientist (Joseph Cotten), a dashing officer (Claudio Cassinelli) and the exquisitely beautiful daughter who makes her first appearance on horseback (Barbara Bach). Throw in a voodoo priestess and the apparently Lovecraft-inspired fish men and you have an entertaining (if derivative) period romp.

Barbara Bach and the fishmen that hold her captive.

The film's budgetary limitations do show through at times, with the fish men looking rather cheap and plastic. However, the cast performs well, with Johnson turning in a wonderfully villainous performance. Veteran director Sergio Martino clearly has a flair for this kind of classic adventure story, and he keeps things moving along at a decent pace. Along with *The Great Alligator* (1979), it's probably the best of his later films. A belated sequel—entitled *The Fishmen and their Queen*—arrived in 1995, once again directed by Martino.

U.S. distributors New World Pictures felt that the film wasn't quite right for the drive-in market, so new footage starring Cameron Mitchell and Mel Ferrer was shot. Kim Newman claims Joe Dante directed this extra material, but other sources attribute it to Miller Drake. Whatever the truth, the new sequences add little to the film. Apparently New World thought so too, since they went on to create a trailer that included scenes that were not actually in the movie. Movie patrons were not impressed, and New World edited the spurious footage into the film, renaming the movie *Screamers* or *Something Waits in the Dark*.

Killer Fish (1979)
Aka: Agguato sul fondo, Deadly Treasure of the Piranha

Director: Antonio Margheriti; Story/Screenplay: Michael Rogers, Giovanni Simonelli; Producer: Alex Ponti; Special Effects/Makeup:

Augusto Possanzo, Waldimiro Reis; Music: Guido De Angelis, Maurizio De Angelis

Starring: Lee Majors (Lasky), Karen Black (Kate Neville), Margaux Hemingway (Gabrielle), Marisa Berenson (Anne), James Franciscus (Paul Diller), Roy Brocksmith (Ollie), Dan Pastorini (Hans), Frank Pesce (Warren)

A gang of professional jewel thieves take refuge at a holiday resort after pulling off a major heist and stashing the proceeds at the bottom of a lake. Predictably, certain members are not happy with sharing the results of their hard work, and try to recover the jewels before the appointed time. Unfortunately for them someone else is interested in keeping the jewels for themselves, and they've stocked the lake with vicious piranhas to safeguard the treasure. It's up to Lasky, the leader of the thieves—with the help of supermodel Gabrielle—to find out who is controlling the bloodthirsty creatures.

As the alternate titles suggest, *Killer Fish* is an Italian take on Joe Dante's horror spoof *Piranha* (1978). Antonio Margheriti claimed that

Dante's film came out *after* his own, but such claims are common in an industry that thrives upon other people's ideas. Margheriti is a genuinely talented individual with a number of worthy films to his name, but *Killer Fish* is not one of them.

Made to cash in on the recent popularity of Lee Majors and *The Six Million Dollar Man*, *Killer Fish* started shooting with an incomplete script that was changed day by day. Even with a decent (and completed) script, several things hampered the film. For a start, Majors has a certain charisma on the small screen, but he isn't a particularly competent actor. Faced with such poor material, he's reduced to a one-note performance. His co-star, model Margaux Hemingway, doesn't fare much better. The Italian cast is made up of B-movie regulars who work through the script as best they can.

At his best Margheriti is a decent special effects director, but this isn't one of those occasions. His miniature work looks obvious and clumsy, while the piranhas themselves are less than impressive. Given the limited budget and preparation time, it's a wonder the effects are as good as they are, but that doesn't make them any easier to watch.

Lacking the spirit and pace of Sergio Martino's *The Great Alligator* and hamstrung by poor acting and a derivative script, *Killer Fish* will probably only be of interest to Italian exploitation enthusiasts or fans of the film's main stars. It's certainly better than *Piranha II: The Spawning* (1981), but that's not saying much.

The Killer Is Still Among Us (1985)
Aka: L'assassino e' ancora tra noi

Director: Camillo Teti; Story: Camillo Teti, Giuliano Carnimeo; Screenplay: Ernesto Gastaldi, Camillo Teti; Special Effects: Roberto Pace; Music: Detto Mariano
Starring: Mariangela D'Abbraccio, Giovanni Visentin, Riccardo Perrotti, Luigi Mezzanotte, Yvonne D'Abbraccio, Francesco Capitano, Oreste Rotundo, Silvia D'Agostini, Fabio Carfora, Franco Adducci, Marco Bertini, Anna Pera, Giuseppe Pelli, M. Rosario Tizzano, Roberto Sanna

A female student's investigations into a series of brutal murders attract the attention of the murderer.

The Killer Is Still Among Us is one of a number of Italian films based on the crimes of The Monster of Florence, a real-life killer responsible for some 32 murders between 1968 and 1985. When Teti's film came out in 1986, the fiend was still at large, giving the scriptwriters a wonderful opportunity to play on a very real public fear.

Leaving aside the dubious historical relevance for a moment, the film is a competently made and entertaining effort. Not as flashy or stylish as the best *gialli*, but it's still respectable enough. However, the film secured itself an unpleasant reputation, thanks to at least one scene of sickening and graphic brutality. The main scene occurs toward the film's conclusion, where we are treated to a detailed and exceptionally graphic demonstration of the killer's favored mutilations. Unsurprisingly it's the same brand of sexualized violence that appears in other *gialli* like *Giallo a Venezia* (1979) and *The New York Ripper* (1982). What makes these scenes more potent is that they are based on real-life crimes, down to each sickening detail. Recycling real-life atrocities always has been a staple of Italian exploitation, but it's no more palatable here than it is in *Gestapo's Last Orgy* (1976), making *The Killer Is Still Among Us* the worst kind of sleaze. *Il Mostro di Firenze*, a 1986 film directed by Cesare Ferrario, deals with the same events.

Killing Birds (1987)
Aka: Raptors, Zombie 5–Killing Birds

Director: Claude Milliken [Claudio Lattanzi], Aristide Massacessi [uncredited]; Story: Claude Milliken [Claudio Lattanzi], Sheila Goldberg; Screenplay: Daniel Ross [Daniele Stroppa]; Special Effects: Harry Harris III, Martin Schwerk, Robert Gould; Makeup: Frank Moore, Don Gligor; Music: Carlo Maria Cordio
Starring: Lara Wendel (Anne), Timothy W. Watt (Steve), Leslie Cummins (Mary), James Villemaire (Paul), Sal Maggiore, Jr. (Brian), James

Sutterfield (Rob), Lin Gathright (Jennifer), Robert Vaughn (Dr. Fred Brown)

A group of students head off into the Louisiana bayou to look for rare birds. They get lost and end up spending the night in a ramshackle old building, unaware that their arrival has disturbed the restless dead.

Killing Birds is a strange effort: part Italian zombie film, part Hitchcock rip-off, part American teen movie. This schizophrenic attitude gives the film some rarity value—after all, it's not every day audiences get to see a psycho Vietnam veteran, homicidal birds and the living dead in the same 90 minutes. In many ways *Killing Birds* is a typical late 1980s Italian horror film, and it possesses a certain druggy charm that makes it more entertaining than some of its contemporaries. The film is ponderously slow in places, for a start. Several scenes are padded out with footage of the main characters socializing, having fun and romping through the country to the strains of some pleasing elevator music. Plenty of nature footage is inserted, too. The corresponding lack of dialogue—barely a word is spoken in the first 10 minutes—adds to the film's somnambulistic feel, giving it a definite dreamlike quality. Even when the zombies appear and begin to attack, their slow, jerky movements and the accompanying wreaths of dry ice suggest the whole film is little more than a dream.

Ultimately this atmosphere is probably for the best, since Massacessi's films are not known for their energetic pace. The script, such as it is,

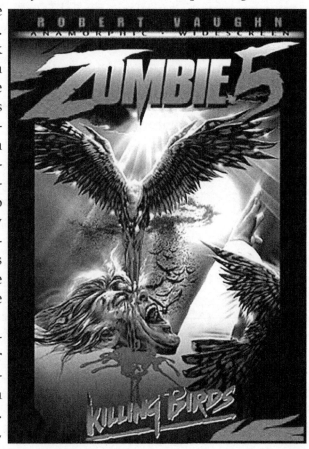

is pretty basic and clichéd, much like the acting. Robert Vaughn does his best to inject some emotion into the role, but it's a wasted effort. His presence is welcome nonetheless. A reasonable amount of graphic gore appears, but it's poorly done and consists mostly of the same technique viewed from different angles. *Killing Birds* is never going to be a rediscovered classic or even a minor cult gem, but if audiences can appreciate the leisurely pace and drugged-out atmosphere, it's an entertaining enough film.

Trivia note: According to Massacessi *Killing Birds* was originally to have been directed by Michele Soavi. However, he chose to direct *The Church* (1989), and the job was given to Lattanzi, Soavi's assistant director on *Stagefright* (1987).

The Last Shark (1980)
Aka: L'ultimo squallo, The Great White

Director: Enzo G. Castellari; Story / Screenplay: Mark Princi; Producer: Maurizio Amati, Ugo Tucci; Special Effects: Giorgio Ferreri, Giorgio Pozzi, Antonio Corridori; Makeup: Gianni Morosi; Music: Guido De Angelis, Maurizio De Angelis
Starring: James Franciscus (Peter Benton), Vic Morrow (Ron Hamer), Micky Pignatelli [Micaela Pignatelli] (Jenny Benton), Joshua Sinclair (Mayor Wells), Timothy Brent [Giancarlo Prete] (Bob Martin), Stefania Girolami (Gloria Benton), Gian Marco Lari, Massimo Vanni (Jimmy)

Plans to open a beach resort are disrupted by the arrival of a giant great white shark. The mayor wants to keep the resort open so it's up to a local expert and an old fisherman to stop the creature.

Of all the European monster movies inspired by Steven Spielberg's *Jaws* (1975), Enzo G. Castellari's *The Last Shark* is probably the best known. Paradoxically, it's also one of the hardest to find, thanks to a lawsuit from Universal, who felt it was a little too similar to their blockbuster. The Italian film was withdrawn from American theaters and never made it to video.

It's curious that Universal didn't try to get it removed from European cinemas too, given that it was released in Germany under the title *The Last Jaws*. Since then it has become a much sought after film, only available in the world of gray-market bootlegs.

The Last Shark attacks his latest victim.

Universal's reaction was perhaps a little strong, for although the film possesses some decent acting and Castellari's typically strong direction, *The Last Shark* is crippled by poor special effects and the unfortunate use of stock footage. Inserting animal footage from nature documentaries might work when one is producing a dead-in-the-water piece of trash like *Hell of the Living Dead* (1981), but *The Last Shark* has loftier ambitions. The footage is poorly chosen, often depicting sharks that are a different color than the mechanical shark used for the attack sequences. During the central helicopter scene the actor hanging from the runners is clumsily replaced by a dummy, so not a drop of blood is spilt when the dummy's legs are severed.

As stated before, *The Last Shark* boasts a decent cast, including James Franciscus (*The Cat O'Nine Tails*, 1971; *Killer Fish*, 1978), Joshua Sinclair (*Hitch Hike*, 1977) and the great Vic Morrow, star of Kinji Fukasaku's *Message from Space* (1978) and *Humanoids from the Deep* (1980). Morrow delivers a fine performance in an accent that veers between Scottish and Irish, probably helped by the actor's notorious drinking habits. It's obviously based on Robert Shaw's performance in *Jaws*, but it's still great to watch.

Ultimately—and unsurprisingly—*The Last Shark* doesn't compare to *Jaws*, but it's still an entertaining movie. It's also one of the best of the Italian *Jaws* rip-offs.

Luna di sangue (1989)
Aka: Fuga dalla morte

Director: Enzo Milioni; Story/Screenplay: Enzo Milioni, Giovanni Simonelli; Producer: Luigi Nannerini, Antonio Lucidi; Music: Paolo Gatti, Alfonso Zenga

Starring: Annie Belle, Alex Berger, Barbara Blasko, Zora Kerova [Zora Keslerova], Jessica Moore [Luciana Ottaviana], Jacques Serna, Pamela Prati

A series of murders focus on a rich woman.

[Notes: Part of the *"Lucio Fulci presents…"* collection. Clips from this film were used in Lucio Fulci's *Nightmare Concert* (1990). Synopsis taken from *Spaghetti Nightmares* (see bibliography).]

Macabre (1980)
Aka: Macabro, Frozen Terror

Director: Lamberto Bava; Story/Screenplay: Pupi Avati, Roberto Gandus, Lamberto Bava, Antonio Avati; Producer: Gianni Minervini, Antonio Avati; Special Effects: Tonino Corridori [Antonio Corridori], Angelo Mattei; Music: Ubaldo Continiello
Starring: Bernice Stegers (Jane Baker), Stanko Molnar (Robert Duval), Veronica Zinny (Lucy Baker), Roberto Posse (Fred Kellerman), Ferdinando Orlandi (Mr. Wells), Fernando Pannullo (Leslie Baker), Elisa Kadiga Bove (Mrs. Duval)

After Jane's daughter drowns her son, and her adulterous lover is killed in a traffic accident, Jane is confined to a mental institution. Upon her release she moves into her former love nest to nurse her obsession for her dead lover.

Lamberto Bava's directorial debut is a twisted little drama built around some of Italian horror's favorite topics: murder, mutilation, obsession and perverted sex. Using only a small cast—including an obsessive mother, her psychopathic daughter and a neurotic blind man—he manages to weave a complex and increasingly bizarre tale that show-cases the very worst qualities of mankind. With the pseudo-New Orleans locations and a languid jazz score, *Macabre* closely resembles the sleazy *gialli* of the 1970s.

Based on a newspaper article and co-scripted by respected director Pupi Avati, *Macabre* is an auspicious debut. Bava's direction shows the influence of his father Mario, with more emphasis on style than substance. The camera keeps moving, making the most of the limited locations and the small rooms. However, there's plenty of substance here anyway, with a decent cast making the most of their roles. Ve-ronica Zinny (sister of Karl Zinny from *Demons*, 1985) gives a great performance as the quietly murderous Lucy. Unfortu-nately the plot builds relatively slowly, often leaving lengthy periods when little happens. Such minor plot points gain sig-nificance later on, but this tendency only becomes evident on repeated viewings.

The film's only truly sour note is the ending, which mimics *Carrie* (1976) and *Friday the 13th* (1980). Up until that point, *Macabre* plays like a grimly fascinating soap opera. Even with the unfortunate ending, it's an exploitation classic and a great start to Lamberto Bava's career. For the next few years, he would be at the top of his game. After *Demons 2* (1986), Bava's career pretty much went downhill. Trivia note: Michele Soavi was considered for the role of Robert, but Bava chose Stanko Molnar. Both Soavi and Molnar appeared in Bava's next film, *A Blade in the Dark* (1983).

Madhouse (1981)
Aka: There Was a Little Girl

Director: Ovidio G. Assonitis; Story / Screenplay: Stephen Blakely, Ovi-dio G. Assonitis, Peter Shepherd, Robert Gandus [Roberto Gandus]; Producer: Ovidio G. Assonitis, Peter Shepherd; Music: Riz Ortolani Starring: Trish Everly (Julia), Michael McRae (Sam), Dennis Robertson (Father James), Morgan Hart (Helen), Jerry Fujikawa (Kimura), Alison

Biggers (Mary), Edith Ivey (Amatha Boregard), Don Devendorf (principal), Huxsie Scott (secretary), Richard Baker (Sacha Robertson, Jr.), Doug Dillingham (Golden), Jamie Baker (Sacha's mother), Joe Camp (hospital nightwatchman)

A woman suspects that her insane and disfigured sister is going to try to kill her on her next birthday.

This relatively obscure film attracted a certain amount of attention thanks to its inclusion on the infamous U.K. "video nasties" list. Without a presence on the list, *Madhouse* would have disappeared without a trace. However, the film became sought after based on the strength of a few notorious splatter scenes, most notably the use of a power drill to kill a dog, the most brutal scene in the film. Director Assonitis tried to create an American-style film, primarily by using an American cast, but in terms of atmosphere and style this is very much a low-budget Italian film.

Unfortunately the rest of the movie is not quite so interesting. A decent plot concerning two sisters is introduced, with some unpleasant details and suspicious elements thrown in for good measure. How-ever, the build-up is far more successful than the climax, which will leave most viewers disappointed. The annoying musical score by Riz Ortolani does not help much, for his music makes far too much use of clichéd nursery rhyme melodies.

With a handful of decent gore scenes, and some early promise, *Madhouse* can't be considered a total failure, but better Italian horror films from the turn of the decade are easily found. "Video nasty" collectors will need to see this for the sake of completion, but others will not be quite so interested.

Malabimba (1979)

Aka: The Malicious Whore, Possession of a Teenager

Director: Andrew White [Andrea Bianchi]; Story/Screenplay: Piero Regnoli; Producer: Gabriele Crisanti; Music: Elsio Mancuso, Berto Pisano
Starring: Katell Laennec (Daniela "Bimba" Karoli), Patrizia Webley [Patrizia De Rossi] (Nais), Enzo Fisichella (Andrea), Giuseppe Marrocu (Andrea's brother), Elisa Mainardi (the medium), Giancarlo Del Duca (Giorgio), Pupita Lea (Andrea's mother), Maria Angela Giordano (Sister Sofia)

A demon possesses a young girl. She proceeds to seduce everyone around her, male and female, family included.

Malabimba is another cheap sex-and-horror slice of exploitation from producer Gabriele Crisanti. This time there's none of the extreme gore that colored *Giallo a Venezia* (1979), *Patrick Still Lives* (1980) and *Burial Ground* (1981); instead we have hardcore pornography. Aside from that, it's business as usual—terrible acting, a non-existent script, shaky camerawork and yet another scintillating performance from Maria Angela Giordano.

The whole film looks like it was shot in a couple of days with one take per scene. As with most Italian films, dialogue and sound were added at a later date, although clearly without any real effort. The final scene, featuring Sister Sofia's demise, shows Katell Laennec with a completely straight face, yet the soundtrack consists of extensive moaning and groaning. Apparently, grief sounds much the same as sex. Two versions of *Malabimba* exist, one with hardcore inserts. They're sloppily edited—every so often the camera cuts away to an anonymous penis—but that's in keeping with the rest of the film.

For those viewers that like their sleaze, *Malabimba* will be perfect viewing. Demonic possession, masturbation, graphic sex, incest and even teddy-bear abuse are all on display here. Everyone else should stay away.

The Man Who Didn't Want To Die (1988)
Aka: L'uomo che non voleva morire

Director: Lamberto Bava; Story/ Screenplay: Gianfranco Clerici, Giorgio Scerbanenco; Producer: Lamberto Bava, Andrea Piazzesi; Makeup: Franco Casagni; Music: Simon Boswell
Starring: Keith Van Hoven, Martine Brochard, Gino Concari, Lino Salemme, Stefano Molinari, Peter Pitsch, Jacques Serna, Igor Zalewsky

[Notes: Made for television. Part of the "*Alta tensione*" series.]

Manhattan Baby (1982)
Aka: Possessed, Eye of the Evil Dead

Director: Lucio Fulci, Story/Screenplay: Elisa Livia Briganti, Dardano Sacchetti; Producer: Fabrizio De Angelis; Makeup: Maurizio Trani; Music: Fabio Frizzi
Starring: Christopher Connelly (Professor George Hacker), Martha Taylor (Emily Hacker), Brigitta Boccoli (Susie Hacker), Giovanni Frezza (Tommy Hacker), Cinzia De Ponti (Jamie Lee), Laurence Welles [Cosimo Cinieri] (Adrian Marcato), Andrea Bosic (optician), Carlo De Mejo (Luke), Vincenzo Bellanich, Mario Moretti, Antonio Pulci

While her father explores an Egyptian tomb, Susie receives an amulet from a peddler. The family returns to New York after a blue light inside the tomb blinds Susie's father, and the girl becomes the focus for supernatural activity.

Manhattan Baby is a curious film. Although it bears similarities to the Lucio Fulci films that immediately preceded it, the film is something of a departure. *Manhattan Baby* seems to be an attempt to make a more overtly commercial film, strongly reminiscent of *The Awakening* (1980) and *The Exorcist* (1973), not to mention *The Omen* (1976) and *Poltergeist* (1982). Unfortunately the attempt was not a great success and failed to find favor with critics or fans. It was Fulci's last film to be released theatrically in the U.S.

From the title onward (what exactly does *Manhattan Baby* refer to?), the film is a confusing mess. Few works of art conceived from contractual obligations turn out well, and *Manhattan Baby* is no exception. Producer Fabrizio De Angelis wanted an Egyptian prologue—something that had not been in the script—in order to cash in on the moderate success of *The Awakening*. After ordering this extra material, he then cut the budget by more than two thirds, angering the director further.

Perhaps in an effort to assert his status as a serious director, Fulci chose to include little of his characteristic violence and gore. Unfortunately, what little pace and kinetic energy exist in films such as *Zombie* (1979) and *The Beyond* (1981) are derived primarily from the threat of impeding bloodshed and ultraviolence. Without the regular appearance of grisly special effects, the movie rests on story alone, a serious problem for films as thinly plotted and poorly developed as *Manhattan Baby*. What is left is a soporific occult tale that fails to evoke any interest from its audience and relies too heavily on devices plundered from other, more successful films. Plenty of Fulci trademarks appear here,

Supernatural terror from ancient Egypt in *Manhattan Baby*

including mystically inclined children and endless eye-related symbolism. However, viewers will be less likely to put up with Fulci's annoying facial close-ups in a film as tame and unchallenging as *Manhattan Baby*. Even the score is boring: It's made up of elements taken from other Fabio Frizzi scores, including *The Beyond*.

Ultimately *Manhattan Baby* is a dull film that is unlikely to impress fans of the director's earlier films. It's competently made, but lacks the fire and inventiveness of his finest works. Even so, it's still a cut above some of the dross that followed—an indication of just how low Fulci's career would sink in years to come and not an endorsement of *Manhattan Baby*. The director has a brief cameo as Dr. Forrester.

Massacre (1989)

Director: Andrea Bianchi; Story/Screenplay: Andrea Bianchi; Producer: Luigi Nannerini, Antonio Lucidi; Makeup: Pino Ferranti [Giuseppe Ferranti]; Music: Luigi Ceccarelli
Starring: Gino Concari, Patrizia Falcone, Silvia Conti, Pier Maria Cecchini, Robert Egon, Danny Degli Espositi, Marcia Furgiuele, Lubka Lensi, Anna Maria Placido, Maria Grazia Veroni, Christina Lynn, Piero Pieri, Paul Muller, Maurice Poli

Violent murders plague a horror film shoot.

Here is another sleazy splatter flick from the director of *Malabimba* (1979) and *Burial Ground* (1980). Unfortunately Andrea Bianchi doesn't produce anything quite as interesting as *Burial Ground*'s incest-and-gore themes (or *Malabimba*'s hardcore sex scenes), but the movie's still a cut above the usual tame late-1980s fare. Producers Nannerini and Lucidi were probably the busiest men in Italian horror at the end of the decade, and like their other films from the period, *Massacre* bears the credit "*Supervised by Lucio Fulci.*" Fulci's *Nightmare Concert* contains clips from this film

Typically for this kind of film, the characters are a hateful bunch whose grisly deaths are definitely welcomed. When the cast is not being killed off, most of them are engaging in some kind of sexual activity, from lesbianism to voyeurism. This provides plenty of opportunities for nudity, the film's other selling point, along with some gratuitous and brutal (but also amateurish and cheap) special effects.

Bianchi's directing style hasn't improved much since *Burial Ground*, limited to master shots with a minimum of camera movement. There's a film-within-a-film plot, but it's more than likely there to pad out the running time rather than provide some kind of reflexivity. Luigi Ceccarelli provided the score for a number of 1980s exploitation films, but his work here is pretty bad and clearly designed to emulate Simon Boswell or Claudio Simonetti.

If audiences are looking for a cheap sex-and-splatter flick, *Massacre* is perfect. It's more enjoyable than the majority of gutless made-for-television movies released around the time, but it's not a patch on earlier attempts. There's nothing new here, but *Massacre* still entertains in a jaded sort of way.

Massacre in Dinosaur Valley (1984)
Aka: Nudo e selvaggio, Amazonas, Cannibal ferox 2, Cannibal Massacre in Dinosaur Valley, Stranded in Dinosaur Valley

Director: Michael E. Lemick [Michele Massimo Tarantini]; Story/ Screenplay: Michael E. Lemick [Michele Massimo Tarantini]; Makeup: Waldir Cota
Starring: Michael Sopkiw (Kevin Hall), Susane Carvall [Suzane Carvalho] (Eva Ibanez), Milton Morris, Martha Anderson, Joffrey Soares (José), Gloria Cristal, Susie Hahn, Mary Reis, Andy Silas, Leonid Baker, Carlos Imperial, Samuca, Ney Pen, Albert Silva, Jonas Dalbecchi, Paul Sky, Paul Pacelli, Morton Kays, Indio Xin, Robert Roney

A passenger plane crashes in the Amazon jungle. It's up to dinosaur hunter and adventurer Kevin Hall to make sure the passengers avoid the cannibals, the crocodiles and the quicksand (amongst other things) and make it out alive.

Many films are described as being so bad they're good, but for the most part a bad film remains just that. Generally such movies are a chore to watch and an unrewarding experience. Once in a while, however, a film comes along that genuinely benefits from zero budget, awful production values, absurd story and terrible cast. Such a movie is *Massacre in Dinosaur Valley*.

For starters, there's no massacre, no dinosaurs and not even a valley. We do have a party of third-rate actors stranded in some unconvincing jungle terrain, menaced by cannibals; the actors stumble around like crippled gorillas and end up in all sort of trouble. They're lead by Michael Sopkiw, a generic Indiana Jones-type paleontologist who looks suitably intense and comes up with bad one-liners as often as possible. Most of the women in the film take every opportunity

to shed their clothes, and a few soft-core sex scenes abound, including one with Suzane Carvalho being ravished by a female slave. The fake blood is spread about pretty enthusiastically, but clearly the budget didn't allow much in the way of special effects, except for a dodgy looking piranha-savaged leg (and only one piranha). Mercifully no animal slaughter appears, although Michael Sopkiw does throw a bored looking snake across a clearing.

With better production values and a little more time and effort, *Massacre in Dinosaur Valley* would have been a completely dull film. In its current form it's so amateurish and badly made that audiences can't help but laugh. If people are looking for typical Italian cannibal fare, they will be very disappointed, but if you're are in the mood for cheap laughs and an even cheaper plastic crocodile, *Massacre in Dinosaur Valley* is the way to go.

Maya (1989)

Director: Marcello Avallone; Story/Screenplay: Marcello Avallone, Andrea Purgatori, Maurizio Tedesco; Producer: Maurizio Tedesco; Special Effects/Makeup: Rosario Prestopino, Franco Casagni; Music: Gabriele Ducros
Starring: Peter Phelps (Peter), William Berger, Mariella Valentini (Lisa), Cyrus Elias, Mariangelica Ayala, Mirella D'Angelo, Antonello Fassari, Erich Wildpret

Lisa arrives in Venezuela to investigate the death of her father. Together with local beach bum Peter, she endeavors to uncover the connection between the recent murders and the rituals that took place in the area centuries ago.

Maya is something of a curiosity. Despite being released by Reteitalia, the company responsible for most of the tame made-for-TV movies released in the late 1980s, the film includes a substantial amount of nudity and gore, as well as some great cinematography and decent locations. The idea of ancient rituals requiring blood sacrifices is an old one, but the theme is handled effectively.

The most striking aspect of the film is the smoky, atmospheric visuals. Cinematographer Silvano Ippolito's pastel shades give the Venezuelan locations a hazy beauty that complements the stifling heat and languid sexuality depicted in the script. The script itself is fairly derivative, but it manages to effectively contrast the simplistic, wholesome lifestyle of the villagers with the sleazy decadence of those who didn't grow up in the area; all Peter and his friends want to do is drink and engage in casual sex. Not surprisingly, it is the outsiders who are the main target of the supernatural entity. The murders themselves are inventive and laced with typical Italian cruelty, particularly the bathtub scene.

Unfortunately the film's meandering and inconclusive script works heavily against it. After an impressive build-up, *Maya* enters erotic thriller territory and loses pace sharply. While the murder scenes are effective and tense, too much time is wasted on the hotelier's failing marriage. The exact reason for the murders is glossed over too quickly, and the film's conclusion is tame compared to earlier scenes. With tighter plotting and a decent ending, *Maya* would probably have been one of the better films of the period. It remains an entertaining movie though, and proof that the failing Italian horror scene of the late 1980s could still produce interesting results.

Monster Dog (1985)
Aka: Il signore dei cani, Leviatán

Director: Claudio Fragrasso; Story/Screenplay: Claudio Fragrasso, Carlos Aured; Producer: Carlos Aured; Special Effects/Makeup: Carlo De Marchis; Music: Alice Cooper
Starring: Alice Cooper (Vincent Raven), Victoria Vera (Sandra), Carlos  Santurio (Frank), María José Sarsa (Marilou), Pepita James (Angela), Emilio Linder (Jordan), Ricardo Palacios (Sheriff Morrison), Luis Maluenda (Deputy), Bernabe Barta Barri (old man)

A rock star returns to his hometown to shoot a video and finds the town terrorized by a pack of wild dogs.

This creaky Spanish-Italian co-production is probably the worst rock star horror movie ever made. *Monster Dog* is supposed to be a werewolf movie, although most viewers will be left wondering where's the werewolf. The monster dog model broke almost immediately, so these scenes involving the troubled machine were rewritten. All we're left with is a handful of dodgy rubber masks and an exceptionally poor film. Alice Cooper was much better in John Carpenters' *Prince of Darkness* (1987).

Monster Shark (1984)
Aka: Shark (rosso nell'oceano), Devilfish,
Devouring Waves, Red Ocean

Director: John Old, Jr. [Lamberto Bava], Story: Lewis Coates [Luigi Cozzi], Dean Lewis, Martin Dolman [Sergio Martino]; Screenplay: Gianfranco Clerici, Frank Walker, Dardano Sacchetti, Hervè Piccini; Producer: Mino Loy; Special Effects: German Natali, Ovidio Taito (shark); Makeup: Victor Basil [Guiseppe Ferranti]; Music: Antony Barrymore [Guido De Angelis, Maurizio De Angelis]
Starring: Michael Sopkiw (Peter), Valentine Monnier (Dr. Stella Dickens), John Garko [Gianni Garko] (Sheriff Gordon), William Berger (Professor Donald West), Iris Peynado (Sandra Hayes), Dagmar Lassander (Sonja West), Cinthia Stewart [Cinzia De Ponti] (Dr. Janet Bates), Lawrence Morgant (Dr. Bob Hogan), Paul Branco (Dr. Davis)

A giant monster is devouring swimmers off the Florida coastline. A team of oceanologists sets out to determine the nature of the beast and hopefully destroy it.

It's difficult to say exactly why *Monster Shark* was made. By the time it came out, the *Jaws* franchise produced three entries, and it was clear that the public was no longer particularly interested in giant sharks. Unsurprisingly, *Monster Shark* wasn't a great success, but it's pretty entertaining despite—well, because of—the obvious flaws.

Predictably, the screenwriters looked to Peter Benchley for inspiration and cribbed a few ideas from his novel *White Shark*. The uninspired plot is the result of no less than seven credited screenwriters, which also accounts for the general lack of cohesion within the film. Michael Sopkiw and the cast are generally competent, but the script contains too many holes to make their efforts worthwhile.

Even so, Bava is a skilled director and the end result is probably as good as it could have been. No amount of directorial skill can hide the fact that the monster itself is a shabbily built contraption with only the most basic of mechanical functions. With a second-rate script and a monster that looks like it came from a theme park rather than a special effects studio, *Monster Shark* is a fun movie when spoofed on *Mystery Science Theater 3000*, but it's a long way from being included among the better Italian efforts of the period.

Murder-Rock Dancing Death (1984)
Aka: Murderock – Uccide a passo di danza, The Demon is Loose

Director: Lucio Fulci; Story: Gianfranco Clerici, Vincenzo Mannino, Lucio Fulci; Screenplay: Gianfranco Clerici, Vincenzo Mannino, Roberto Gianviti, Lucio Fulci; Producer: Augusto Caminito; Makeup: Franco Casagni; Music: Keith Emerson
Starring: Olga Karlatos (Candice Norman), Ray Lovelock (George Webb), Claudio Cassinelli (Dick Gibson), Cosimo Cinieri (Lieutenant Borges), Giuseppe Mannajuolo (Professor Davis)

Someone is murdering dancers at a prestigious dance academy. Suspicion falls on the students competing for a lucrative television position.

After a couple of non-horror efforts—*Conquest* (1983) and *The New Gladiators* (1984)—Lucio Fulci turned once more to the *giallo* for his next film. Even so, it's not as brutal and uncompromising as *The New York Ripper* (1982) and contains many indications of Fulci's desire to create a more mainstream brand of horror film. He would later describe *Murder-Rock* as a perfect American television movie, although it's unlikely many people would see that as a compliment.

Despite a reasonable plot and a decent cast, the setting—a modern dance school—and the lengthy scenes of people in leotards and leg warmers dancing to Keith Emerson's absurd disco tunes, hampers *Murder-Rock*. Clearly the Italian Godfather of Gore was hoping to hop on the *Fame* bandwagon, something that makes the film horribly dated to anyone

The Godfather of Gore takes on the Kids From Fame in *Murder-Rock*.

watching after 1985. Emerson's music is painful to hear and is worlds away from his bombastic, intrusive yet mostly acclaimed work on Dario Argento's *Inferno* (1980). Beneath the awful 1980s gloss lies a worthwhile plot, fueled by well-rounded characters, such as Candice Norman, the teacher whose life and sanity are unraveling quickly in the wake of the killings. Some judiciously placed blood and gore would have enlivened the story, but here Fulci goes for a discreet method of killing and a general sense of restraint.

In terms of plot and characterization, *Murder-Rock* is a decent enough film, but its hard to escape the feeling that this is Fulci running at half speed. The attempts at Americanization do not suit a characteristically Italian director, and such missteps mark the film as another misbegotten effort from the great man's declining years.

The Murder Secret (1989)
Aka: Non aver paura della zia Marta, The Broken Mirror,
Don't Be Afraid of Aunt Martha

Director: Robert Martin [Mario Bianchi]; Story/Screenplay: Robert Martin [Mario Bianchi]; Producer: Luigi Nannerini, Antonino Lucidi; Makeup: Guiseppe Ferranti; Music: Gianni Esposito
Starring: Adriano Rosso, Gabriele Tinti, Anna Maria Placido, Jessica Moore [Luciana Ottaviani], Maurice Poli, Massimiliano Massimi, Edoardo Massimi, Sacha Maria Darwin

Aunt Martha returns home from a mental hospital, so her family decides to visit. When they arrive at the house the caretaker tells them that she isn't there, but will return tomorrow. They are invited to stay in the house until she returns, as long as they don't go in the cellar…

The Murder Secret is one of several horror films produced by Luigi Nannerini and Antonino Lucidi in the late 1980s. A deal with Lucio Fulci allowed these films to carry the heading *"Lucio Fulci Presents…"* without any actual contributions from the aging director. Unsurprisingly, the presence of Fulci's name has allowed *The Murder Secret* a longer lease on life than would have been otherwise possible given the poor script, creaky acting and generally dull atmosphere.

The association with Fulci is surprisingly appropriate because *The Murder Secret* does indeed resemble one of the director's films, especially his later works. It starts off well and sets up a fairly interesting scenario. Unfortunately this soon gives way to clichéd plot twists and standard horror film red herrings. After 40 minutes the film begins to pick up speed, throwing in some genuinely gruesome murders. Sadly, the director exhausts his entire supply of victims, and we're back to the derivative plot. Eventually we're treated to a conclusion that should induce groans from even the most tolerant of viewers.

Aside from a handful of decent gore scenes, *The Murder Secret* is a substandard film. Even the editing—by longtime Fulci collaborator Vincenzo Tomassi—is lifeless and amateurish. Fulci's *Nightmare Concert* (1990) quotes *The Murder Secret*'s standout scene, but audiences are not missing much if that's all they see. This kind of Italian splatter film might have done okay 10 years before, but by 1989 the interest in such movies had largely faded.

The New York Ripper (1982)
Aka: Lo squartatore di New York

Director: Lucio Fulci; Story: Gianfranco Clerici, Vincenzo Mannino, Lucio Fulci; Screenplay: Gianfranco Clerici, Vincenzo Mannino, Lucio Fulci, Dardano Sacchetti; Producer: Fabrizio De Angelis; Makeup: Franco Di Girolami, Rosario Prestopino; Music: Francesco De Masi Starring: Jack Hedley (Lt. Fred Williams), Almanta Keller (Fay Majors), Howard Ross [Renato Rossini] (Mickey Scellenda), Andrew

Painter [Andrea Occhipinti] (Peter Bunch), Alexandra Delli Colli (Jane Forrester Lodge), Paolo Malco (Dr. Davis), Cinzia De Ponti (Rosie), Laurence Welles [Cosimo Cinieri] (Dr. Lodge), Daniela Doria (Jenny/Kitty), Babette New (Mrs. Weissburger), Zora Kerowa [Zora Keslerova] (Eva from the sex show), Barbara Cupisti

A maniac is brutally murdering women in New York. In an effort to track down the killer, the police consult a psychologist.

The New York Ripper is undoubtedly Lucio Fulci's most notorious film and one of the more infamous titles in the Italian exploitation canon. It also marks the end of the director's so-called golden age that began with 1979's *Zombie*. Does an unrecognized classic lurk behind all the accusations of misogyny and sensationalist violence, or is *The New York Ripper* just another piece of unsavory trash?

The answer is probably somewhere in between the two, although it leans toward the latter. The film is a well-constructed and good-looking effort. This is probably thanks to cinematographer Luigi Kuveiller, who worked on Fulci's 1971 *giallo*, *A Lizard in A Woman's Skin*, as well as Dario Argento's *Deep Red* (1975). Kuveiller's roving camera keeps things interesting and gives us gruesome close-ups of the murders. The green-tinted episode in the back room of the strip club is perhaps the standout scene in terms of visual appeal. Veteran composer Francesco De Masi—a mainstay of the Italian exploitation scene since the early 1960s—provides an excellent score that's firmly entrenched in 1970s cop thriller territory.

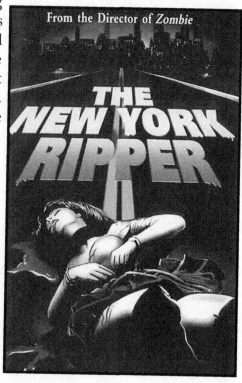

On the downside, the question of the film's misogynistic violence is hard to avoid. Although women have been poorly treated in many of Fulci's films—as they are in most horror films, to be fair—the violence in *The New York Ripper* seems to go one step further with

nipples being slashed by razors and women being stabbed in the crotch with broken bottles. Fulci's difficult relations with the female gender are well documented, but few of his films have been quite so explicit in their disgust for women and feminine sexuality. Is Fulci responsible for these elements? He did contribute to the script, but so did Gianfranco Clerici and Vincenzo Mannino, a writing team known for the excessive sexual violence of their scripts. Ultimately it is perhaps unfair to criticize the director for including such things in his films, since they have been a regular feature—perhaps in a less explicit form—of Italian horror since the 1950s. Other directors such as Mario Landi and Andrea Bianchi have included sexually violent scenes regularly in their films, but it's a shame to see a director as talented as Fulci descending to the level of his less-than-worthy compatriots.

Other flaws abound in *The New York Ripper*, however. It's isn't particularly well scripted, with Paolo Malco's little psychological insights coming across as trite and clichéd, not to mention inaccurate. However, poor scripting can't compare with the exceptionally ill-advised decision to have the killer quack like a duck during the killings. It ruins the suspense, provoking giggles rather than fear, and the plot doesn't even support this quirk. What could have been a grim and nihilistic *giallo* is turned into a farce by that one decision. *The New York Ripper* would never have been a masterpiece, but losing the absurd quacking could only improve the film. Fulci makes a cameo appearance as a senior cop.

Nightmare City (1980)
Aka: Incubo sulla città contaminata, City of the Walking Dead

Director: Umberto Lenzi; Story/Screenplay: Antonio Cesare Corti, Luis María Delgado, Piero Regnoli; Producer: Diego Alchimede, Luis Méndez; Special Effects: Franco Di Girolami; Makeup: Guiseppe Ferranti, Antonio Corridori; Music: Stelvio Cipriani
Starring: Hugo Stiglitz (Dean Miller), Mel Ferrer (General Murchison), Laura Trotter (Dr. Ann Miller), Maria Rosaria Omaggio (Sheila), Fran-

cesco Rabal (Major Warren Holmes), Sonia Viviani (Cindy), Eduardo Fajardo (Dr. Kramer), Stefania D'Amario (Jessica Murchison), Ugo Bologna (Mr. Desmond), Sara Franchetti (Liz), Manolo Zarzo (Colonel Donahue), Tom Felleghi (Lieutenant Rafeman), Pierangelo Civera (Jessica's Husband)

An unmarked plane makes an emergency landing at an airport. As security forces surround the plane, a door opens and a horde of disfigured zombies burst out, attacking the waiting soldiers. As the creatures spread out across the city, groups of survivors try to reach the relative safety of the countryside.

Shortly after the release of *Burial Ground*, writer Piero Regnoli prepared yet another zombie script, this time in partnership with Antonio Corti. Spanish producer Diego Archimede commissioned the work as part of a joint Spanish/Italian/Mexican venture. Bizarrely enough, the completed script was first offered to Enzo G. Castellari, who declined, and the job went to the prolific Umberto Lenzi. He immediately suggested that the script be altered, losing the traditional zombies in favor of fast-moving intelligent creatures, disfigured and driven insane by nuclear radiation. *Nightmare City* thus became the first Italian zombie film to move away from the usual mystical, voodoo-influenced territory.

Until the hackneyed plot twist turns up at the end, *Nightmare City* is a surprisingly entertaining film, even though it's obviously not a classic. Naturally the story contains second-rate mate-

rial, but Lenzi has enough sense to keep things moving quickly. The frenzied, gun-wielding zombies rampage through the streets and buildings, glossing over plot holes and continuity errors. Daniele Alabiso's competent editing helps the film seem a lot shorter than it really is, which is a definite bonus. Alabiso started work in the early 1960s, and managed to work on every kind of exploitation film—Westerns, *peplums*, *Emmanuelle* clones, *gialli*, women-in-prison flicks, not to mention Deodato's *Jungle Holocaust* (1977).

Despite the director's objections, the co-producers insisted that Hugo Stiglitz, a popular Mexican actor, play the lead role. Unfortunately he's incredibly wooden and manages to make it through most of the film without displaying a trace of emotion, even when faced with scenes of carnage and destruction. It's nice to see genre favorites like Mel Ferrer, but it would be good to see him in a larger role, since he's better than most of the actors here. The mixed Spanish-Italian players are generally competent, but they're not asked to do much more than strip off and/or get killed.

Makeup men Giuseppe Ferranti and Antonio Corridori both had fairly illustrious careers. Ferranti worked on both *The Bird with the Crystal Plumage* (1970) and *The Cat O'Nine Tails* (1971), and he later provided the gruesome makeup for Lenzi's *Cannibal ferox* (1981). He would go on to work with Lamberto Bava, Bruno Mattei and Lucio Fulci. Corridori assisted on *Phenomena* (1985) and *Opera* (1987). All of which makes it all the more puzzling—why do the zombies in *Nightmare City* look so bad? Apparently it took over an hour to apply the makeup for each of the zombies, but I'm at a loss to see why smearing brown shoe polish on an actor's face should take quite so long. Stelvio Ciprani does provide a great score, however, even if it is oddly reminiscent of several more famous scores from his past.

Nightmare City has the distinction of being one of the few zombie movies to have its basis in real events. In July 1976, in the Seveso Oak Forest near the town of Meda in northern Italy, a valve broke at an unmanned chemical factory, releasing around 3,000 kilos of chemical material into the atmosphere. The effects were devastating. Although nobody was killed, some 37,000 people were affected, and 80,000 farm animals had to be slaughtered to avoid contaminated meat. The symptoms included immune system problems, neurological disorders and spontaneous miscarriages. Perhaps the most curious effect was the change in the gender ratio; after the accident, the male-to-female birth ratio altered from the usual 1:1 to 1:2, leaving a generation of children that contained roughly twice as many females as males.

The accident at Seveso brought the dangers of chemical pollution to the attention of the people of Italy, and Lenzi decided that it would be wise to capitalize on this new fear. The creatures of *Nightmare City* might look comical compared to the real horrors presented by Chernobyl (for example), but the director should perhaps be given credit for trying to give his film a more contemporary feel. George Romero had previously suggested that radiation or pollution was responsible for the dead returning to life—*Biohazard*, the Japanese title for *Dawn of the Dead*, is particularly suggestive[5]—but until that point, Italian filmmakers had always resorted to pre-Romero explanations.

Nightmare Concert (1990)
Aka: Un gatto nel cervello (I volti del terrore), A Cat in the Brain

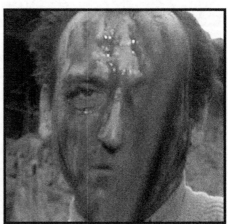

Director: Lucio Fulci; Story / Screenplay: Lucio Fulci, John Fitzsimmons, Antonio Tentori; Producer: Luigi Nannerini, Anthony Clear [Antonino Lucidi]; Makeup: Pino Ferrante [Giuseppe Ferranti]; Music: Fabio Frizzi
Starring: Lucio Fulci (Dr. Lucio Fulci), Brett Halsey (The Monster), Ria De Simone (The Soprano), Sasha Darwin (Woman in Microwave Oven), Robert Egon (Second Monster), David I. Thompson (Professor Egon Schwarz), Melissa Lang [Malisa Longo] (Katya Schwarz), Shilett Angel (Filipo, the Producer), Jeffrey Kennedy (Gabrielli, the Producer), Judy Morrow (Lilly, the Nurse), Paul Muller (Man crushed by Wheelchair), Maurice Poli

(Newsreader), Paolo Cozzo (Psychiatrist's assistant), Vincenzo Luzzi (Man with Chainsaw)[uncredited]

A splatter film director (called Lucio Fulci, bizarrely enough) is having difficulty distinguishing between real life and the violent movies he makes. In an effort to resolve the issue, he visits a psychiatrist. Unfortunately the shrink is a little unstable himself, and sets Lucio up to take the fall for his own killing spree.

It's safe to say that *Nightmare Concert* is Lucio Fulci's worst film. It's not an exaggeration to describe it as one of the worst horror films ever made. Even in his declining years, the director managed to pull one or two redeeming features out of the bag, even if the film as a whole wasn't up to the standards of his earlier work. *Nightmare Concert*, however, is a total failure.

Nightmare Concert is a slapdash concoction, a mixture of some badly shot original scenes, with a great deal of material cribbed from other films, including some of Fulci's own. *Ghosts of Sodom* and *Touch of Death* (both 1988) weren't exactly great films in the first place, so the wisdom of recycling them is somewhat questionable. The rest of the clips come from a number of low budget, late-1980s Italian horror films, several of them released under the spurious *"Lucio Fulci presents…"* banner. Obviously it was cheaper for Fulci to secure material taken from films with which he had nominally been involved. More than half of the film's running time is taken up with these clips, which are sloppily edited into the narrative.

The star of the film is Fulci himself, playing a horror film director usually referred to as "Dr. Fulci." He's not a great actor, but then neither is anyone else in *Nightmare Concert*. The story is pretty bland, however, serving mostly as a prop on which to hang the gore scenes.

This wouldn't be so bad, but some of them are patently absurd, especially the death-by-wheelchair episode. The poor quality of the special effects is supposed to reflect the cheap scenes in Dr. Fulci's movies, but that doesn't make them fun to watch.

It's clear from interviews that Fulci considered *Nightmare Concert* one of his better films and a personal triumph. Sadly, not all of his fans agree. For most viewers, the film is a messy, amateurish collection of second-hand splatter scenes with no redeeming qualities. *Nightmare Concert* is the absolute low point of the great man's career.

Nothing Underneath (1983)
Aka: Sotto il vestito niente

Director: Carlo Vanzina; Story: Marco Parma (novel *Sotto il vestito niente*); Screenplay: Enrico Vanzina, Carlo Vanzina, Franco Ferrini; Producer: Achille Manzotti; Special Effects: Corridori [Giovanni & Antonio Corridori]; Music: Pino Donaggio
Starring: Tom Schanley (Bob Crane), Renee Simonsen (Barbara), Nicola Perrin (Jessica Crane), Maria McDonald (Margaux Wilson), Catherine Noyes (Carrie Blynn), Paolo Tomei (hotel porter), Sonia Raule (Christina Landolfi), Cyrus Elias (Giorgio Zanoni), Donald Pleasence (Inspector Danesi)

A Yellowstone park ranger sees his sister murdered in a nightmare, so he heads to Italy, where she is modeling, to make sure she is safe. When he arrives there, he finds she has gone missing. Receiving little help from the police, he tries to find her himself.

While it doesn't rank among the best efforts of the period, *Nothing Underneath* is still a solid, enjoyable example of the *giallo* in the mid-1980s. The flashy, shallow world of international modeling is a perfect backdrop for these films, particularly because it allows for a decent supply of attractive victims. The story is bolstered by the concept of a psychic link between the

CHASING FAME IS MURDER

hero and his sister, the killer's first victim. Thankfully Carlo Vanzina (the son of Steno, one of Italy's most famous comedy directors) is a talented individual able to imbue crucial scenes with a respectable level of tension. Very little gore appears, but the murder scenes are nicely orchestrated and suspenseful.

A few aspects of the film probably seemed like a good idea at the time (disco tunes by Murray Head and Gloria Gaynor, the characteristically 1980s fashion show), but these touches dated rapidly and will probably elicit groans or laughs from a modern audience. Nonetheless, *Nothing Underneath* is an entertaining example of a style of film soon to be replaced by dull erotic thrillers or one-note slasher movies. An appearance from Donald Pleasence is always welcome, but he doesn't have much to do here.

The Ogre (1988)
Aka: La casa dell'orco, The Ogre: Demons 3, Demons III: The Ogre

Director: Lamberto Bava; Story: Dardano Sacchetti; Screenplay: Dardano Sacchetti, Lamberto Bava; Producer: Lamberto Bava; Special Effects: Angelo Mattei; Makeup: Fabrizio Sforza; Music: Simon Boswell
Starring: Paolo Malco (Tom), Virginia Bryant (Cheryl), Sabrina Ferilli, Stefania Montorsi, Patrizia Vinci, Alice Di Giuseppe, Davide Flosi, Alex Serra

A writer, plagued by nightmares as a child, rents a villa in the countryside to complete her next novel. When she and her family arrive, she discovers that it's the same villa from her childhood nightmares, and suspects there may be something evil lurking in the cellar. Needless to say, her husband doesn't agree.

Although frequently marketed as the second *Demons* sequel, *The Ogre* is in fact a made-for-TV movie and part of Lamberto Bava's *Brivido Giallo* series. The other films in the series are *Graveyard Disturbance* (1987), *Until Death* (1987) and *Dinner with a Vampire* (1988). This gore free and lifeless offering will disappoint audiences expecting something in the same vein as *Demons* (1985). Like the other films in the series, *The Ogre* is poorly scripted and cheaply made. The competent cast makes the most of the material, but even the most talented of actors would have a hard time making this script sound good. The central premise—a horror novelist discovers that the nightmares she was plagued with as a child actually took place in the Italian castle where she is now spending her holidays—is seriously undermined by the fact that the creature from her nightmares is a man in a wobbly rubber suit that pads around the underground chambers like a pantomime villain. With such an unconvincing monster, it's hard to take the woman's increasingly fragile mental state seriously, not to mention her husband's brutish responses.

Plot holes and poor scripting aside, *The Ogre* is a surprisingly good-looking film. Gianfranco Transunto's camerawork is excellent, and the locations are great, especially the castle's dusty corridors and the junk-filled cellar. A shame these fine locations could not have been used more effectively. Simon Boswell's stately score is effectively creepy, but the effort is wasted. Like most of Lamberto Bava's television movies, this one is best avoided. The director has a brief cameo as one of the card players in the café.

Opera (1987)
Aka: Terror at the Opera

Director: Dario Argento; Story: Dario Argento; Screenplay: Dario Argento, Franco Ferrini; Producer: Dario Argento; Special Effects: Renato Agostini, Sergio Stivaletti, Antonio Corridori, Giovanni Corridori, Germano Natali; Makeup: Rosario Prestopino, Franco Casagni; Music: Brian Eno, Roger Eno, Claudio Simonetti
Starring: Christina Marsillach (Betty), Ian Charleson (Marco), Urbano Barberini (Inspector Alan Santini), Daria Nicolodi (Mira), Coralina Cataldi Tassoni (Julia), Antonella Vitale (Marion), William McNamara (Urbano), Barbara Cupisti (Albertini), Antonia Juorio, Carola Stagnaro, Francesca Cassola (Alma)

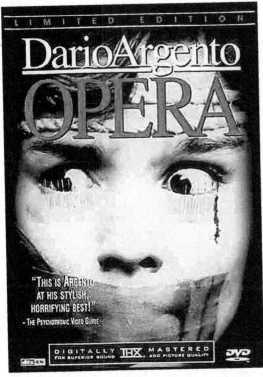

Betty, a young opera singer, is thrust into the spotlight when the star is involved in an accident. Unfortunately, a maniac is killing off the cast and crew, and he seems to be fixated on the young star.

After the lukewarm reception given to *Phenomena* (1985), Argento returned to more reliable territory with the excellent *Opera*. The film contains none of the fantasy elements that seemed so out of place in its predecessor, concentrating here on the director's established trademarks: innovative cinematography, well-constructed shots and exceptionally violent murders. While not as highly regarded as Argento's best works, *Opera* is still fine piece of Italian cinema.

Unfortunately, a string of annoying incidents dating back to the film's inception cursed the production. Producers offered Argento the opportunity to direct an opera, something the director had always wanted to do. He accepted the offer and proposed a version of Verdi's *Rigoletto*, a notoriously dark and tragic opera that originally featured a vampire. The producers objected, telling Argento to select a more traditional opera; he objected, and the projected was scrapped. The director then chose to construct a *giallo* around a production of Verdi's *Macbeth*, to star Vanessa Redgrave. However, the veteran actress fell out with the director and left the set acrimoniously. Ian Charleson was involved in a serious automobile accident and halted production of *Opera*. He returned before he had fully recovered, but work was delayed for several weeks. Tragically, Argento's father passed away during the shoot; however, the director elected to continue work.

Given the difficult circumstances, it's perhaps surprising that *Opera* is quite as good as it is. Traces of all these tragic incidents appear in the film, however; in the opening scene, the diva storms off the stage, suggesting that the director—who is attempting to create his first opera—return to his "crummy movies" (she's then hit by a car while crossing the street). Later the director's labeled as a good-for-nothing peddler of cheap horror movies. It's not difficult to see where Argento got the inspiration for these scenes.

Visually, *Opera* is stunning. Argento's camera—guided by acclaimed cinematographer Ronnie Taylor—stalks through the opera house like a snake. The scenes where the camera assumes the point of view of the circling crows is magnificent and required complex machinery to pull off. In the end this cinematography looks fluid and natural, and ranks among the best scenes of Argento's career. During the murders we are given close-ups of the victims, seeing their deaths in graphic detail. Due to the film's main plot device, these scenes are almost unbearably tense.

Crucially, Argento assembled a good cast. Christina Marsillach is excellent as the naïve understudy thrust against her wishes into both the limelight and the killer's perilous gaze. Noted British actor Ian Charleson gives a cool performance as the beleaguered director. Sadly, it would be one of his last roles; he died in 1990. Many of the lesser roles contain familiar Italian exploitation actors, including Urbano Barberini (*Demons*, 1985), Coralina Cataldi Tassoni (demonized in *Demons 2*, 1986, and wasted in *Evil Clutch*, 1988) and Barbara Cupisti (*Stagefright*, 1986; *Dellamorte Dellamore*, 1994). The director's ex-fiancée Daria Nicolodi has a small role, but it doesn't allow her to show her considerable talents.

A number of problems stop *Opera* from being an example of Argento at his best. As with *Phenomena*, the director mixes a sophisticated score—here provided by Brian Eno and Claudio Simonetti—with annoying heavy metal songs that detract from the tension of the movie. Far more damaging, however, is the somewhat elliptical ending. After a climatic scene in the opera house, we're transported to the Swiss Alps for an unnecessary and confusing epilogue that does nothing to improve the film. It's desperately out of keeping with the rest of the film and raises more questions than it answers.

Without the ill-advised end sequence (and the dumb heavy metal), *Opera* would rank not far behind *Tenebrae* (1982) in terms of quality. Unfortunately it takes its place among Argento's inconsistent later works as a worthwhile but ultimately unsuccessful film. However, there's plenty to enjoy, and the movie is certainly better than many late 1980s Italian horror films.

The Other Hell (1980)
Aka: L'altro inferno, Guardian of Hell

Director: Stefan Oblowsky [Bruno Mattei]; Story: Bruno Mattei, Claudio Fragrasso; Screenplay: Claudio Fragrasso; Producer: Arcangel Picchi; Makeup: Giuseppe Ferranti; Music: Goblin

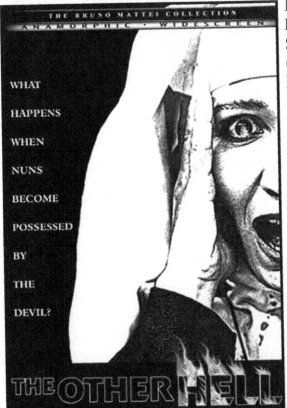

Starring: Franca Stoppi (Mother Superior), Carlo De Mejo (Father Valerio), Francesca Carmeno, Susan Forget, Frank Garfeild [Franco Garofalo], Paola Montenero, Sandy Samuel, Andrew Ray [Andrea Aureli]

A priest investigates a case of demonic possession at a convent.

Here Bruno Mattei and Claudio Fragrasso—the team that gave the world the execrable *Hell of the Living Dead* (1981)—step into the world of nunsploitation horror. And the results are about the same—a low-budget monstrosity with few redeeming features. Well, only one redeeming feature: the score, lifted from the superior *Beyond the Darkness* (1979).

Nunsploitation has only one real purpose—to present nuns in a variety of offensive or shocking activities. Granted it's difficult to shock the modern horror fan, but the material on display here is terrible. The closest we get to a shocking nun scene is the introduction, where a crazy nun stabs a dead nun in the crotch. After that, all we get is scared nuns and endless speeches about possession, sex and Satan. The film's most gratuitous moment isn't even nun-related and features the actual death of a chicken.

Mattei and Fragrasso rely upon first-timers for most of their cast, but a couple of decent actors appear here. Franca Stoppi is fine as the deranged Mother Superior, and while her performance isn't as good as her excellent turn in *Beyond the Darkness*, it's still the best thing about the film. Carlo De Mejo, a Fulci regular, does his best as a young priest sent to investigate the strange goings-on, but he's not able to make too much out of the terrible script.

The Other Hell was shot at the same time as another nunsploitation film, *The True Story of the Nun of Monza*. With Mattei and Fragrasso working on two films at once, often utilizing the same cast and crew, it's hardly surprising that neither film is particularly good. This one is for nasty nun completists only.

Paganini Horror (1989)
Aka: Il violino che uccide, The Killing Violin

Director: Lewis Coates [Luigi Cozzi]; Story: Raimondo Del Balzo; Screenplay: Daria Nicolodi, Luigi Cozzi; Producer: Fabrizio De Angelis; Special Effects: Paolo Ricci; Makeup: Franco Casagni, Rosario Prestopino; Music: Vince Tempera Starring: Daria Nicolodi (Sylvia Hackett), Jasmine

Jasmine Main falls under the spell of the *Paganini Horror*.

Main, Pascal Persiano, Maria Christina Mastrangeli, Michele Kilipp-stein, Pietro Genuardi, Luana Ravagnini, Roberto Giannini, Giada Cozzi, Elena Pompei, Perla Constantini, Donald Pleasence (Mr. Pickett)

An all-girl rock band finds a lost piece of sheet music written by Paganini, and decides to craft their next hit around it. They hire an old mansion in which to shoot the video, but the music summons a demonic presence that proceeds to kill them off, one by one.

Venice may be one of the most beautiful cities in Europe, but it's the kiss of death for Italian horror films. Nicholas Roeg managed to shoot the excellent *Don't Look Now* (1973) there, but it's also been the backdrop for trash like *Giallo a Venezia* (1979), *Vampire in Venice* (1988) and *Paganini Horror*, a third-rate Satanic thriller from the incomparable Luigi Cozzi.

Where to begin? Everything about this movie is flawed, amateurish and downright silly, from the plot to the acting to the special effects and all stops in between. Besides the awful rock songs, we're treated to some of the worst dialogue ever: "No one's ever done it before, except for Michael Jackson's *Thriller* with its fantastic video clip!" Many of the voices are incompetently dubbed, and Donald Pleasence clearly didn't stick around long enough to record his own part, so we don't even have the benefits of his familiar croaky rasp. The rest of the actors overact horribly and throw themselves into hysterics wherever possible. At first this is amusing, but it quickly becomes very tiresome. I'm still not sure why Daria Nicolodi agreed to appear in the film. Ordinarily I'd say it was because she also co-wrote the script, but that's not something you'd want to admit.

It's said that every film has at least one positive feature; in the case of *Paganini Horror*, it's probably the brief glimpses of Venice. But there's still no reason to sit through the whole 93 minutes of hell.

Patrick Still Lives (1980)
Aka: Patrick viva ancora, Patrick Is Still Alive

Director: Mario Landi; Story/Screenplay: Piero Regnoli; Producer: Gabriele Crisanti; Special Effects/Makeup: Vincenzo Napoli, Rosario Prestopino; Music: Berto Pisano
Starring: Sacha Pitoeff (Professor Herchell), Gianni Dei (Patrick Herschell), Maria Angela Giordano (Stella Randolph), Carmen Russo (Cheryl Cough), Paolo Giusti (David Davies), Franco Silva (Lyndon Cough), John Benedy (Peter Suniak), Anna Veneziano (Lidya Grant)

A young man is comatose after a traffic accident. Although unable to move or communicate, he possesses considerable psychic power. Years later the boy's father invites a group of people to stay at his health spa. One of them is responsible for Patrick's accident, and his father is determined to have his revenge.

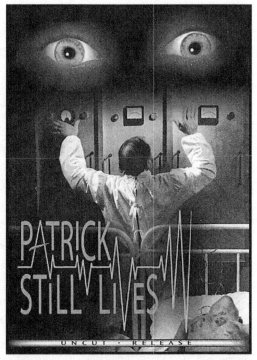

The curse of the unofficial sequel has led to some odd movies, but perhaps the strangest is *Patrick Still Lives*. An alleged follow-up to the minor Australian thriller *Patrick*, it's hard to say why this film was made, since the original wasn't exactly a box office smash. The extremely violent and sexual nature of the film made it unlikely that it would reach a particularly wide audience but such attributes ensured it a certain degree of notoriety.

Those viewers familiar with producer Gabriele Crisanti's other films from this period—*Malabimba, Giallo a Venezia* (both 1979) and *Burial Ground* (1980)—

will know exactly what is in store here: extreme violence, graphic (and twisted) sex and at least one memorable scene featuring Crisanti's then-wife, Maria Angelo Giordano. Here she has the pleasure of being impaled—through the crotch—by a psychically guided fireplace poker. It's the most violent and notorious scene in the film, but the others aren't far behind. Masturbation, decapitation, boiling and dog attacks also appear, all portrayed in graphic detail, even if the special effects are largely poor.

The sole intention of *Patrick Still Lives* is to shock and titillate, so it's hardly surprising that Mario Landi's direction is virtually nonexistent and Piero Regnoli's script crass and pointless. The cast members, many of whom appeared in other Crisanti films, are low-grade exploitation types that recite their lines in a wooden fashion and are killed off with equal flair. This was veteran Sacha Pitoeff's last film, an ignoble end to a career that started 30 years before and included a central role in Dario Argento's *Inferno* (1980).

Gorehounds and the exceptionally jaded might find something to appreciate in *Patrick Still Lives*, although it's more likely to involve laughing at the film rather than celebrating its excesses. Not as gory as *Burial Ground* but more interesting than *Giallo a Venezia*, the film remains a curious footnote to Italian exploitation cinema.

Phantom of Death (1988)
Aka: Un delitto poco comune, Off Balance

Director: Ruggero Deodato; Story: Gianfranco Clerici, Vincenzo Mannino; Screenplay: Gianfranco Clerici, Vincenzo Mannino, Gigli-

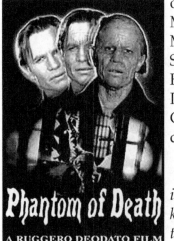

ola Battaglini; Producer: Pietro Innocenzi; Makeup: Fabrizio Sforza, Franco Schioppa; Music: Pino Donaggio
Starring: Michael York (Robert Dominici), Edwige Fenech (Hélène Martell), Donald Pleasence (Inspector Datti Downey), Mapi Galan (Susanna), Giovanni Lombardo Radice (Giuliano)

A renowned pianist, driven to the brink of insanity by a rare aging disease, embarks on a killing spree, taunting the police and challenging them to catch him before he dies.

Phantom of Death
A RUGGERO DEODATO FILM

Phantom of Death marked a return to form for Ruggero Deodato after the disappointing *Body Count* (1986) and an ill-advised foray in *Conan*-style mayhem with *The Barbarians* (1987). The same team that wrote Lucio Fulci's *New York Ripper* (1982) penned the script here, but Deodato's film is superior in almost every respect. Here we have a killer suffering from a rare aging disease making it almost impossible to recognize him, and add to this mix a detective who is on the verge of retirement but determined to crack the case. While not as graphically violent as *Cannibal Holocaust* (1979)—or even *Cut and Run* (1985)—*Phantom of Death* includes enough gore to please fans of the red stuff.

Veterans Donald Pleasence and Michael York take the central roles—detective and murderer—and York turns in his best performance in years. Neither role breaks new territory, but it's a pleasure to see two talented actors making the most of a well-written script. The lovely Edwige Fenech—in a break from her usual comedy roles—appears as York's girlfriend, struggling to work out what is happening. Even with a respectable cast, the credibility of the whole film hangs on Fabrizio Sforza's makeup, and thankfully his work is excellent. York's transformation from boyishly good-looking middle age to moribund decrepitude is smooth and realistic.

Unfortunately the second half of the film is too leisurely, failing to maintain the appropriate level of suspense. The killer's motives are not adequately explained, something that casts a shadow over the whole movie. With more exposition and tighter scriptwriting, *Phantom of Death* could have been a classic *giallo*. Even with these flaws, it's one of the director's best films; it's essential viewing for anyone who thinks Deodato is only good for cannibal tales and Amazonian adventures.

Phenomena (1985)
Aka: Creepers

Director: Dario Argento; Story/Screenplay: Dario Argento, Franco Ferrini; Producer: Dario Argento; Special Effects: Sergio Stivaletti, Tonino Corridori [Antonio Corridori], Luigi Cozzi; Makeup: Pierantonio Mecacci; Music: Goblin, Simon Boswell
Starring: Jennifer Connelly (Jennifer Corvino), Daria Nicolodi (Mrs. Bruckner), Dalila Di Lazzaro (headmistress), Patrick Bauchau (Inspector Rudolf Geiger), Donald Pleasence (Dr. John McGregor), Fiore Argento (Vera Brandt), Federia Mastroianni (Sophie), Fiorenza Tessari (Gisela Sulzer), Mario Donatone (Morris Shapiro), Francesca Ottaviani (nurse), Michele Soavi (Kurt), Franco Trevisi (real estate agent)

Jennifer Corvino, the daughter of an American film star, is sent to study at a Swiss college. She is not a normal girl. On her first night at the school she sleepwalks and witnesses a brutal murder, and she also has the power to communicate with and control insects. When she befriends a wheelchair-bound entomologist, they combine their respective talents to try to catch the killer.

Phenomena is one of Argento's most-discussed films, and fans tend to fall into one of two camps—those who view it as a magical and sensuous journey through fairy tale territory, and those who see it as an overblown mish-mash of half-formed elements and ideas, thrown together with the minimum of effort.

Being fair to the director, *Phenomena* is a great-looking film. His sense of color and contrast is as good as it ever was, meaning the film is not without interest. Unfortunately it's saddled with an absurd plot, poor dialogue, a generally lackluster cast and a sometimes intrusive musical score.

As Argento's first film to be shot entirely in English, it's hardly surprising that some linguistic difficulties exist. However, that doesn't really excuse the atrocious dialogue. The most famous example is the oft-quoted line, "It's perfectly normal for insects to be slightly telepathic," but several other groan-inducing moments appear. A skillful cast can sometimes overcome script problems, but aside from the reliable Donald Pleasence, few of the cast appear to be interested in their roles. Daria Nicolodi turns in one of her worst performances ever, while central star Jennifer Connelly (later in the award-winning drama *A Beautiful Mind*, 2001) seems wooden and shallow.

The plot itself seems to be an attempt to graft more fantastic elements onto a *giallo* framework. So we end up with a teenager who has a telepathic link with insects investigating a series of murders at an isolated girl's school, aided by a wheelchair-bound Scots entomologist and a sympathetic chimpanzee. There are the usual scenes of extreme cruelty and violence, leading at least one commentator to suggest Argento had descended to the level of Fulci. However, on this charge at least the director is innocent, since the scenes in *Phenomena* are no worse than others in *Deep Red* (1976) or *Inferno* (1980). Nonetheless, the plot is far-fetched and cumbersome, impeding the necessary suspension of disbelief.

Having already demonstrated his love of heavy metal in Lamberto Bava's *Demons* (1985), Argento chose to display it once again in *Phenomena*. Songs from some of the biggest names in music—Motorhead and Iron Maiden—are interspersed with cuts from lesser acts such as Andi Sex Gang. Unfortunately the scenes involved would be better suited to Claudio Simonetti's synth-based ambience rather than Iron Maiden's overblown rock histrionics, which are simply intrusive and annoying.

Phenomena is the work of a director trying to break new ground rather than merely rehash his older work over and over. While that's a respectable ambition, the film is ultimately a failure. With some work on the script and a motivated cast, it could have been a decent—if unspectacular—effort, but in its current form it doesn't really compare to the rest of Argento's pre-*Trauma* catalogue.

Piranha II: The Spawning (1981)
Aka: Piranha paura, Piranha II: Flying Killers

Director: James Cameron, Ovidio G. Assonitis [uncredited]; Story/
Screenplay: H.A. Milton; *producers* Ovidio G. Assonitis, Chako van
Leeuwen, Jeff Schechtman; Special Effects: Giannetto De Rossi, Gil-
berto Carbonari, Antonio Corridori; Makeup: Maurizio Trani; Music:
Steve Powder [Stevio Cipriani]
Starring: Tricia O'Neal (Anne Kimbrough), Steve Marachuk (Tyler
Sherman), Lance Henriksen (Steve Kimbrough), Ricky G. Paull (Chris
Kimbrough), Ted Richert (Raoul), Leslie Graves (Allison)

*Genetically engineered flying piranhas start attacking tourists at a Ca-
ribbean resort.*

History has seen fit to categorize *Piranha II* as one of the worst
sequels ever made— not to mention one of the worst *films*. Although
Joe Dante's 1978 hit *Piranha* was a successful and popular film, this
cheap Italian sequel is dull, derivative and frustrating. After fighting
in the courts to gain control of the original, producers van Leeuwen
and Schechtman headed to Italy, where the cost of filmmaking is considerably lower, and the results sometimes terrible. Aside from the

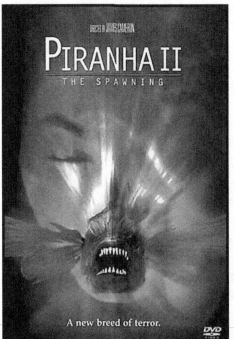

A new breed of terror.

two producers, none of the cast and
the crew from Dante's film worked
on the sequel.

It's not clear whether a competent crew could have made something more of the film, since the
script is so bad. Undoubtedly written by a hack using a pseudonym
(H.A. Milton spells Hamilton), it's
a mass of absurdities and clichés.
The piranhas are now unrecogniz-
able; aside from their ability to fly,
they seem only interested in killing
their victims and their traditional
blood frenzy is entirely absent. The
material is handled completely
straight. The only humorous ele-
ment is the suggestion by the town

sheriff that the deaths are due to ordinary shark attacks, rather than bio-engineered tropical fish.

Piranha II would probably have been lost to the mists of time by now if it weren't for the phenomenal success of the director, James Cameron. At one point Cameron preferred to give the impression that *The Terminator* (1984) was his first film, but he has recently shown a willingness to discuss this earlier film. According to his account, Cameron shot the entire film, but was then fired and barred from the studio, with producer Assonitis removing his name from the project and editing his own version. Assonitis claims that Cameron only shot a week's worth of footage before he was fired. The truth of the matter is largely irrelevant, since little about the film is reminiscent of Cameron's later work. It is fairly

similar to Assonitis' dreadful *Tentacles* (1977), another aquatic monster film that also featured composer Stelvio Cipriani and cinematographer Roberto D'Ettorre Piazzoli.

Almost everything about *Piranha II* is mediocre. Antonio Corridori turns out some fake-looking fish with visible wires, just as bad as the shark monster in Lamberto Bava's *Monster Shark* (1984). Also the usually reliable Giannetto De Rossi and Maurizio Trani fail to provide even decent gore, so viewers can't even enjoy this as a splatter film. None of the cast was particularly experienced at the time, so it's hardly surprising that they struggle with the atrocious script. Lance Henriksen would later become a respected genre actor (starring in some of James Cameron's best films), but this does not rank amongst his finest work. *Piranha II* might be of interest as an example of one of Henriksen's early roles, but few other people are likely to spend time tracking this down.

Porno Holocaust (1981)
Aka: Holocausto Porno

Director: Joe D'Amato [Aristide Massacessi]; Story / Screenplay: Tom Salina [Aristide Massacessi]; Makeup: Massimo Camilleti; Music: Nico Fidenco
Starring: George Eastman [Luigi Montefiore], Dirce Funari [Patrizia Funari]; Annj Goren [Annamaria Napoletano], Mark Shannon [Manlio Cersosimo], Lucia Ramirez, Aristide Massacessi

A group of scientists head off to a tropical island to study the effects of atomic testing years earlier. The island isn't entirely deserted however — a solitary creature, mutated by the radiation, is waiting for them.

Since the early 1970s Aristide Massacessi has been making large amounts of money from softcore porn movies, often combining them with whatever bandwagon was passing at the time: *peplums* (*The Arena*, 1973), jungle / cannibal efforts (*Trap Them and Kill Them*, 1977), *Emmanuelle* clones, *mondo* movies, etc. When the horror movie became popular, aside from his own splatter efforts (*Anthropophagous*, 1980, etc.), Massacessi experimented with combining hardcore sex with horror. *Porno Holocaust* is one such attempt, shot at roughly the same

time as *Erotic Nights of the Living Dead* (1981), using many of the cast and crew members.

If readers pardon the pun, he screws it up pretty badly. Sex scenes are interrupted by the arrival of a huge zombie that is more interested in oral sex than cannibalism. Without going into too much detail, the film is a mess. Hardcore porn stars can't act, and Massacessi's script is porn movie bad. The horror elements are pretty muted, with none of the rampant blood and gore that colored his other genre efforts. This is unlikely to please fans of either horror or hardcore. Most will just smirk at the title and move on.

The Prince of Terror (1988)
Aka: Il maestro del terrore

Director: Lamberto Bava; Story: Ira Goldman; Screenplay: Dardano Sacchetti; Producer: Lamberto Bava, Andrea Piazzesi; Special Effects: Sergio Stivaletti, Ditta Corridori; Makeup: Franco Casagni; Music: Simon Boswell
Starring: Tomas Arana (Vincent Omen), Carole André, David Brandon (Paul Hilary), Ulisse Minervini, Joyce Pitti, Marina Viro, Virginia Bryant, Pascal Druant, Augusto Poderosi

A maniac holds a notorious horror film director and his family hostage. It isn't long before the director turns the tables on his attackers.

Throwaway scripts and a lack of contentious material usually hamper Lamberto Bava's television movies, which is to say there's very little violence and no sex. *Prince of Terror* is different, however. Not only does it boast a fairly decent story, but the film is also very gruesome in places. The death of the family dog is particularly nasty, demonstrating that directors can still squeeze some life out of the old horror film clichés.

Most of the film takes place in the director's isolated house, allowing for a suitably tense atmosphere as the victims end up playing cat-and-mouse with the killer. A strong performance from Tomas Arana as horror director Vincent Omen helps to counterbalance some deficiencies in the script, while the knife-wielding maniac is straight out of the David Hess school of acting really nasty. Thankfully Sacchetti throws in a few twists to keep things from growing stale. Such twists are not particularly innovative, but they're still welcome. The conclusion is silly, but *The Prince of Terror* is definitely Bava's best film since *Demons 2* (1986). Unlike most of his made-for-television movies, it's interesting, gory and at times quite unpleasant.

The Ratman (1988)
Aka: Quella villa in fondo al parco

Director: Anthony Ascott [Giuliani Carnimeo]; Story/Screenplay: David Parker, Jr. [Elisa Livia Briganti]; Producer: Maurice Matthew [Fabrizio De Angelis]; Special Effects: Franco Giannini; Music: Stefano Mainetti
Starring: David Warbeck, Janet Agren, Nelson De La Rosa, Eva Grimaldi, Luisa Menon, Werner Pochath

A monster terrorizes a group of fashion models. The sister of one of the models teams up with a writer to track down and destroy the creature.

The Ratman is confirmed exploitation trash and also something of a guilty pleasure. Taken as a straight film, it's pretty awful, but it's very entertaining in an Ed Wood sort of way. David Warbeck and Janet Agren are always good to see, with Warbeck playing the lantern-jawed hero as usual. If audiences watch this film under its English title then the creature responsible will be immediately obvious, but it's fun watching the cast play amateur detective anyway.

Typically for an Italian exploitation flick, plenty of nudity and gore's on display. Franco Giannini's effects aren't always great, but the sight of Nelson De La Rosa—at 72 c.m., the world's smallest actor—dressed up in claws and rat makeup is absolutely priceless. De La Rosa appears to be having great fun with the role, despite the heavy makeup. It's a shame that *The Ratman* has not seen an official release in English, because an audience exists for this one-of-a-kind splatter film.

Rats: Night of Terror (1984)
Aka: Rats—Notti di terrore

Director: Bruno Mattei; Story: Bruno Mattei; Screenplay: Claudio Fragrasso, Hervé Piccini; Special Effects/Makeup: Giuseppe Ferranti; Music: Luigi Ceccarelli

Starring: Richard Raymond [Ottaviano Dell'Acqua] (Kurt), Janna Ryann [Geretta Giancarlo] (Chocolate), Alex McBride [Massimo Vanni] (Taurus), Richard Cross (Video), Ann Gisel Glass (Myrna), Christopher Bretner [Jean-Christophe Brétigniere] (Lucifer), Tony Lombardo [Fausto Lombardi] (Deuce), Henry Luciani (Duke), Cindy Leadbetter (Diana), Chris Fremont (Noah), Moune Duvivier (Lilith)

In a post-apocalypse world, a group of motorcycle-riding scavengers search for food and water. While poking around a deserted town thousands of rats attack them and the scavengers must fight off the rat hordes.

Bruno Mattei has stated that *Rats: Night of Terror* is his favorite film, and it's not hard to see why. It's definitely one of his most entertaining efforts. As with most post-apocalypse movies, *Rats* is heavily influenced by *Mad Max* (1979) and *Mad Max 2: Road Warrior* (1981). Leather-clad motorcycle gangs mix with biker chicks sport-

ing big 1980s hairdos and heavily applied makeup. Stock footage of desolate areas of the United States creates the imagery of the futuristic world.

The cast consists of mostly minor players on the Italian exploitation scene. Massimo Vanni and Ottaviano Dell'Acqua both appeared in many Bruno Mattei films, and they're perfect for the low-budget horror/action efforts the director churned out for most of the decade. Neither of them are brilliant actors, but they have the sense to play the roles straight. Mattei himself is in fine form and handles the direction surprisingly well. Nothing's particularly adventurous here, but Mattei moves the film along at a decent pace that makes it a little easier to overlook the script deficiencies.

The film's greatest flaw is the rats themselves. For a start, they're not rats. Rats were apparently too hard to handle, so hundreds of guinea pigs were brought in and painted up to resemble their larger rodent cousins. Needless to say, the creatures don't look much like rats, and they don't act like them either. Unfortunately the guinea pigs are treated pretty badly during the film, and it does appear that a number of them were killed.

Perhaps the single most entertaining aspect of *Rats* is the climax. It's not certain whether Mattei and Fragrasso intended the film's big twist to be hilarious, but that's how it turned out. It's an unforgettable scene, and sure to leave viewers slack-jawed in disbelief. Even if audiences don't enjoy the rest of the movie, it's worth seeing for the jaw-dropping finale.

The Red Monks (1988)
Aka: I frati rossi

Director: Gianni Martucci; Story: Luciana Anna Spacca; Screenplay: Pino Buricchi, Gianni Martucci; Producer: Pino Buricchi; Music: Paolo Rustichelli
Starring: Gerardo Amato, Lara Wendel, Malisa Longo, Richard Brown, Claudio Pacifico, Mary Maxwell, Ronald Russo, Ludovico Dello Jojo

After a chance meeting in a forest, a young woman and a wealthy noble-man are married. Once she moves into the family mansion, the woman begins to suspect that her new husband has sinister designs upon her.

This dull occult sex thriller is one of the infamous *"Lucio Fulci presents..."* films. Producer Pino Buricchi bought the right to include the aging director's moniker on his own film, which would certainly have sunk without a trace were it not for Fulci's name. *The Red Monks* is not really worthy to be associated with Fulci, even during the director's declining final years.

It's hard to escape the fact that *The Red Monks* was shot on a very small budget. The killings are either off-screen, or perfunctory and brief, while the director pads out the running time with a lengthy rape scene. The scene is rendered even more distasteful by the fact that the victim seems to end up enjoying the experience and bears the rapist no outward malice. There is very little in the way of special effects, except for a ridiculous-looking spider that rivals the library scene in *The Beyond* (1981) for groan-inducing mediocrity. All these events are hung on a derivative plotline that doesn't

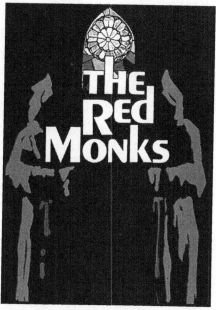

stand up to close scrutiny. Aside from Lara Wendel (*Tenebrae*, 1982; *Killing Birds*, 1987; *Ghosthouse*, 1988), no familiar faces appear in the cast. Even Eurohorror fanatics will find it hard to find something worth watching in this dismal effort, and less interested parties should give it a wide, wide berth. Director Gianni Martucci also helmed the minor-league *giallo Trhauma* (aka *Thrauma*, 1979).

The School of Fear (1989)
Aka: Il gioco

Director: Lamberto Bava; Story: Roberto Gandus, Dardano Sacchetti, Giorgio Stegano; Screenplay: Roberto Gandus; Producer: Lamberto Bava, Andrea Piazzesi; Special Effects: Franco Casagni; Music: Simon Boswell
Starring: Alessandra Acciai, Jean Herbert, Daria Nicolodi, Viola Simoncioni, Morena Turchi, Fabio Jellini, Stefano De Sando

Malicious students torment a new teacher.

[Notes: Made for television. Part of the *"Alta tensione"* series. Synopsis taken from internet sources.]

The Scorpion with Two Tails (1980)
Aka: Assassinio al cimitero Etrusco,
Murder in an Etruscan Cemetery

Director: Christian Plummer [Sergio Martino]; Story: Ernesto Gastaldi, Dardano Sacchetti; Screenplay: Ernesto Gastaldi, Maria Chianetta, Jacques Leitienne; Producer: Luciano Martino; Special Effects: Paolo Ricci; Music: Fabio Frizzi
Starring: Elvire Audray (Joan Barnard), Paolo Malco (Mike Grant), Claudio Cassinelli (Paolo Domelli), Marilu Tolo (Maria), Luigi Rossi, Van Johnson (Mulligan), Sonia Viviani (Contessa Maria Volumna), John Saxon (Arthur Barnard), Jacques Stany

After seeing his death in a dream, a young woman travels to Italy to find her archaeologist husband. She uncovers a labyrinthine plot involving Satanism, drug smuggling and murder.

The Scorpion with Two Tails is a condensed version of a seven-part miniseries, reworked into a feature film. The result is less than successful, combining flat acting, a terrible script and a noticeable shortage and blood and violence. For a supposed *giallo*, it's a very tame effort. The scenery is quite pleasant, but Martino fails to capitalize on the possibilities presented by the Etruscan ruins. He does know a good score when he hears one, though, but he clearly liked Fabio Frizzi's work on Lucio Fulci's *City of the Living Dead* (1980) because he recycles several parts of it here.

The cast is fun to watch, if only because of the many familiar faces. Cassinelli, a Martino regular, was in *The Island of the Fishmen* and *The Great Alligator* (both 1979). Paolo Malco appeared in both *The House by the Cemetery* (1981) and *The New York Ripper* (1982), while Elvira

Audray went on to star in *Amazonia* (1986), although that is not necessarily anything for which to be proud. Unfortunately John Saxon has only a small role, but it's good to see him anyway.

If audiences can cope with the absurd (and somehow still not interesting) plot twists, they will be rewarded with the equally senseless ending. However, sitting through the whole film is a thankless task, best left to insomniacs and completists.

The Sect (1991)
Aka: La setta, Demons 4, The Devil's Daughter

Director: Michele Soavi; Story/Screenplay: Dario Argento, Giovanni Romoli, Michele Soavi; Producer: Mario and Vittorio Cecchi Gori, Dario Argento; Special Effects: Massimo Cristofanelli; Makeup: Rosario Prestopino; Music: Pino Donaggio
Starring: Kelly Curtis (Miriam Kreisl), Herbert Lom (Gran Vecchio), Maria Angela Giordano (Kathryn), Michel Hans Adatte (Franz), Carla Cassola (Dr. Pernath), Angelika Maria Boeck (Mrs. Heins), Giovanni Lombardo Radice (Martin Romero), Niels Gullov (Mr. Henri), Tomas Arana (Damon)

After assisting an old man, a schoolteacher finds herself drawn into a nightmare world of murder and Satanic cults, with a local doctor her only ally.

Often released in English-speaking countries under the misleading title *The Devil's Daughter*, Michele Soavi's third film is a slow-moving and atmospheric tale of Satanic conspiracies. Forgoing the dazzling multi-colored visuals of his earlier films in favor of a quieter, more ethereal approach, *The Sect* is often overlooked. While it isn't as exciting as *The Church* (1989) or as unique as *Cemetery Man* (1994), it's a rewarding film that deserves more attention.

Although two opening scenes promise violence and moments of extreme gore, the rest of the film prefers to in-

Kelly Curtis begins her nightmare journey in *The Sect*.

dulge in quietly naturalistic images and dream-like moments seemingly inspired by *Alice in Wonderland*. Images of animals abound, whether it's the bizarre, TV-watching white rabbit, the room full of insect sketches, or the children wearing animal masks. The few scenes of violence are strikingly effective against this pleasant, pastel-colored background. Another scene appears to be a bizarre homage to Clive Barker's *Hellraiser* and Terry Gilliam's *Brazil*[6] (both 1985), as the cult members remove a victim's face using long hooks.

The plot, while not entirely relevant in *The Church*, is even less important here. Several scenes appear to have nothing whatsoever to do with the story, something that can be both fascinating and infuriating. At nearly two hours in length, *The Sect* is too long to maintain this kind of rambling approach, but it's worth putting up with if viewers have the patience. The curiously enigmatic ending creates far more questions than it answers, which is perhaps in keeping with the film. Sadly, this lack of cohesion throughout is largely what stops *The Sect* from being a great horror film. However, the film's still an interesting experience, and rewarding too to see a talented director growing and evolving.

Specters (1987)
Aka: Spettri

Director: Marcello Avallone; Story/Screenplay: Marcello Avallone, Andrea Purgatori, Dardano Sacchetti, Maurizio Tedesco; Producer:

Maurizio Tedesco; Special Effects: Sergio Stivaletti; Makeup: Dante Trani; Music: Lele Marchitelli, Danilo Rea Starring: John Pepper (Marcus), Katrine Michelsen [Trine Michelsen] (Alice), Donald Pleasence (Professor Lasky), Massimo De Rossi (Matteo), Riccardo De Torrebruna (Andrea), Lavinia Grizzi (Barbara), Riccardo Pariso Perrotti

Donald Pleasence deciphering clues in *Specters*.

While exploring catacombs beneath Rome, a group of archaeologists unwittingly release a demon.

Specters is another of Reteitalia's made-for-TV movies that eventually received a video release overseas. It's a little better than most of their efforts, boasting a half decent cast and some good locations, but the film is still hampered by the standard half-hearted Reteitalia approach.

From start to finish, *Specters* is a mess of half formed ideas and lackluster performances. Donald Pleasence seems largely uninterested in his role and delivers only a fraction of what he's capable. The younger cast members do slightly better—including former Miss Denmark Trine Michelsen—but they can't overcome the inherent script problems. Even Sergio Stivaletti's animatronics and special effects seem sloppy and amateurish, although it's impossible to say whether that's because of budgetary restrictions or a general lack of interest on the artist's part (I suspect a mixture of both). A few of the earlier scenes manage to generate some suspense, but it's not enough to sustain interest. Marcello Avallone's talents are much better illustrated in *Maya* (1989), his next film, but *Specters* is a definite non-starter.

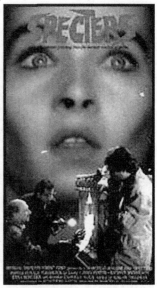

Trivia: Dardano Sacchetti claims he had no part in the preparation of the script. According to an interview printed in *Spaghetti Nightmares*, he claimed that he was hired to write a script for Marcello Avallone to film, but Avallone chose to use one of his own scripts and left Sacchetti's name in the credits to generate foreign interest.

Spider Labyrinth (1988)
Aka: Il nido del ragno

Director: Gianfranco Giagni; Story: Tonino Cervi; Screenplay: Riccardo Aragno, Tonino Cervi, Cesare Frugoni, Gianfranco Manfredi; Producer: Tonino Cervi; Special Effects: Sergio Stivaletti; Music: Franco Piersanti
Starring: Roland Wybenga (Professor Alan Whitmore), Paola Rinaldi, Marghareta Von Krauss, Claudia Muzii, William Berger, Stéphane Audran, Valeriano Santinelli, Massimiliano Pavone, Arnaldo Dell'acqua, Lazlo Sipos, Lote Attila, Bob Holton, Bill Bolender, John Morrison

An American professor goes to Budapest to make contact with a fellow academic. Shortly after he arrives, the other man is found dead, leaving the professor to uncover the mystery behind his death.

This little-known curiosity is one of the more interesting Italian horror films of the late 1980s. It doesn't resemble a modern horror film at all; it has more in common with the works of Mario Bava than Lamberto Bava. More classic Italian Gothic than teen horror. The setting is Budapest, an ancient city that (in the film, at least) doesn't seem to have changed much in the last century. The local inhabitants, who wear antiquated clothing and drive cars at least 40 years out of date, create the film's prior history feel. Franco Piersanti's excellent score sounds reminiscent of Bernard Hermann's work, contributing to the impression that *Spider Labyrinth* is a film from the 1950s rather than the 1980s.

Despite this carefully planned air of obsolescence, the film's greatest single influence is undoubtedly *Suspiria* (1977). Giagni is no Argento—his attempts to emulate the other director's impeccable sense of color and style come across as flat and uninspired—but his tale of an American adrift in a different country surrounded by increasing malevolence is surprisingly entertaining. The director wisely holds off on the gore until the final 15 minutes, when the film takes a definite turn for the bizarre. Sergio Stivaletti's gruesome stop-motion effects have been criticized for their out-of-date feel, but here they seem oddly reminiscent of the work of recent Czech animators such as Jan Svankmajer.

The film may not be particularly original, but *Spider Labyrinth* is a technically well-made horror film that deserves to be better known. If fans do manage to find a copy of this minor gem, it is worth acquiring. Surely a DVD release is on the horizon.

Stagefright (1987)
Aka: Deliria, Stage Fright—Aquarius, Bloody Bird

Director: Michael [Michele] Soavi; Story/Screenplay: Lew Cooper [Luigi Montefiore]; Producer: Aristide Massacessi, Donatella Donati; Music: Simon Boswell
Starring: David Brandon (Peter), Barbara Cupisti (Alicia), Don Fiore, Robert Gligorov (Danny), Mickey Knox, John Morghen [Giovanni Lombardo Radice] (Brett), Clain Parker (Irving Wallace)

A group of dancers, rehearsing for opening night, are locked in a theater. Unknown to them, a murderer escaped from the local mental asylum and slipped into the theater.

After a lengthy apprenticeship serving as assistant or second unit director to Dario Argento, Lamberto Bava and Aristide Massacessi, Michele Soavi released *Stagefright*, his directorial debut. Although often dismissed as a slasher movie, it's a well-constructed and visually impressive film that stands out as one of the highlights of Italian horror in the late 1980s.

Despite the timeworn plot—actors trapped in a theater with a maniac on the loose—Soavi is blessed with a capable cast and a surprisingly well-written script from Luigi Montefiore. The characters are mostly hateful and bitchy, with Radice and Brandon delivering wonderfully waspish performances. Barbara Cupisti's

heroine comes across as a little insipid in comparison to the other, stronger characters, but no real need exists for a classic *Final Girl* here. Instead Soavi allows his cast to run around like headless chickens, trying one unlikely plan after another, in a suitably theatrical fashion. The killer remains a lurking, shadowy presence that never seems quite real, an effect enhanced by the bizarre bird mask he wears throughout much of the film. It's a lot more memorable than Jason's hockey mask.

Not every aspect of *Stagefright* has aged well. The concept of a modern dance version of the Jack the Ripper story now seems horribly camp and absurd, but thankfully the film doesn't dwell on it for long. Simon Boswell provides a decent enough score, but it is unfortunately anchored in mid-1980s sensibilities. Even so, *Stagefright* is a striking debut that manages to effectively combine elements of the *giallo* with aspects of the slasher movie.

The Sweet House of Horrors (1989)
Aka: La dolce casa degli orrori

Director: Lucio Fulci; Story: Lucio Fulci; Screenplay: Vincenzo Mannino, Gigliola Battaglini; Makeup/Special Effects: Guiseppe Ferranti; Music: Vince Tempera
Starring: Jean Christophe Bretigniere (Carlo), Cinzia Monreale (Marcia), Lubka Civalova (Mary), Lino Salemme (Guido), Franco Diogene (Mr Coby), Alexander Vernon Dobtcheff (the exorcist), Giuliani Gensini (Marco), Ilary Blais (Sarah), Dante Fioretti (Father O'Toole), Pascal Persiano (Roberto)

During a home invasion, a married couple are brutally murdered, and their two children are sent to live with an aunt and uncle. Soon the household is subjected to ghostly disturbances that seem to have a special significance for the children.

The Sweet House of Horrors is one of two films directed by Lucio Fulci as part of a TV series entitled *Le case del terrore* (*Houses of Doom*). Umberto Lenzi directed the other two films. Italian made-for-TV movies are usually pretty poor, but *Sweet House* is actually one of the best films from Fulci's later years. It boasts a fairly good script (Vincenzo Mannino also co-wrote *New York Ripper*, 1982, and *Murder-Rock Dancing Death*, 1984) and some gore-soaked violence, as well as a decent performance from the lovely Cinzia Monreale (*Beyond the Darkness*, 1979; *The Beyond*, 1981).

Fulci's influence on the script appears to be extensive, and it boasts two of his favorite motifs: a house that has been the scene of violence and death and children whose connection to the supernatural events taking place is unclear, all mixed in with extreme violence and graphic special effects. The blood 'n' guts approach is certainly out of keeping with the standards of most television horrors—observe the bland and inoffensive nature of Lamberto Bava's made-for-TV films—but the *Houses of Doom* series seems to been intentionally gory. It's hard to see why else Reteitalia and Dania Film would hire two directors with reputations for extreme violence. Unfortunately, *Sweet House* is cursed by the same lackluster direction that colors most of Fulci's later films. For a lesser director it would probably have been a moderate success, so it's perhaps unfair to criticize. The rest of the series is generally poor, but  this contribution from Fulci contains some of the best moments of his later career.

Tenebrae (1982)
Aka: Sotto gli occhi dell'assassino, Shadow, Tenebre, Unsane

Director: Dario Argento; Story: Dario Argento; Screenplay: Dario Argento, George Kemp; Producer: Claudio Argento; Special Effects: Giovanni Corridori; Music: Claudio Simonetti, Fabio Pignatelli, Massimo Morante

Starring: Anthony Franciosa (Peter Neal), Christian Borromeo (Gianno), Mirella D'Angelo (Tilda), Veronica Lario (Jane Micarro), Ania Pieroni (Elsa), Eva Robins (Girl on beach), Carola Stagnaro (Inspector Altieri), John Steiner (Christiano Berti), Lara Wendel (Maria Alboretto), John Saxon (Bulmer), Daria Nicolodi (Anne), Giuliano Gemma (Detective Germani)

An American writer visits Italy to promote his latest murder-mystery novel. When he arrives he discovers that a maniac is using his novel as the inspiration for a series of real-life murders. With the police hampered by a lack of evidence, the writer attempts to find the killer himself.

After the Gothic excesses of *Suspiria* (1977) and *Inferno* (1980), Dario Argento returned to the *giallo* in style. *Tenebrae* is not only one of Argento's finest films, it's also among the best examples of this characteristically Italian genre. Inspired by death threats the director received from a fan, *Tenebrae* builds upon themes close to Argento's heart—most notably the artist's culpability for acts of violence inspired by his work. The central character—a writer—is accused of portraying extreme violence and misogyny for purely sensationalist reasons, a criticism that has been frequently leveled at Argento himself.

Unlike *Suspiria* and *Inferno*, *Tenebrae* is heavily plot-driven. Red herrings and half-clues abound, with several sharp twists thrown in to obscure the truth. The various plot developments become increasingly unlikely, but semi-fantastic storylines are a staple of Argento's work, and it doesn't detract from the film's entertainment value.

Argento once again shows his flair for extreme violence, particularly in *Tenebrae*'s notorious climax. Censors on both sides of the Atlantic targeted these scenes, stripping the film of its most shocking moments. To make matters worse, the American version—released as *Unsane*—featured a Kim Wilde song as the closing theme which hampered the production further. Thankfully later versions have restored the original score.

While his Gothic horrors were a riot of color and form, *Tenebrae* is almost muted in comparison. It is, however, no less stylish and impressive. Here, Argento utilizes pastel shades and a brilliant white as his backdrop. The intense Roman sunshine, reflected back from the bright white surfaces, is almost dazzling. It's also the perfect background for bloody murder, as the arcs of vivid arterial blood leap out from the white background. Blood red is also used on a few other occasions, particularly in the dream-girl's lipstick and high-heeled shoes. The choice of color is clearly intentional, doubling as an omen of the violence to come.

As with most *gialli*, the victims here are unsympathetic. None of them seem to be particularly nice people, and most of them have some kind of sexual quirk. We have adulterers, promiscuous girls, lesbians and bisexuals, giving rise to accusations that Argento is misogynistic and cruel. However, his victims are often male, and the director is only following the Italian tradition of sex, sleaze and murder. These are here purely for audience interest, just like the lusty teenagers of the American slasher movie; no one is seriously suggesting kids who indulge in premarital sex should be slaughtered, and Argento isn't promoting violence toward women. He even playfully

In Argento's films the black-gloved hands of the killer are often the director's own.

inserts a scene where a female reporter criticizes the writer for the apparently misogynistic tone of his work. In keeping with Argento's over-the-top sensibilities, the reporter is also a jealous lesbian, soon to be one of the killer's victims. Argento favors beautiful women for his victims, and *Tenebrae* includes several of them, most notably well-known transsexual and television host Eva Robins.

Although mocked in recent years, *Tenebrae* is blessed with a great score from three members of Goblin. Combining disco and rock themes with electronic instrumentation, their work complements the film perfectly. The musicians are not listed in the credits as Goblin, because drummer Agostino Marangolo was not present, but the score remains some of the group's finest work.

After *Tenebrae*, Argento's work became increasingly erratic. Each of the films that followed (*Phenomena*, 1985; *Opera*, 1987; *Two Evil Eyes*,

One of *Tenebrae*'s less graphic moments...

1990; *Trauma*, 1993) contained moments of genius and confirmed the abilities of the director, but none were as consistently outstanding as *Tenebrae*. Given the patchy nature of his later work, it's safe to say that this is Argento's last genuine classic and one of the best Italian horror films of the decade.

Trivia: Actress Theresa Russell dubbed Dario Nicolodi's part in the English-language version. Look out for cameos by assistant directors Lamberto Bava (an elevator repairman) and Michele Soavi (a young man on a bike).

Touch of Death (1988)
Aka: Quando Alice ruppe lo specchio, When Alice Broke the Mirror

Director: Lucio Fulci; Story/Screenplay: Lucio Fulci; Producer: Luigi Nannerini, Antonio Lucidi; Special Effects: Angelo Mattei; Makeup: Pino Ferranti [Giuseppe Ferranti]; Music: Carlo Maria Cordio
Starring: Brett Halsey (Lester Parson), Ria De Simone (Alice Shogun), Pier Luigi Conti (Randy), Sasha Darwin [Sacha Maria Darwin] (Maggie MacDonald), Zora Ulla Kesler [Zora Keslerova] (Virginia Field), Marco Di Stefano (the tramp)

Lester Parson is a psychopath who kills women and steals their savings. When another killer moves into the area, Lester suspects his livelihood might be threatened.

Touch of Death has often been labeled Lucio Fulci's worst film, although one commentator suggested that it's one of his best. Being fair, fans of *The New York Ripper* (1982) and devotees of the director's implacable taste for gore will be satisfied. And *Touch of Death* is certainly gory, probably more so than any of Fulci's films since *Ripper*. In the first half alone the audience experiences cannibalism and a *very* graphic dismemberment. All of this is the work of Lester Parson, a schizophrenic psychopath desperately trying to keep his activities secret, as well as avoid the attentions of local thugs eager to reclaim some gambling losses. So far, so good.

Unfortunately, *Touch of Death* is supposed to be a *comedy*. A blacker-than-black comedy, but a comedy nonetheless. The splatter film has frequently been combined with humor (Peter Jackson's incredible *Dead Alive* is probably the best example), but Fulci's humor misfires at every turn. Lester Parson's murderous activities are presented as a chore and

a drudge, with the killer matter-of-factly dispatching his victims and setting about the mutilations with an air of resignation. But he's not some middle-aged, middle-management civil servant, bowed under the weight of his work but lacking the ambition and resolve to break free; he's simply a serial killer. He's killing people because that's his job and he can't escape his responsibilities. I know we're supposed to derive a few belly laughs from the sight of a victim that *just won't die*, with Lester forced to beat her into a bloody pulp to stop her moving, but there's no genuine humor in sight. I'm sure trying to pass a corpse off as a living person was funny once, but the gag was old hat by the time it appeared in *Weekend at Bernie's* (1989), a film that's a lot more palatable than *Touch of Death*. I won't get started on Fulci's attempts to make the audience hate Parson's victims, but they provide plenty of ammunition to those who suggest the director had a serious grievance against women.

In short, *Touch of Death* is a moronic, misbegotten, offensive film with an atrocious score tacked on. This *might* be of interest to dedicated Fulci fans, but somehow I doubt many of them will be happy to sit through it more than once.

Trauma (1993)

Director: Dario Argento; Story: Franco Ferrini, Gianni Romoli, Dario Argento; Screenplay: Dario Argento, T.E.D. Klein; Producer: Dario Argento; Special Effects/Makeup: Tom Savini; Music: Pino Donaggio Starring: Christopher Rydell (David Parsons), Asia Argento (Aura

Petrescu), James Russo (Captain Travis), Laura Johnson (Grace), Hope Alexander-Willis (Laura), Sharon Barr (Hilda Volkman), Frederic Forrest (Dr. Judd), Piper Laurie (Adriana Petrescu), Brad Dourif (Dr. Lloyd)

An artist befriends a young anorexic girl who saw her mother murdered by a serial killer. Together they attempt to identify the killer, who strikes when it rains and decapitates his victims using an electronic noose.

Trauma was the first Dario Argento film to be shot entirely in the United States, probably with the intention of making his mainstream breakthrough. The finished film was a definite mixed bag—too mainstream and Americanized to please his hardcore fans and too European to prove a hit across the Atlantic. Even so, it's an interesting film that doesn't deserve the poor reputation that it has among fans.

Central to the film is Asia Argento's respectable performance as the anorexic Aura Petrescu. She certainly looks the part, pale and sallow, and manages to be convincing as the unstable teenager caught in the unpleasant mystery. The director attracted criticism for filming his daughter in a topless scene (the same criticism followed *The Phantom of the Opera*, 1998), but such comments aren't worthy of rebuttal. American actor Christopher Rydell does well as a reformed drug addict, but James Russo and Piper Laurie deliver hackneyed performances, particularly Laurie, who recycles her role from *Carrie* (1977).

The most prominent absentee from the film is Argento's characteristic scenes of graphic violence. Since the killer's *modus operandi* is to decapitate

his victims with a wire, there are plenty of opportunities for blood and gore, particularly with Tom Savini at the helm. However, while not entirely free from gore, *Trauma* is easily Argento's most restrained film. This isn't a flaw so to speak, but the film is severely undermined by Savini's unusually poor special effects. The severed heads are definitely not up to his usual standards.

Trauma has a strong visual side, with hallucinatory images prevailing, reinforced by the many drug references. Once again a handful of animal images appear, including a gruesome lizard close-up and an impressive butterfly's-eye-view sequence. Cinematographer Raffaele Mertes is the film's hidden star, and he does a wonderful job at creating a dimly lit and mysterious atmosphere (as he did in Michele Soavi's *The Sect*, 1991) that foreshadows David Fincher's *Seven* (1995). Pino Donaggio provides a competent score, but it isn't among his best work.

For any other director, *Trauma* would be considered a success, but Argento raised the bar so high with *Suspiria* (1977) and *Tenebrae* (1982) that the inevitable low points seem more significant than they really are. As long as audiences do not expect a *giallo* to rival the director's earlier work, *Trauma* is an enjoyable film that's still head-and-shoulders above the majority of serial killer-thrillers released in the past 10 years.

Troll 2 (1990)
Aka: Trolli, Trolls

Director: Drago Floyd [Claudio Fragrasso], Aristide Massacessi [uncredited]; Story/Screenplay: Drago Floyd [Claudio Fragrasso]; Producer: Brenda Norris, Aristide Massacessi [uncredited]; Makeup: Maurizio Trani; Music: Carlo Maria Cordio
Starring: Michael Stephenson, George Hardy, Margo Prey, Connie Young, Robert Ormsby, Deborah Reed, Jason Wright

Young Joshua Waits and his family head off to the rural town of Nilbog to spend their vacation. Joshua's dead grandfather appears to him as a ghost and warns him of the danger surrounding the family. The town is home to a large number of goblins, and it's up to Joshua (and his dead grandfather) to save his family.

Widely considered to be one of the worst films ever made, *Troll 2* is one of the many low-budget films produced by Massacessi's Filmirage company during the late 1980s and early 1990s, the majority of which were aimed squarely at the U.S. market. Despite the title it bears no relation to John Carl Buechler's *Troll* (1986), and it doesn't feature any trolls either.

Being fair to the film, it's reasonably well constructed, and veteran cinematographer Giancarlo Ferrandi manages to make it look considerably better than the zero-budget rubbish it really is. Not that it matters, since the script is quite possibly the worst thing Fragrasso has ever put his name to, contradicting itself on numerous occasions and making desperate attempts at humor that inevitably fall flat. The cast is made up of amateurs, including a local dentist. They're uniformly terrible, and constantly fluff the line readings. Maurizio Trani's make-up is far from his best, and the goblin costumes themselves are taken from other Filmirage projects.

Connoisseurs of bad movies have elevated *Troll 2* to the status of a cult classic, but everyone else is advised to stay away. And is there *anyone* who didn't realize that Nilbog is goblin spelled backward?

Two Evil Eyes (1990)
Aka: Due occhi diabolici

—The Facts in the Case of Mr. Valdemar

Director: George Romero; Story: E.A. Poe; Screenplay: George Romero; Producer: Achille Manzotti; Special Effects/Makeup: Tom Savini; Music: Pino Donaggio
Starring: Adrienne Barbeau (Jessica Valdemar), Ramy Zada (Dr. Robert Hoffman), Bingo O'Malley (Ernest Valdemar), Jeff Howell (policeman), E.G. Marshall (Steven Pike), Tom Atkins (Detective Grogan)

A wife and her lover hypnotize her husband and make him sign his estate over to her. Still hypnotized, he dies and is trapped between life and death, not fully dead and not fully alive.

—The Black Cat

Director: Dario Argento; Story: E.A. Poe; Screenplay: Dario Argento, Franco Ferrini; Producer: Achille Manzotti; Special Effects/Makeup: Tom Savini; Music: Pino Donaggio
Starring: Harvey Keitel (Roderick Usher), Madeleine Potter (Annabel), John Amos (Detective Legrand), Sally Kirkland (Eleonora), Kim Hunter (Mrs. Pym), Holter Ford Graham (Christian), Martin Balsam (Mr. Pym), Julie Benz (Betty)

A photographer kills his girlfriend's cat but finds it isn't quite so easy to dispose of the creature. Soon his life is spiraling out of control.

Two Evil Eyes was originally intended to be a four-part film, including segments directed by George Romero, Dario Argento, Wes Craven and John Carpenter, but the plans fell through and only the first two parts were ever filmed. It marked Dario Argento's return to directing after his move to production following *Opera* (1987). Edgar Allan Poe's short stories became the inspiration for the two-episode screenplay.

George Romero's contribution, *The Facts in the Case of Mr. Valdemar*, has much in common with his own *Creepshow* (1982). Both works are heavily influenced by the old E.C. comics' style and starred Adrienne Barbeau. Despite good performances from the cast and some interesting camerawork, the episode is flat and uninvolving. Perhaps the story is too familiar—it holds no real surprises and feels more like a story from the resurrected *Twilight Zone* series.

Argento's film, on the other hand, is grim and brutal. Harvey Keitel is excellent as Roderick Usher, a photographer with a preference for the macabre and disturbing. The story provides plenty of opportunities for Tom Savini to show off his abilities: dissected corpses, mutilations, brutal murders, and a scene that is oddly reminiscent of *Cannibal Holocaust* (1980). Savini even makes a brief appearance as a murderer in a bit that references yet another Poe story, *Bernice*. The director is in fine form, coaxing solid performances from his cast and keeping the film visually interesting, with complex set-ups and fluid tracking shots. With a short, tightly arranged story, very little opportunity exists for the self-indulgence that sometimes marred Argento's later work. Without a doubt, it's one of his best works of the 1990s.

The idea of two influential, talented directors tackling stories by one of horror's most important icons should have been a dream project. Sadly, the first episode is not as strong as the second, but Argento's contribution is enough reason to seek this out.

Until Death (1987)
Aka: Per Sempre, The Changeling 2 – The Revenge

Director: Lamberto Bava; Story: Dardano Sacchetti; Screenplay: Dardano Sacchetti, Lamberto Bava; Makeup: Fabrizio Sforza; Music: Simon Boswell

Starring: Gioia Scola, David Brandon, Guiseppe De Sando, Roberto Pedicini, Marco Vivio, Urbano Barberini

A wife and her lover conspire to poison her husband and bury his corpse in a shallow grave. Six years pass, and the couple now own a restaurant. A handsome stranger turns up one night asking for shelter and offering to work as a handyman. They hire him, but the wife begins to think he looks oddly like her dead husband.

After 1988's *Prince of Terror*, this supernatural take on *The Postman Always Rings Twice* is probably Lamberto Bava's best made-for-television movie, although it doesn't compare to his early theatrical work. Like his other television movies, no real gore appears, but it's a little more hard-edged, being built around the themes of adultery, murder, cruelty and revenge. Predictably, the film has no connection whatsoever to Peter Medak's 1980 chiller, *The Changeling*.

The core players in this film are all pretty good in their roles, particularly David Brandon, who sneers and scowls all the way through the film, occasionally erupting into violence. Since he is usually cast in more cerebral parts, it's nice to see him get a chance to flex his acting muscles a little. Gioia Scola is fine as the adulterous and ultimately murderous wife, and Urbano Barberini makes the most of his limited screen time. The young son played by Marco Vivio from *Demons 2* (1987) is pretty irritating and unsympathetic, but that is possibly because of the substandard dubbing. Simon Boswell's score is fairly good but not exceptional, which is better than nothing. Bava fans might have some fun with this above-average television movie, but it's too derivative and predictable to entertain more mainstream film fans.

Vampire in Venice (1986)
Aka: Nosferatu a Venezia, Nosferatu in Venice

Director: Augusto Caminito, Klaus Kinski [uncredited], Luigi Cozzi [uncredited]; Story: Alberto Alfieri, Leandro Lucchetti; Screenplay:

Augusto Caminito; Producer: Augusto Caminito; Makeup: Sergio Angeloni, Franco Corridori, Luigi Rocchelli; Music: Luigi Ceccarelli Starring: Klaus Kinski (Nosferatu), Christopher Plummer (Professor Catalano), Barbara De Rossi (Helietta), Elvire Audray (Ute Barneval), Donald Pleasence (Don Alvise), Yorgo Voyagis (Dr. Barneval), Anne Knecht (Maria)

Nosferatu stalks the Venice carnival, looking for fresh victims.

Vampire in Venice was intended to be a sequel to Werner Herzog's 1979 film *Nosferatu*, but the project seems to have been doomed from the start. Two directors had been removed prior to shooting, while a third—genre veteran Mario Caiano—quit on the first day. Producer Caminito eventually took the reins but left after disputes with the notoriously erratic Kinski, who tried to complete the film himself. Luigi Cozzi was then drafted to try to turn the uneven results into a film. Not surprisingly, the finished effort is somewhat unsatisfactory.

It's a shame that the film's production was a shambles, for the concept has a few things in its favor. At his best Kinski is a great performer, while Christopher Plummer and Donald Pleasence are both fine character actors. Unfortunately Kinski seems to have been less than happy with the role, since his performance is rarely better than pedestrian. The film would have benefited from the excellent makeup Kinski wore in Herzog's film, but the actor refused to wear it a second time. The rest of the talented cast seems to know what a turkey they've been handed and choose not to waste too much energy over it.

The ancient city of Venice should be the ideal setting for any Gothic horror,

but here it's another wasted opportunity. In the hands of a talented and committed director, the script could have been turned into a decent film. With six irons in the fire and a temperamental leading man, *Vampire in Venice* is mediocre at best.

The Visitor (1979)
Aka: Stridulum

Director: Giulio Paradiso; Story: Ovidio G. Assonitis, Giulio Paradiso; Screenplay: Lou Comici, Robert Mundy; Producer: Ovidio G. Assonitis; Special Effects: Bob Shelley, Vernon Hyde; Music: Franco Micalizzi
Starring: Joanne Nail (Barbara Collins), Paige Conner (Katy Collins), Lance Henriksen (Raymond Armstead), Glenn Ford (Detective Jake Durham), John Huston (Jerzy Colsowicz), Shelley Winters (Jane Phillips), Mel Ferrer (Dr. Walker), Sam Peckinpah (Dr. Sam Collins), Franco Nero (Jesus)

Satan fights for control of a woman who carries the evil gene allowing her to produce Satanic children. With her daughter Katie already drawn to the dark side, Satan employs human agents and extraterrestrials (!) to secure the birth of a son.

Ovidio G. Assonitis was one of the great Italian exploitation producers of the 1970s and 1980s, responsible for many cheap knock-offs like *Beyond the Door* (1975) and *Tentacles* (1977). *The Visitor* is perhaps his most interesting film. It's very silly and sometimes verges on incoherency, but it's never dull and often more entertaining than the official sequels to *The Exorcist* (1973) and *The Omen* (1976), two of the many films it copies.

The Visitor's biggest selling point is undoubtedly the fantastic cast. We have well-respected actors from Hollywood's heyday like Glenn Ford and Shelley Winters, European favorites Mel Ferrer and Franco Nero and two famous directors,

John Huston and Sam Peckinpah. On top of that add Lance Henriksen, fresh from his role in *Damien: Omen II* (1978), and soon to become a popular cult actor. Clearly Assonitis was keen to assemble as much star power as possible, and he seems to have succeeded.

It's safe to say that *The Visitor* is in a class of own, cribbing elements from a wide variety of sources, from *Close Encounters of the Third Kind* (1977) through *Village of the Damned* (1960) and on to *Rosemary's Baby* (1968). In keeping with other devil movies, plenty of suspicious deaths occur, several inspired by *The Omen*. A handful of bird attacks appear as well, courtesy of Ray Berwick, who worked on both *The Birds* (1963) and *Omen II*. Given the talent involved it's a little surprising that the birds are rather unrealistic. Poor special effects also hamper several other scenes, most notably the alien insemination episode and the spacecraft itself.

The film's best scene is the very last one. Having kidnapped Katie and turned her into a white-robed, bald-headed alien child, John Huston parades her in front of Jesus (played by Franco Nero!) who smiles beatifically, implying that the good guys have indeed won. The film ends there, with several plots unresolved and a host of questions unanswered, most likely leaving the viewer stunned by the sheer stupidity of it all. This is a unique movie that deserves to be seen.

Voices from Beyond (1991)
Aka: Urla dal profondo, Voci dal profondo

Director: Lucio Fulci; Story: Lucio Fulci, Daniele Stroppa; Screenplay: Lucio Fulci, Piero Regnoli; Makeup: Pino Ferranti [Giuseppe Ferranti]; Music: Stelvio Cipriani
Starring: Diulio Del Prete (Giorgio Mainardi), Karina Huff (Rosie Mainardi), Pascal Persiano (Mario Mainardi), Lorenzo Flaherty [Laurence Flaherty] (Tommy/Gianni), Frances Nacman (Hilda Mainardi), Paolo Paoloni (Grandpa Mainardi), Sacha Darwin [Sacha Maria Darwin] (Doria), Antonella Tinazzo (Rita), Damiano Azzos, Rosamaria Grauso

A wealthy patriarch suspects his family of poisoning him. After his death, his spirit tries to communicate with his one loyal daughter. At her father's request, she begins to investigate the circumstances of his death. There is a time limit however — as his corpse rots, his ability to communicate with the living disappears.

The low-key chiller has been described as one of the best films of Lucio Fulci's declining years, and it certainly has a lot to recommend it. The story (a ghost contacts his daughter to try to find out who was responsible for his death) may not be particularly original, but it's handled considerably better than the more adventurous plot of something like *The House of Clocks* (1988). By imposing a time limit on the ghost's existence, Fulci manages to add some tension to the story. Only a few hints of the much-vaunted Fulci gore appear, including several close-ups of the ghost's rotting corpse and a welcome cameo by a handful of zombies. On the whole though, the film trades on suspense and chills rather than splatter.

Voices from Beyond would have been a much better movie with a more competent crew. Cinematographer Sandro Grossi displays little or no imagination, resorting to static master shots throughout much of the film, while the lighting is pedestrian and bland. It seems odd that Fulci would settle for such substandard efforts, but perhaps the director no longer had the energy to involve himself in every aspect of the filmmaking process. Whatever the truth may be, *Voices from Beyond* remains an interesting film hampered by poor craftsmanship.

Washing Machine (1993)
Aka: Vortice mortale

Director: Ruggero Deodato; Story/Screenplay: Luigi Spagnol; Producer: Corrado & Alessandro Canzio; Music: Claudio Simonetti
Starring: Philippe Caroit (Inspector Alexander Stacev), Ilaria Borrelli (Maria "Sissy" Kolba), Kashia Figura (Vida Kolba), Barbara Ricci (Ludmilla Kolba), Laurence Bruffaerts (Nikolai), László Porbély, Claudia Pozzi (Irina), Yorgo Voyagis (Yuri Petkov)

A woman reports a dead body in her washing machine and a police inspector comes to her home. When he arrives, the corpse has vanished. During the investigation that follows, the inspector finds himself deeply involved with the woman and her two sisters.

Despite the faintly ludicrous title, *Washing Machine* is a neatly twisted erotic thriller. While not as interesting or exciting as Ruggero Deodato's best work, it's still a worthy attempt at a modern *giallo*. The film's biggest handicap is arguably the plot; dozens of erotic thrillers have tried to squeeze new life from the clichéd story of a cop getting sexually involved with murder suspects. However, there's enough malice and perversion here to lift the film above the mass of similar efforts. Lesbianism, voyeurism and sadomasochism are just a few of the things on display, and a definite feeling of *sleaze* underscores much of the movie.

Deodato manages to coax strong performances from the central characters, although most of the female leads are only required to look seductive and/or frightened. Philippe Caroit's Inspector Stacev is clearly modeled on various Mickey Rourke characters, but he remains believable throughout. Unfortunately the script is meandering and sometimes confusing, indulging in flashbacks and hallucinations that only serve to obscure the plot.  To the writer's credit, the climax brings the story to a satisfying (if predictable) conclusion.

Washing Machine is unlikely to find an audience with lovers of Deodato's more violent films, but most *giallo* fans should find something to appreciate. It's certainly better than *Dial: Help* (1988) and the majority of American erotic thrillers. To date it remains the director's last theatrical work.

Welcome to Spring Break (1988)
Aka: La spaggia del terrore, Nightmare Beach

Director: Harry Kirkpatrick [Umberto Lenzi]; Story: Harry Kirkpatrick [Umberto Lenzi], Vittorio Rambaldi; Screenplay: Harry Kirkpatrick [Umberto Lenzi]; Producer: William J. Immerman; Special Effects:

Alex Rambaldi, Gary Bentley; Makeup: Mayte Nardo; Music: Claudio Simonetti
Starring: Nicolas De Toth (Skip), Sarah Buxton (Gail), Rawley Velverde (Ronnie), Lance Le Gault (Reverend Bates), Michael Parks (Doc Willet), John Saxon (Strycher), Luis Valderama, Fred Buck (Mayor Loomis), Debra Gallagher (Rachael), Turk Harley (Malcolm), Christina Kier (Kimberley), Ben Stotes (Al), Kristy Lachance (Lori), Gregg Todd Davis (Ralph), Yamilet Hidalgo (Trina), John Baldwin

A psycho biker is electrocuting teens at a Florida resort. With a corrupt mayor and a twisted police captain trying to make life difficult for him, Skip Banacek has to stop the killings.

This third-rate slasher movie is a belated attempt to cash in on the brief craze of spring break-related movies. It's obvious from the start that we're dealing with a low-budget, zero-effort production. Check

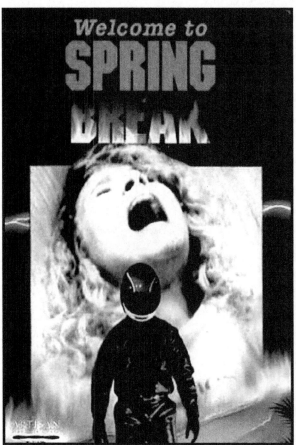

out the beautiful young things on the beach, trying to look sexy, despite the gray skies and strong winds that indicate the film was shot off-season.

Nothing new's here. John Saxon plays the nasty sheriff who's got it in for the kids, but he can't be bothered to deliver a decent performance and doesn't come across as dangerous. Nicolas De Toth is terribly earnest and serious, but few of the cast put any effort into the roles. Being fair, the script is mundane and clichéd so it's unlikely they could have done anything decent with their performances. Alex Rambaldi (son of

Carlo) and Gary Bentley provide the special effects, sometimes the only saving grace of such films, but they're amateurish at best and laughable at worst.

Welcome to Spring Break was clearly part of a two-film deal. Harry Kirkpatrick and the Rambaldi brothers also collaborated on *Primal Rage* (1988), which featured many of the same cast and crew. *Primal Rage* is another teen-oriented horror flick, but it's gorier than this effort and more entertaining. Claudio Simonetti provides the scores for both films, but they're basic, throwaway efforts. In *Welcome to Spring Break* the standard pop-metal soundtrack overshadows his work. This time it's not faceless acts that you've never heard of—there's a few names here that should be familiar to fans of the 1980s rock scene, including Bobby Rondinelli, Ronnie James Dio and former Ted Nugent guitarist Derek St. Holmes. However, it's not enough to recommend the film to most viewers, who will still find *Welcome to Spring Break* mind-numbingly tedious.

Witch Story (1989)
Aka: Streghe

Director: Alessandro Capone; Story: Alessandro Capone; Screenplay: Alessandro Capone, Rosario Galli, Jeff Moldovan; Producer: Mauro Morigi, Giuseppe Pedersoli, Alessandro Capone; Special Effects: Vince Montefusco; Makeup: Rick Gonzales; Music: Carlo Maria Cordio Starring: Ian Bannen (Father Matthew), Christopher Peacock (Ken), Michelle Vannucchi (Carol Hayes), Amy Adams (Susan), Jeff Bankert (Michael), Charon Butler (Gloria), Todd Conatser (Virgil), Gary Kerr (Ed Hayes), Jason M. Lefkowitz (Paul), Nancie Sanderson (Simona), Deanna Lund (Helena), Suzanne Law (Rachel Hayes)

Teens staying at an old house are possessed by the murderous spirit of a witch, burned to death on the site centuries before.

Witch Story is a typical 1980s horror film, heavily indebted to American efforts such as *The Amityville Horror* series and similar teen-oriented shockers. It so closely resembles an American film that, were it not for the opening credits, audiences would never know Italians made the film. This is not really a bad thing; of all the attempts made by Italian filmmakers to produce a film that could be easily sold across the Atlantic, *Witch Story* is perhaps the most successful.

It helps greatly that the film was shot in the United States, so a cast of American actors was readily available, rather than the usual amateurs that got roped into Italian films because they happened to live in the vicinity of the shooting location. The performers are not always great, but they deliver their lines on time, scream in all the right places and seem to have some idea of what they're doing. Nancie Sanderson is great as Simona, the cousin who seems to know more than she's letting on. The late great Ian Bannen, who delivers an eccentric performance as the drunken priest, supports the youthful cast. Before his death in 1999 Bannen appeared in dozens of films, including *Gandhi* (1982) and *Braveheart* (1995).

Plenty of gore and lingerie is on display here. Most of the characters meet an unpleasant end, as they're supposed to in films like this. Alessandro Capone manages to inject some suspense into the death scenes, even if the eventual outcome is hardly a surprise. The obligatory tacked on epilogue introduces the possibility of a sequel that never materialized. It's not really necessary anyway. Although it doesn't win any awards for originality, *Witch Story* is a competently made 1980s-style horror film that deserves to be rediscovered.

Witchcraft (1988)
Aka: La casa 4, Evil Encounters, Ghosthouse 2, Witchery

Director: Martin Newton [Fabrizio Laurenti]; Story/Screenplay: Daniel Davis [Daniele Stroppa]; Producer: Peter Newton [Aristide Massacessi]; Special Effects/Makeup: Maurizio Trani; Music: Carlo Mario Cordo
Starring: David Hasselhoff (Gary), Linda Blair (Jane Brooks), Catherine Hickland (Linda Sullivan), Annie Ross (Rose Brooks), Leslie Cumming (Leslie), Bob Champagne (Freddie Brooks), Rick Farnsworth (Jerry Giordano), Michael Manchester (Tommy Brooks), Hildegard Knef (The Lady in Black)

A long dead witch returns to collect souls to send to hell.

Despite the alternative titles, this dismal occult thriller is not an official sequel to Umberto Lenzi's *Ghosthouse* (1987), which is also known as *La casa 3*. Aristide Massacessi's Filmirage produced both films, but *Witchcraft* is a sequel in name only. Once again Linda Blair gets to prance around in a white nightgown while mysterious things start happening to her. The obvious selling point is the possibility of sex between Blair and Hasselhoff—she's a virgin and he's a randy photographer—but guests of both the human and supernatural kind constantly interrupt the cozy couple.

The main plot concerns the death of a witch centuries before and her attempts at rein-carnation, with the aid of virgin's blood. Sadly, the film advances at such a crawl that after the first 30 minutes it's hard to keep a focus on the plot. The production costs were minimal and the script is a mess—despite the prot-estations of the cast, there is clearly no storm raging outside, so why doesn't everyone just leave? Has-selhoff and Blair seem to sleepwalk through their parts, and the rest of the  cast are firmly Z-grade. In one sense, *Witchcraft* is unique; however, it's the first film to feature demon rape, long-dead witches and David Hasselhoff's gruesome demise—and still managed to be dull beyond belief. Luigi Cozzi was slated originally to direct.

You'll Die at Midnight (1986)
Aka: Morirai a mezzanotte, Midnight Killer, Midnight Horror

Director: John Old, Jr. [Lamberto Bava]; Story: Dardano Sacchetti; Screenplay: Dardano Sacchetti, John Old, Jr. [Lamberto Bava]; Music: Claudio Simonetti

Starring: Valeria D'Obici (Professor Anna Berardi), Leonardo Treviglio (Nicola Levi), Lea Martino, Eliana Hoppe, Barbara Scoppa, Massimo Baratta, Loredana Romito, Paolo Malco (Inspector Piero Terzi), Lara Wendel (Carol)

A police inspector's wife is murdered, and the suspicion falls upon him. However, he thinks the murder was the work of a serial rapist believed to have died in a fire years before.

Like the later *Body Puzzle* (1991), *You'll Die at Midnight* was a television thriller given a cinematic release against the wishes of the director. Despite the general lack of gore and sleaze that colored theatrical *gialli*, it's an entertaining film that remains one of Lamberto Bava's best made-for-TV films. This is partly due to a competent, attractive cast. Paolo Malco turns in a decent performance as the cop under pressure, relying upon the expertise of psychologist Valeria D'Obici as well as the comforts afforded by his beautiful wife Carol (Lara Wendel). Unfortunately Sacchetti and Bava prepared a mediocre script that starts well but fails miserably when expected to resolve the various threads of the plot, and the climax is a moment worthy of *Scooby-Doo*.

Thankfully Bava himself is in form, and injects the formulaic material with some energy and style. The murders themselves are strongly reminiscent of Dario Argento's work,

which is hardly a criticism. Despite his unhappiness with the project, Bava seems to have put some effort into *You'll Die at Midnight*; it doesn't have the same half-hearted feel that his later television films have, even though it doesn't stand up to his best work. It's still a professionally made film that deserves a wider audience. Trivia note: The director appears briefly as a police photographer.

Zeder (1983)

Aka: Revenge of the Dead, Zeder: Voices from Beyond, Zeder: Voices from the Beyond, Zeder: Voices from the Darkness

Director: Pupi Avati; Producer: Gianni Minervini, Antonio Avati; Story: Pupi Avati; Screenplay: Pupi Avati, Maurizio Constanzo, Antonio Avati; Makeup: Alfonso Cioffi; Music: Riz Ortolani
Starring: Gabriele Lavia (Stefano), Anne Canovas (Alessandra), Paola Tanziani (Gabriela Goodman), Cesare Barbetti (Dr. Meyer), Bob Tonelli (Mr. Big), Ferdinando Orlandi (Giovine), Enea Ferrario (Don Mario)

A journalist receives a secondhand typewriter for his birthday. On the ink ribbon he finds the story of a scientist, Paolo Zeder, who claimed to have found the secret of the K Zones—supernatural locations that have the power to spontaneously revive the dead. He attempts to investigate Zeder's work further, but finds that he isn't the only one.

Although he is now best known for his period dramas, Pupi Avati has also directed a handful of horror movies, most notably *The House with the Laughing Windows* (1975), a stylish and brutal *giallo*. Less well known is *Zeder*, a belated and bizarre contribution to the Italian zombie boom. Early U.S. distributors released the film as *Revenge of the Dead* in a transparent attempt to link it to the earlier zombie movies, but it has nothing in common with them. Instead this is a grim and somber mystery thriller, heavy on atmosphere but short on gore and special effects.

Zeder is pretty much a one-man show. Despite a range of interesting co-stars, much of the film consists of Gabriele Lavia unraveling a string of obscure clues. Lavia is a decent actor but a curiously unemotional one. He's too detached to be convincing as a man obsessed by the desire to solve this mystery, whatever the cost. Much better is Anne Canovas, who plays Lavia's girlfriend, increasingly bewildered by her boyfriend's obsessions. Avati's direction is taut and assured, maintaining a palpable sense of tension throughout. Sadly, two things undermine the director's good work. The first is a weak ending. Viewers familiar with the awful *Pet Sematary* (1989) will recognize the problem: A character tries to bring a loved one back to life knowing that the resurrection will turn the deceased into a monster. It's hard to believe that Stefano would allow his girlfriend to become some kind of undead thing just to have her back. After a skillful build-up, the movie offers a disappointing climax. The second problem is Riz Ortolani's deeply annoying score. Consisting solely of screeching violins overlaid with a loud, discordant bass riff, it crashes in at every available opportunity, regardless of plot significance.

Without those two flaws, *Zeder* would be an above average occult thriller. Even with the poor ending and absurdly bad score, it's still entertaining. Sadly, it doesn't rank among the most noteworthy of Italian horror films from the period, and it is unlikely to impress the viewer looking for more visceral terrors.

Zombie (1979)
Aka: Zombi 2, Zombie Flesh Eaters, Island of the Living Dead

Director: Lucio Fulci; Story/Screenplay: Lucio Fulci, Elisa Briganti [Dardano Sacchetti]; Producer: Fabrizio De Angelis, Ugo Tucci; Special Effects/Makeup: Giannetto De Rossi, Maurizio Trani; Music: Fabio Frizzi, Giorgio Tucci
Starring: Tisa Farrow (Anne Bowles), Ian McCulloch (Peter West), Richard Johnson (Dr. Menard), Al Cliver [Pier Luigi Conti] (Brian Hull), Auretta Gay (Susan Barrett), Stefanio D'Amazio (Nurse), Olga Karlatos (Paola Menard)

A derelict ship floats into New York harbor. A rotting corpse comes to life and attacks the police who try to board her. A journalist finds out who owns the yacht — a doctor who lives on the island of Matool and hasn't been seen for several months. The journalist, accompanied by the doctor's daughter, travels to the Caribbean to try to find him. They find that Matool is infected with an epidemic that causes the victims to come back to life as flesh-eating ghouls.

As is well documented, the worldwide popularity of George Romero's *Dawn of the Dead* (1978) was the catalyst for a wave of European zombie films. The most important of these was Lucio Fulci's *Zombie* (Italian title, *Zombi 2*), cynically painted as a sequel to Romero's film, which was released in Europe as *Zombi*. The commercial success of both films ensured that many later efforts would draw their inspiration equally from Romero and Fulci. *Dawn* provided the apocalyptic themes, the army of the dead concept and the general dynamics of the zombies themselves, while

the Italian film supplied a tropical vs. urban dichotomy, low-budget sensibilities and special effects that went a few steps beyond (and often below) Romero's none-too-subtle standards.

Zombie was the brainchild of producer Fabrizio De Angelis, whose previous work included producing one of Joe D'Amato's spurious *Emmanuelle* clones and an Umberto Lenzi-directed John Saxon crime thriller. Keen to produce a film that would cash in on the success of the Dario Argento-produced *Dawn of the Dead*, De Angelis and his partner Ugo Tucci began to cast around for a suitable writer and director. They hired prolific scriptwriter Dardano Saccheti to write a zombie-filled script. Saccheti was already one of the most important names in Italian genre cinema, having prepared material for Mario Bava and Dario Argento. De Angelis was eager for rising star Enzo G. Castellari to direct the film, but he wasn't interested, so the script—now credited to the writer's wife, Elisa Briganti, although apparently not written by her—was passed on to Fulci, who rewrote several parts and added the

New York scenes. Ironically, Castellari's father, Marino Girolami, would direct *Zombie Holocaust* (1980), one of the first films to cash in on the success of *Zombie*.

Shot in the Dominican Republic in the summer of 1979, *Zombie* boasts an effective synth-based score, courtesy of Fabio Frizzi and Giorgio Tucci. Despite one or two ill-advised moments—the cod-calypso theme is particularly annoying—the gentle ambient tones support both the exotic locations and the atmosphere of menace that builds throughout the film. The casting was not so successful, with only Ian McCulloch and Richard Johnson turning in half-decent performances. Tisa Farrow's portrayal of Anne is lifeless and undistinguished, especially when compared with the vitality that Catriona MacColl brought to the lead roles in Fulci's later films. The other American characters are thin and two-dimensional, and the natives haven't evolved much since the 1930s. Frightened and superstitious, their behavior is generally contrasted against that of the more reasonable and heroic Americans. Johnson manages to tread the line between mad scientist and philanthropic doctor quite well, and his character remains the most interesting person in the film.

Not surprisingly, the special effects and makeup, provided by Giannetto De Rossi and Maurizio Trani, are the real stars of the film. The zombies are almost perfect, with open wounds and decaying flesh presented in great detail. Not all of them are so well done, with the zombie aboard the boat representing the low point. Fulci's characteristic love of maggots isn't always as effective as it's supposed to be, but these are minor complaints. On the whole, Fulci's zombies are the best ones of the whole Italian zombie boom. The gore effects are excellent, in particular the infamous eyeball puncturing scene that remains one of the most memorable episodes in Fulci's deranged catalogue. Flesh-tearing effects are usually fairly poor, but De Rossi and Trani do a great job here, and they create enough close-up shots of open wounds to keep any gore fan happy.

Cinematographer Sergio Salvati manages to portray the great natural beauty of the Caribbean, providing a stunning backdrop to the disturbing scenes that take place in the film. Together, Fulci and Salvati present a world where man is the intruder and death is a part of the natural order. For all their otherworldly horror, the zombies seem to fit the environment much better than the visitors, and any incursions that civilization makes into the natural world are temporary at best.

Clearly Fulci's film owes a significant debt to the films of George Romero, but *Zombie* is far more than a pale *Dawn of the Dead* clone. The Caribbean setting is reminiscent of the early zombie classics, *White Zombie* (1932) and *I Walked with a Zombie* (1943); the latter movie was an acknowledged influence on Fulci. Odd touches like the conquistador zombies give the film a sense of history, and Paola Menard's small compound looks like an old mission house, or the wooden-walled slave owner mansions of the Deep South. Menard himself has a shade of Bela Lugosi in his character, and for a brief while it looks like he may have something to do with the problems himself. This is quickly dispelled as despair sets in and Menard comes to look like a defeated old man rather than a mad scientist.

Perhaps the most significant difference between Romero and Fulci's separate films is the presentation of the zombies. In *Dawn of the Dead* the connection between the living and the dead is heavily emphasized, and the fact that the zombies are simply repeating activities from their former lives is one of their central characteristics. Fulci's zombies have no humanity left. Whereas the shopping mall zombies have little more than a gray-green pallor to indicate their necrotic state, the zombies of Matool are a mass of open sores and decayed, maggot-ridden flesh, walking depictions of the ravages of decomposition. Even the more recently dead have empty eye sockets and fresh wounds. They no longer resemble human beings, and their one desire—to feed—is more animalistic than anything else. Fulci might be overstating the point, but his zombies symbolize Death in its worst incarnation; Romero's are intended to reflect life and human society.

The friendships formed during the making of *Zombie* became brief, but fruitful, alliances. Fabrizio De Angelis, Saccheti, Frizzi, Salvati and De Rossi all worked on Fulci's finest films, and it would be fair to say that

One of the decaying zombie inhabitants of Matool

they played no small part in the groundbreaking efforts that followed *Zombie*. After 1982's *Manhattan Baby* the partnerships were dissolved; only editor Vincenzo Tomassi—who had previously worked on Jorge Grau's *The Living Dead at the Manchester Morgue* (1974), along with De Rossi—continued to work with Fulci.

Although disliked by mainstream critics, *Zombie* became a hit at European theaters in late 1979 and early 1980. In some countries it seemed to equal the success of *Dawn of the Dead*. Fulci was certainly fond of claiming that his film was more popular than Romero's, with some justification. By the end of 1980 it had also conquered North America, introducing Fulci's brand of mayhem to a new generation of appreciative horror fans. Some countries did not respond so well, demanding that the film be cut or banned outright, although few territories have retained such a ban to the present day. Cuts of varying lengths are still in circulation, making purchasing the movie a potential minefield. It remains one of the most significant Italian horror films of all time, however, and it's a necessary acquisition for any self-respecting horror buff.

Zombie 3 (1987)
Aka: Zombi 3, Zombie Flesh Eaters 2

Director: Lucio Fulci, Bruno Mattei, Claudio Fragrasso [uncredited]; Story/Screenplay: Claudio Fragrasso; Producer: Franco Gaudenzi; Special Effects/Makeup: Franco Di Girolami; Music: Stefano Mainetti
Starring: Deran Serafian (Kenny), Beatrice Ring (Patricia), Richard Raymond [Ottaviano Dell'Acqua] (Roger), Alex McBride [Massimo Vanni] (Bo), Ulli Reinthaler (Nancy), Marina Loy (Carole), Deborah Bergamimi (Lia), Mike Monty [Michael O'Donahue] (General Morton), Robert Marius (Professor Holder)

Terrorists inadvertently unleash a biological weapon on an island in the Philippines, causing the inhabitants to turn into rotting zombies. The government steps in to stop the spread of infection—at any cost. A group of travelers find themselves fighting against both the living dead and the government troops.

Having failed to score a critical or commercial hit since *Manhattan Baby* in 1982, it's not surprising that Lucio Fulci eventually succumbed to the pressure to create a sequel to his most successful movie, *Zombie* (1979). Without the support of a talented production team, the project was essentially doomed from the outset.

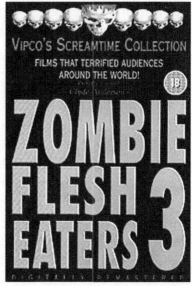

Predictably the shoot was a troubled affair. After a couple of weeks, Fulci returned home, either because of illness or frustration. Bruno Mattei, the man responsible for the awful *Hell of the Living Dead* (1981), was brought in to finish the picture. Feeling out of his depth, Mattei recruited his regular screenwriter and asked Claudio Fragrasso to help with the direction. After shooting a few extra scenes, the pair simply strung together the best of the material and moved on to other projects. It's hard to piece together a definitive account of the shoot, since so many of the statements conflict. What is certain is that none of the directors employed were particularly happy with the assignment, with the obvious consequences. *Zombie 3* is a mess of unresolved threads, illogical plot devices and poor scripting. At least the script problems can be laid squarely at the feet of Claudio Fragrasso, the sole scriptwriter. The recycling of a plot device from *Return of the Living Dead* (1985)—a film designed to spoof such old-school zombie movies—indicates just how out of touch Fragrasso was.

Without the presence of a makeup genius such as Giannetto De Rossi, *Zombie 3* cannot even be relied upon for some decent zombie action. Franco Di Girolami is a competent technician, but too much time is spent trying to replicate the makeup and special effects from Lamberto Bava's *Demons* (1985). A case in point is the scene where a zombie in the abandoned building attacks Beatrice Ring. Not only does the creature's makeup resemble Rosario Prestopino's work on *Demons*, but also the location is flooded with dry ice and green lighting. In an exceptionally ill-advised move, the fight scene is sped up, possibly to make it resemble the frenetic action that characterized Bava's film.

Not everything in the movie is an embarrassing failure. For the most part, *Zombi 3* is well edited, with the hyperactive zombies helping to build up the film's pace, and it's certainly a more entertaining film than Mattei's own *Hell of the Living Dead*. Compared to the original *Zombie*—or any of the films that immediately followed—it's distinctly unimpressive. Given the state of Italian horror in 1987, it's perhaps surprising that it turned out quite as well as it did. Even so, it remains one of the most disappointing sequels in the history of Italian horror films.

Zombie Holocaust (1980)
Aka: Zombi Holocaust, Dr. Butcher, M.D.,
La regina dei cannibali, Queen of the Cannibals

Director: Frank Martin [Marino Girolami]; Story: Fabrizio De Angelis; Screenplay: Walter Patriarca, Romano Scandariato; Producer: Fabrizio De Angelis, Gianfranco Couyoumdjian; Special Effects/Makeup: Maurizio Trani, Rosario Prestopino; Music: Nico Fidenco, Walter E. Sear
Starring: Ian McCulloch (Peter Chandler), Alexandra Cole [Alexandra Delli Colli] (Laurie Ridgeway), Sherry Buchanan (Susan Kelly), Peter O'Neal (George Hooper), Donald O'Brien (Dr. Abrero)

Dr. Ridgeway discovers that an orderly is stealing body parts and organs from the hospital where they work. Although the suspect is killed before the police can question him, evidence suggests he came from the Caribbean island of Kito, where in the past cannibalism had been reported. Accompanied by police investigator Peter Chandler, Dr. Ridgeway heads off to Kito to track the source of the organ theft ring.

In March 1980, the first of many films inspired by *Zombie* (1979) appeared. Once again, Fabrizio De Angelis, eager to repeat the success of Lucio Fulci's film, was the motivating factor. Having devised a similar story, De Angelis hired scriptwriter Romano Scandariato to write it and veteran filmmaker Marino Girolami to direct. Two associates of Giannetto De Rossi, Maurizio Trani and Rosario Prestopino, were brought on board to handle the special effects. Ian McCulloch returned to play another New Yorker, this time a health department official. The ac-

tor who played Dr. Me-
nard's native assistant in
Zombi appears—bizarrely
enough—as Dr. Obrero's
assistant.

In many respects *Zom-
bie Holocaust* is an inferior
copy of *Zombie*. The plot is
similar—four New York-
ers head off to an exotic
location, traveling by boat
and Jeep—and many of
the locations seem to have
been chosen for their similarity to ones used in Fulci's original film. Obrero's
laboratory, for example, is
rumored to be the hospital
from *Zombie*, and the two
buildings certainly look
the same. Whereas Fulci
shot his Caribbean scenes

near Santo Domingo, *Holocaust* was filmed 35 miles outside Rome,
near the town of Latina. Unfortunately this distinctly non-tropical
location boasts well-kept lawns and thick European foliage, with
only the occasional palm tree to represent the film's intended location. Scenes deleted from the final cut clearly show Ian McCulloch
wading through dead leaves beneath autumnal trees, an uncommon
sight around the equator.

Despite the presence of Maurizio Trani and Rosario Prestopino,
both competent artists, the special effects in *Zombie Holocaust* are
substantially worse than those in *Zombie*. For the most part makeup
is only applied to the head, leaving arms, legs and torso noticeably
free of rotting flesh. The heads themselves are nothing special—thick
masks with little of the sickening detail that characterized Fulci's zombies. The other effects consist almost entirely of standard cannibalistic
touches—lumps of bright red flesh and intestine—but there's enough
on show to please most gore fans.

Aside from *Zombie*, this film is clearly indebted to that other Italian exploitation favorite, the cannibal movie. It's worth mentioning

Starring IAN MCCULLOCH · ALEXANDRA DELLI COLLI
SHERRY BUCHANAN
Produced by GIANFRANCO COUYDUVOVIAN
Released by ...

at this point that Girolami's film was the first one to combine both zombies and cannibals into one gory mess. The cannibals as presented here are of the usual variety—scrawny, crouching figures covered in ashen face paint. Unlike the films of Umberto Lenzi and Ruggero Deodato, these cannibals aren't accompanied by naked tribeswomen and no sleazy masturbation/rape episodes appear here. The cannibals seem fixated on the naked body of Alexandra Delli Colli, in scenes possibly intended to mimic Ursula Andress in *She* (1965) and *Mountain of the Cannibal God* (1978). The discovery of cannibal cults at large in New York seems to echo the opening of Lenzi's *Eaten Alive* (1980); given the cannibalistic nature of Italian genre writers, it's entirely possible.

Zombie Holocaust was transported to the big screen in March 1980, where it proved popular. Not as popular as *Zombie*, it earned enough to make it a profitable venture. In the United States Terry Levene, head of Aquarius Releasing, Inc., acquired the film; ARI was a frequent distributor of European and Asian exploitation movies. Discovering he did not have the rights to the film's title, Levene approached independent filmmaker Roy Frumkes, with the intent to buy some footage from him. Some time before, Frumkes had set about producing an anthology of horror stories, featuring a variety of directors including Wes Craven and Brendan Faulkner. The project, titled *Tales That'll Rip Your Heart Out*, had finally run out of money before it could be completed, leaving behind a large amount of never-to-be-seen footage. For a relatively small fee, Levene arranged to buy three minutes of footage to serve as a new title sequence for *Zombie Holocaust*. This new material was edited—not especially well—into the film, which was subsequently released as *Dr. Butcher, M.D.* Roy Frumkes went on to produce *Street Trash* (1986) and *Document of the Dead* (1989).

Essential Italian Horror Film Directors, Screenwriters, Special Effects Technicians and Makeup Artists

Dario Argento (b. 09/07/1940, Rome, Italy)

Dario Argento is Italy's most successful director of horror movies. While the domestic horror film has largely faded away, Argento is still able to secure theatrical releases for his films, many of which perform well at the box office. His international reputation is excellent, even though he is little known outside the horror community.

The son of noted film producer Salvatore Argento, Dario Argento was exposed to film from an early age. He began writing about movies in his teenage years, eventually becoming a journalist after leaving school. Soon afterward Argento started to experiment with scriptwriting. During the mid-1960s he penned a number of B-movie scripts, mostly Westerns and war movies for established directors such as Tonino Cervi, Armando Crispino and Umberto Lenzi. His most significant achievement was co-writing Sergio Leone's acclaimed *Once Upon a Time in the West* (1968).

Having gained considerable experience as a scriptwriter and assistant director, Argento released his debut feature, a stylish and complex thriller called *The Bird with the Crystal Plumage*, in 1969. Although released to little fanfare, it quickly began to attract the attention of critics and audiences alike. Argento followed this early success with two other *gialli*, *The Cat O'Nine Tails* and *Four Flies on Grey Velvet* (both 1971). Both were moderately successful. His next film, a historical drama, did not fare so well, receiving no international release and being largely ignored in Italy.

After a couple of television projects, Argento returned to the *giallo* in style with *Deep Red* (1976), one of the best Italian horror films of the decade. *Deep Red* showed a definite progression for Argento, emphasizing the film's visual and aesthetic appeal over the plot and characterization. Although not particularly successful across the Atlantic (perhaps due to savage editing), *Deep Red* proved popular with Italian audiences. His next film, a supernatural chiller called *Suspiria* (1977), was his most successful film so far, as well as his finest achievement. A nightmarish vision backed by a disturbing avant-garde score, *Suspiria* was truly a unique film, confirming Argento's status as horror's premiere stylist. A follow-up, 1980's *Inferno*, built on *Suspiria*'s themes, but failed to find critical acceptance.

The 1980s were a difficult time for Argento. *Inferno* and *Tenebrae* (1982)—another brutal *giallo*—did not receive theatrical releases in the U.S., while his next film, *Phenonema* (1985), starring Donald Pleasence and Jennifer Connelly, was his first serious misstep since *Deep Red*. *Opera* (1987), a troubled production, was also ignored in the U.S. and poorly received at home, leading Argento to angrily withdraw from directing for a few years. Having already produced George Romero's seminal zombie flick *Dawn of the Dead* (1978), Argento turned his attention once again to production. Among other things, he produced Lamberto Bava's lucrative *Demons* movies and two of Michele Soavi's highly regarded films, *The Church* (1988) and *The Sect* (1991).

Argento returned to directing with 1990's *Two Evil Eyes*, a two-part film based on the works of Edgar Allan Poe, with Argento tackling one segment and George Romero handling the other. In 1993 he released *Trauma*, his first American film. The experience was not a happy one, and Argento returned to Italy, vowing never again to make a film specifically aimed at American audiences. Since then his output slowed considerably, with only two more films being released in the 1990s: *The Stendhal Syndrome* in 1996 and his widely criticized reworking of *The Phantom of the Opera* in 1998.

2001's *Sleepless* was generally considered a return to form for Argento, taking him back to the complex and violent mystery thrillers with which he made his name. With *The Card Player* (2004) he tried to move toward a more police-oriented mystery, an idea that did not find favor in all quarters. However, the news that Argento finally intended to complete the trilogy he had begun with *Suspiria* and *Inferno*, nearly a quarter of a century before, tended to galvanize his fans. Perhaps this will represent a real return to form for one of the horror genre's most individual talents.

Lamberto Bava (b. 04/03/1944, Rome, Italy)

The son of Mario Bava, Italy's most famous horror director, Lamberto Bava grew up around movies. From the age of 21 he began assisting his father in the studio, working on films such as *Planet of the Vampires* (1965), *Kill, Baby...Kill!* (1966) and *Bay of Blood* (1972). Lamberto also co-wrote and helped to complete his father's final theatrical film, *Shock*. As an assistant director, he worked with Ruggero Deodato (*Cannibal Holocaust*, 1980) and Dario Argento (*Inferno*, 1980; *Tenebrae*, 1982).

Bava made his directorial debut in 1980 with *Macabre*, a Gothic thriller co-written and produced by Pupi and Antonio Avati. Although critically praised, *Macabre* was not a commercial success. His next film, the violent and bloody *giallo A Blade in the Dark* (1983), cemented his reputation as a talented horror director. The gruesome splatter movie *Demons* (1985) and its sequel would become two of the highest-grossing Italian horror films of the decade.

After the release of *Delirium* in 1987, Lamberto chose to concentrate on television work. He directed several made-for-TV horror movies that enjoyed moderate acclaim. However, Bava's greatest success has been with his fantasy films, including the *Fantaghiro* series and *The Dragon Ring* (1994). He usually assembles distinguished casts, including international stars such as Christopher Lee, Brigitte Nielsen and Ursula Andress, as well as European celebrities like Anna Falchi, Franco Nero and Karel Rodan. Lamberto has become a respected television director in Italy, although he remains best known internationally for his highly regarded horror films. In 1998 announcements proclaimed that Bava would be directing another horror movie, once again written and produced by Pupi and Antonio Avati, but nothing materialized.

Ruggero Deodato (b. 05/07/1939, Potenza, Italy)

Thanks to one film—*Cannibal Holocaust* (1980)—Ruggero Deodato has become one of the most famous (and notorious) figures in the world of horror. Outside of his few cannibal-themed movies, Deodato has shown himself to be a talented director capable of producing spaghetti Westerns, disaster movies, erotic thrillers, brutal *gialli*, television dramas and post-apocalyptic adventures.

Deodato's career began in 1958, when he was hired as third assistant director by acclaimed filmmaker Roberto Rossellini. He quickly became a sought-after assistant director, and a prolific one, too; he worked on a staggering number of films, something in the region of 40 in just nine years. During that period Deodato assisted some of the most prominent Italian directors, including Riccardo Freda, Antonio Margheriti and Sergio Corbucci. By 1968 he was directing his own films, further increasing his reputation.

It wasn't until 1976's *Last Cannibal World* that Deodato began to attract attention outside Italy. Heavily influenced by Umberto Lenzi's *Deep River Savages* (1972), *Last Cannibal World* was a violent adventure that made use of the same graphic gore, sexual violence and real animal slaughter as the earlier film. *Last Cannibal World* paved the way for Deodato's most famous work, and perhaps the most notorious horror film ever made—*Cannibal Holocaust*.

Despite (or perhaps because of) the extreme violence and brutality on display, *Cannibal Holocaust* was an international success. Unfortunately the film's success attracted the attention of censors and concerned parties across the globe. Copies were withdrawn from shelves; the producers were forced to make cuts; Deodato was threatened with legal proceedings in Italy because of the animal cruelty. Before long, his name was synonymous with controversy and extreme cinema. The release of *The House on the Edge of the Park* (1980), a vicious rape-revenge thriller starring David Hess, did nothing to improve the director's image.

216   **Italian Horror**

Deodato spent the best part of a decade trying to shed this negative image and restore his status as a respected filmmaker. His work during the 1980s was erratic, switching between decent efforts like *Phantom of Death* (1988) and trash like the belated sword-and-sorcery flick *The Barbarians* (1987). 1985's *Cut and Run* saw Deodato return to the jungle, but this time there would be less violence, no animal cruelty and no controversy.

After 1993's *Washing Machine*, Deodato moved away from exploitation work and into television. Since then he directed several highly regarded series and become one of the prominent names in Italian television. Deodato is also one of the most sought-after directors of commercials and promotional material, having directed at least 200 clips. Although he hasn't ruled out the possibility of returning to the horror genre, it is clear that Deodato is content to enjoy his newfound (and well-deserved) respectability.

Giannetto De Rossi (b. 08/08/1942, Rome, Italy)

Giannetto De Rossi is widely regarded as Italy's premier makeup artist, a position he has occupied since the early 1980s. He is a third-generation makeup artist, his father and his grandfather having pioneered the art in the early days of Italian cinema (his father Alberto worked on *Once Upon a Time in the West*, 1968). De Rossi is perhaps best known for the excellent zombies he created for Lucio Fulci, on display in *Zombie* (1979) and *The Beyond* (1981).

De Rossi's career started well; the second film he worked on was Joseph L. Mankiewicz' *Cleopatra* (1963), starring Elizabeth Taylor and Richard Burton, where he assisted his father at Rome's acclaimed Cinecittà studios. By the end of the decade De Rossi worked for some of the biggest names in European cinema, including Sergio Leone, Franco Zeffirelli and Pasquale Festa Campanile. In the 1970s he began his long association with the horror genre, providing makeup and effects for Lucio Fulci's *Don't Torture a Duckling* (1972) and Jorge Grau's *The Living Dead at the Manchester Morgue* (1974). His non-horror work included films by Federico Fellini and Bernardo Bertolucci.

After working on Lucio Fulci's best films—as well as Antonio Margheriti's *Cannibal Apocalypse* (1980)—De Rossi was offered the chance to work on a big-budget international picture, David Lynch's troubled rendition of Frank Herbert's *Dune* (1984). Although the production (and the finished film) was beset by many difficulties, the film opened up opportunities for De Rossi. He was soon hired to provide makeup for *Conan the Destroyer* (1984) followed by *The Last Emperor* (1987).

Aside from occasional big-budget action movies like *Rambo III* (1988) and the ill-fated Bruce Willis vehicle *Hudson Hawk* (1991), De Rossi mostly remained in Europe for the last 15 years. He rarely works in the low-budget arena, one notable exception being Alexandre Aja's acclaimed splatter flick *Haute tension* (2003). Most recently, he provided makeup for Uli Edel's retelling of the Ring Saga, *Kingdom in Twilight*, starring Benno Fürmann and Kristanna Loken.

Franco Ferrini (b. 05/01/1944, La Spezia, Italy)

Although he is known primarily as Dario Argento's preferred scriptwriting partner, Franco Ferrini has had a varied and interesting career. He collaborated with Argento on some of his most famous movies, including *Phenomena* (1985), *Opera* (1987) and *Sleepless* (2001).

Ferrini has also worked on the Argento-produced *Demons* (1985) and *Demons 2* (1986), as well as Michele Soavi's *The Church* (1989).

Having studied languages and literature at university, Ferrini's initial ambition was to be a writer. During the 1970s he published many essays and articles, as well as books on the works of Sergio Leone, John Ford and Alain Robbe-Grillet. Ferrini began writing scripts in the late 1970s, making his debut on Michele Massimo Tarantini's *Poliziotti Violente* (1976). Over the next decade he worked with several well-known directors, including Peter Del Monte and Carlo Vanzina. The high point of Ferrini's early career was preparing rewrites for Sergio Leone's acclaimed *Once Upon a Time in America* (1984).

In 1984 Ferrini began his first collaboration with Dario Argento. Although it received mixed reviews, Argento considered *Phenomena* a success, and Ferrini became his most frequent writing partner (only 1998's *The Phantom of the Opera* would not be co-written by him). Since then he has become a highly sought after scriptwriter, both for television and film. Aside from his work with Argento, Ferrini has provided material for Ruggero Deodato (*Dial: Help*, 1988) and Maurizio Ponzi. In 1987 Ferrini directed his first film, a *giallo*-inspired thriller called *Caramelle da uno sconosciuto*.

Lucio Fulci
(b. 06/17/1927, Rome, Italy; d. 03/13/1996, Rome, Italy)

Christened the Italian Godfather of Gore, Lucio Fulci was undoubtedly Italy's premier exponent of the splatter film. During his most commercially successful period (1979-1982), he released a handful of films that rank as some of the country's finest gruesome horror movies. Sadly, Fulci would never again reach that level of quality or commercial success, but those films are enough to confirm his status as one of the great directors of Italian horror.

Fulci's career began the early 1950s. Forsaking his position as a medical student to enroll in film school, the young student impressed his lecturers and quickly gained funding for a handful of documentaries. In 1950 Fulci earned his first position on a feature film, being appointed second unit director on *The Last Days of Pompeii*. It wasn't long before he was working as assistant director and scriptwriter to the great Stefano Vanzina, known as Steno. Steno was a specialist in broad comedies, usually starring the greatest Italian comedian of the day, Totò, and Fulci gained experience from the man's tutelage.

It wasn't until 1966 that Fulci began to move away from comedy. In the years following he tried his hand at many different genres, including spaghetti Westerns and historical dramas. Eventually Fulci seemed to find his feet with 1969's *One on Top of the Other*, a stylish and melodramatic thriller. It was a modest commercial success, so Fulci followed it up with *A Lizard in a Woman's Skin* (1971), a violent *giallo*. Bizarrely, the director found himself accused of killing dogs during the shoot and was dragged into court. Thankfully special effects technician Carlo Rambaldi was able to bring one of the "dogs" before the court and demonstrate how the effect was created. Controversy dogged Fulci's next thriller, the excellent *Don't Torture a Duckling* (1972); it painted an unpleasant picture of rural life and made several scathing comments about the Catholic Church.

Despite his obvious aptitude for violent and perverse thrillers, throughout the 1970s Fulci seemed unsure how to proceed with his career. A couple of belated Westerns and two misguided literary adaptations did little to improve his profile. Fulci's most interesting release, a *giallo* called *The Psychic* (1977), was a commercial flop. In 1978 producer Fabrizio De Angelis approached Fulci with an offer to direct a fairly straightforward horror film. Enzo G. Castellari already turned the script down, which was clearly intended to cash in on the success of George Romero's *Dawn of the Dead* (1978), and Fulci was more than happy to provide his services. *Zombie* was undoubtedly the most significant film of Fulci's career. A massive commercial success, it placed him at the forefront of the Italian horror boom. Working almost exclusively with the same crew, Fulci managed to produce a handful of brutal, stylish and innovative horror films that have overshadowed everything he did before or since. *Zombie, City of the Living Dead* (1980), *The Beyond* and *The House by the Cemetery* (both 1981) are all essential viewing for anyone with an interest in the development of the splatter movie.

Sadly, this golden age could not last forever. By 1983 disputes with his regular producers left Fulci without financial backing and without a reliable crew. The quality of his films began to deteriorate, just as international interest in Italian horror began to wane. His next few releases—an extremely brutal slasher movie, a second-rate sword-and-sorcery flick, even a disco-themed murder mystery—lacked the vitality of his best work, and failed to provoke audience interest. After 1982's dull supernatural thriller *Manhattan Baby*, none of Fulci's films would be given a U.S. theatrical release.

With his fortunes declining, Fulci finally succumbed to pressure to create a sequel to his groundbreaking zombie film. Unfortunately

Zombie 3 (1987) was not the film everyone was expecting. It was sloppy, derivative and stupid, and few people were impressed. After receiving scathing U.S. reviews, the film even failed to do well in Italy, eventually sinking without trace. This outcome was hardly surprising, given that Fulci had left the set well before the end, leaving his film in the hands of Bruno Mattei and Claudio Fragrasso, who slapped together a rough print before heading off to make *Zombie 4–After Death* (1988) in the hope of recouping some of their losses.

His health failing and his commercial potential largely non-existent, Fulci took whatever work he could find. He allowed his name to be added to films he hadn't worked on, he produced a couple of made-for-television movies that never got released and he even stitched together parts of other films with some new material, passing it off as his latest film (*Nightmare Concert*, 1990). The only glimmer of hope came in 1995, when he was hired to direct a remake of the 1953 chiller *House of Wax*. With Dario Argento producing, the project would have decent funding and the publicity necessary to give it at least a chance of being a success. Tragically, Fulci died on March 13, 1996, just as it seemed his career might be getting back on track. Diabetes-related complications led to his demise, although some unanswered questions remain about his death. Nonetheless, Fulci was a genuine pioneer of the splatter film, responsible for some of Europe's finest horror films.

Umberto Lenzi (b. 08/06/1931, Massa Marittima, Grosseto, Italy)

For three decades, Umberto Lenzi was a mainstay of European exploitation cinema. He directed more than 50 films, including cop thrillers, *gialli*, horror films, spaghetti Westerns, war films and historical dramas. While he has not achieved the critical acclaim of some of his colleagues, Lenzi's work proved popular both in Italy and the international market.

Umberto Lenzi on the set of *Hell's Gate*

After studying law and filmmaking at university, Lenzi began writing film reviews and articles while looking for work as a screenwriter and director. In 1961 he made his directorial debut with *Le avventure di Mary Read* (*Queen of the Seas*), the first of many swashbuckling adventures. Following the changing trends, he turned his hand to the *peplum* (sometimes starring Steve Reeves or Richard Harrison), the spy spoof and the spaghetti Western. The revival of interest in the *giallo* in the early 1970s gave Lenzi the opportunity to work in the closest thing to a preferred genre he would come across in his long career. His best film from the period is *Seven Bloodstained Orchids* (1972), but all of his *gialli* are competently made and worth watching.

Throughout the 1970s Lenzi continued to produce films at a prolific rate, with an emphasis on crime thrillers and war films. He found his greatest commercial success (and a degree of notoriety) with his cannibal adventures. The Italian film industry began to wind down in the 1980s, and Lenzi's output dwindled. By the late 1980s he was primarily making low-budget horror movies such as *La casa 3* (*Ghosthouse*, 1989) and *Nightmare Beach* (1989), as well as a handful of made-for-TV horrors.

In the mid-1990s Lenzi entered semi-retirement, bored with trying to compete for space on the Italian market with bigger-budgeted, more popular American movies. It seems unlikely that a man with such a love of filmmaking and cinema in general would withdraw from the industry entirely, but for now Lenzi is content to observe the rediscovery of many of his films (thanks to DVD) and enjoy his status as one of the few remaining godfathers of Italian exploitation.

Aristide Massacessi
(b. 12/15/1936 Rome, Italy; d. 01/23/1999 Rome, Italy)

Aristide Massacessi, most familiar to horror audiences as "Joe D'Amato" (one of more than two dozen pseudonyms), is probably the most notorious—and prolific—figure in the field of Italian exploitation. Although much of his later career was devoted to porn films, he has directed a number of key horror films, as well as founding the influential production company Filmirage.

The son of a studio electrician, Massacessi was exposed to the film industry at an early age. After leaving school he found work as a cameraman, assistant scriptwriter or electrician, depending on what the job required. Throughout the 1960s Massacessi found regular employment as an assistant cameraman, working on films by well-known directors such as Carlo Lizzani (*L'oro di Roma*, 1961), Franco Zeffirelli (*La bismetica domata*, 1967) and Umberto Lenzi (*Paranoia*, 1970). He was also becoming well known for his skills as a cinematographer, working on several spaghetti Westerns in the 1960s and early 1970s. His best work in that field is probably Massimo Dallamano's acclaimed *giallo*, *What Have You Done to Solange?* (1971), although he also worked with Alberto De Martino on *L'assassino...è al telefono* (1972) and *The Tempter* (1974).

Massacessi graduated to directing in the early 1970s, although he continued to serve as cameraman and cinematographer on other films. His first notable effort is the bizarre Gothic chiller *Death Smiles on a Murderer* (1972), starring Klaus Kinski and Giacomo Rossi Stuart. Soon after that he discovered the profits that could be made in pornography and began releasing his many *Emmanuelle* clones. Most of them starred Laura Gemser, a Javanese model who first appeared in *Emmanuelle 2* (1975), although not in a starring role. Massacessi's *Emanuelle* films (note the alternative spelling, used to avoid legal action) also featured a fair amount of violence and gore as well as hardcore porn material. The most notorious is the snuff-themed *Emanuelle in America* (1977), one of the most extreme exploitation films available at the time.

Aside from the porn films, Massacessi also began to dabble in straight splatter movies. His first attempt, *Buio omega* (*Beyond the Darkness*, 1979)—a remake of Mino Guerrini's *Il terzo occhio* (1966)—attracted attention for its graphic displays of cannibalism and necrophiliac themes. Nonetheless, it's a stylish and moody film that ranks as Massacessi's best movie. He courted controversy once again with *Anthropophagous* (1980), in particular the scene where a cannibal monster devours an unborn baby. Controversial material aside, both *Anthropophagous* and the follow-up *Absurd* (1981) were popular with the exploitation fans.

Throughout the 1980s Massacessi continued to release many porn films, a handful of sword and sorcery films and a couple of post-apocalyptic, sub-*Escape from New York* efforts. He devoted much time in the late 1980s to production, mostly through his company Filmirage. His best film as producer was Michele Soavi's debut feature *Stagefright* (1987), but he also produced Lucio Fulci's last film, *The Door to Silence* (1991), as well as movies by Claudio Fragrasso, Luigi Montefiore, Fabrizio Laurenti and Umberto Lenzi.

With the Italian horror film industry in decline during the 1990s, Massacessi concentrated on his lucrative straight-to-video porn films. He died of a heart attack on January 23, 1999, at the age of 63. During his lifetime he was one of the key figures of Italian exploitation, responsible for at least one *bona fide* classic (*Beyond the Darkness*). His son Daniele is a respected cameraman, best known for his work on Ridley Scott's *Black Hawk Down* (2001) and Martin Scorsese's *Gangs of New York* (2002).

Dardano Sacchetti (b. 06/27/19 , Rome, Italy)

It's no understatement to say that Dardano Sacchetti is one of the most prolific scriptwriters working today. He's provided scripts for some of the most famous Italian horror films ever made, from Argento's *Cat O'Nine Tails* (1971) to Fulci's *Zombie* (1979) and Lamberto Bava's *Demons* films. By the mid-1980s Sacchetti's name was synonymous with Italian horror; he was even approached by several producers who wanted to use his name on scripts he hadn't written, as a guarantee of quality and commercial potential.

Like many of his contemporaries, Sacchetti started his career as critic and essayist, as well as a poet. In 1970 he tried to approach Dario Argento with some movie ideas, confident that he would not be able to contact him. To his surprise, Argento expressed an interest in seeing his ideas. Sacchetti went home and quickly typed out a single page treatment, which he then handed to Argento. That single-page became the basis for the director's next film, *Cat O'Nine Tails*, and Sacchetti earned his first screen credit. Shortly afterward he prepared the script for Mario Bava's underrated *Bay of Blood* (1972), as well as a seemingly endless stream of cop thrillers, mostly directed by Umberto Lenzi and Stelvio Massi.

In 1977 Sacchetti began the first of many collaborations with Lucio Fulci. He would serve as scriptwriter on Fulci's most successful films, including *The Beyond* (1981) and *New York Ripper* (1982). These gore-soaked and controversial films secured Sacchetti a reputation as a hard-working and competent writer with a talent for quickly knocking existing material into shape. For the rest of the 1980s he would be rarely without work, sometimes writing as many as five or six films each year. An attempt at writing for American companies fell through, although one of his scripts—reworked by Tommy Lee Wallace—eventually became *Amityville II: The Possession* (1982).

In the 1990s Sacchetti became less prolific as the Italian film industry began to lose pace. Like many of his contemporaries he found work in television, providing scripts for most of Lamberto Bava's made-for-television horror films, as well as lecturing in film studies at Italian universities. Since then Sacchetti wrote several television series, frequently in the cop/thriller genre. His vast legacy—he has written or co-written nearly 100 films—remains an essential part of the history of the Italian horror film.

Michele Soavi (b. 07/03/57, Milan, Italy)

Since his emergence in the early 1980s, Michele Soavi has been hailed as the future of Italian horror. At a time when the genre market was flooded with inferior made-for-television efforts and poor copies of American movies, Soavi released a handful of films that combined the best elements of the past with a fresh and original viewpoint. Although he only made four theatrical films, they are enough to ensure his place among the best Italian horror film directors.

Soavi grew up in an artistic household—his stepfather was a well-known painter—and Soavi initially intended to become an artist. In his late teens he decided to become an actor instead and signed up for acting lessons at Fersen Studio, following his graduation. While honing his acting abilities Soavi also discovered a passion for directing. A brief turn as an extra led to his first job behind the camera, as assistant director on Marco Madugno's *Bambulè* (1979). Soon he was able to secure larger acting roles, appearing in films by established directors such as Enzo G. Castellari (*Il giorno del cobra*, 1980) and Lucio Fulci (*City of the Living Dead*, 1980; *The New York Ripper*, 1982). Soavi also struck up a friendship with Aristide Massacessi (aka Joe D'Amato), leading to several appointments as cameraman, scriptwriter and assistant director.

Soavi's early attempts at scriptwriting attracted the attention of Dario Argento, who asked him to sign on as second assistant director (working behind Lamberto Bava) on his new film *Tenebrae* (1982). He would go on to assist Argento on both *Phenomena* (1985) and *Opera* (1987), while appearing in Bava's *A Blade in the Dark* (1983) and *Demons* (1985). His friendship with Argento and his growing talent led to his first directorial assignments, a Bill Wyman rock video for *Phenomena* and a documentary on Argento himself, *Dario Argento's World of Horror* (1985).

In 1986 Massacessi offered Soavi a shot at directing his first feature film. A stylish *giallo* written by Luigi Montefiore, *Stagefright* was an international success, although it did not fare so well on the domestic market. More importantly, it demonstrated the young director's considerable talent as well as stating his commitment to genre cinema. Among Soavi's international admirers was Terry Gilliam, who was impressed enough to hire him as assistant director on his multi-million dollar production, *The Adventures of Baron Munchausen* (1988).

The Church, Soavi's second feature, was released in 1989. Originally intended to be a third installment in Bava's *Demons* series, *The Church* was produced and co-written by Dario Argento. With a much bigger budget, Soavi was able to give his imagination free rein, making *The Church* a truly grandiose production, as opposed to *Stagefright*'s limited locations. Critics complained that neither *The Church*, nor Soavi's next film, *The Sect* (1991, also produced by Argento), paid enough attention to plot and characterization, an accusation often leveled at Dario Argento.

After an unsuccessful attempt to branch out into different genres, Soavi returned with his finest effort, 1994's *Dellamorte dellamore*. Combining traditional Italian splatter with cynical comedy and existential philosophy, *Dellamorte dellamore* is one of the most highly regarded Italian horror films of the past 20 years, confirming Soavi's status as one of Italy's most talented directors. Tragically, his son's illness forced him to withdraw from the industry for several years. In recent years he has returned to the director's chair, specializing in polished television dramas, including the popular *Ultimo* series. Although he currently has no plans to return to theatrical filmmaking, Soavi remains one of the most respected Italian directors.

Sergio Stivaletti (b. 03/15/1957, Rome, Italy)

Since the mid-1980s Sergio Stivaletti has been one of the most important names in Italian special effects, earning worldwide acclaim for his stunning animatronic work. He began his association with the movie industry in 1976, when he contributed a few self-made *object d'art* to the set of Pupi Avati's Gothic thriller *The House with the Laughing Windows*. After an unsuccessful attempt to secure work on Riccardo Freda's *Fear* (1980), Stivaletti was hired to provide effects for Dario Argento's *Phenomena* (1985), having impressed the producers with the quality of his work and ideas.

From then on, Stivaletti became a frequent collaborator with Argento, working on several of the great director's films, including *The Stendhal Syndrome* (1996) and *Sleepless* (2001). His association with Argento led to collaborations with Lamberto Bava on his successful *Demons* films and with Michele Soavi. His work for Soavi includes the stunning demon head that appears at the end of *The Church* (1989) and the zombie effects in the acclaimed *Dellamorte dellamore* (1994). Outside of Italy Stivaletti has worked on *Titus* (1999), starring Anthony Hopkins.

Stivaletti made his directorial debut in 1997, with the Argento-produced *Maschera del cera* (*The Wax Mask*). The film was well received, adding another string to this talented individual's bow. He continues to be a sought-after technician throughout Europe, and hopes to be able to bring his dream of a new cinematic version of *The Golem* to life fairly soon.

Bibliography

Directors

Cannibal Holocaust & the Savage Cinema of Ruggero Deodato, Harvey Fenton, Julian Grainger & Gian Luca Castoldi (FAB Press, 1999)
Beyond Terror: The Films of Lucio Fulci, Stephen Thrower (FAB Press, 1999)
Lucio Fulci: Beyond the Gates, Chas. Balun (Blackest Heart Books, 1996 & Fantasma Books, 1997)
Art of Darkness: The Cinema of Dario Argento, Chris Gallant (FAB Press, 2000)
Broken Mirrors/Broken Mind: The Dark Dreams of Dario Argento, Maitland McDonagh (Citadel Trade, 1994)

Italian Horror

Eaten Alive! Italian Cannibal and Zombie Movies, Jay Slater (Plexus Books, 2002)
Spaghetti Nightmares, Luca M. Palmerini, Gaetano Mistretta (Fantasma Books, 1996)
The Delerium Guide to Italian Exploitation Cinema 1975-1979, ed. Adrian Luther-Smith (Media Publications, 1997)
Blood & Black Lace, Adrian Luther-Smith (Stray Cat Publications, 1999)

General

The Psychotronic Video Guide, Michael J. Weldon (Titan Books, 1996)
Nightmare Movies, Kim Newman (rev. ed. Bloomsbury, 1988)
The Zombie Movie Guide, Peter Dendle (McFarland & Co., 2001)
Splatter Movies, John McCarty (St. Martin's Press, 1984)

Index of Alternate Titles

La casa 5 see Beyond Darkness
La casa con la scala nel buio see A Blade in the Dark
La casa del anime erranti see The House of Lost Souls
La casa dell'orco see The Ogre
La casa del sortilegio see The House of Witchcraft
La casa del tappeto giallo see The House of the Yellow Carpet
La casa del tempo see The House of Clocks
A Cat in the Brain see Nightmare Concert
Cemetery Man see Dellamorte dellamore
A cena col vampire see Dinner with a Vampire
The Changeling 2–The Revenge see Until Death
La chiesa see The Church
City of the Walking Dead see Nightmare City
Contamination—Alien arriva sulla terra see Contamination
Creepers see Phenomena

Dark Waters see Dead Waters
Deadly Treasure of the Piranha see Killer Fish
Deliria see Stagefright
Delirio di sangue see Blood Delirium
Dèmoni see Demons
The Demon Is Loose see Murder-Rock Dancing Death
Dèmoni 2 see Demons 2
Dèmoni 2…L'incubo ritorna see Demons 2
Demoni 3 see Black Demons
Demons 2…The Nightmare Returns see Demons 2
Demons 3 see The Church
Demons III: The Ogre see The Ogre
Demons 4 see The Sect
Demons 5 see The Devil's Veil
Demons 6: De profondis see The Black Cat (1989)
Demons '95 see Dellamorte dellamore
De profondis see The Black Cat (1989)
Devilfish see Monster Shark
Devil's Daughter see The Sect
The Devil's Honey see Dangerous Obsession
Devouring Waves see Monster Shark
Dr. Butcher, M.D. see Zombie Holocaust
La dolce casa delgi orrori see The Sweet House of Horrors
Don't Be Afraid of Aunt Martha see The Murder Secret

Doomed to Die see Eaten Alive!
Due occhi diabolici see Two Evil Eyes

Eaten Alive by the Cannibals see Eaten Alive!
The Emerald Jungle see Eaten Alive!
E tu vivrai nel terrore—L'aldilà see The Beyond
Evil Encounters see Witchcraft
Extrasensorial see Blood Link
Eye of the Evil Dead see Manhattan Baby

I fantasmi di sodoma see Ghosts of Sodom
The Farm see The Curse
The Fishmen see The Island of the Fishmen
Il fiume del grande caimano see The Great Alligator
Forest Slave see Amazonia
Formula per un assassino see Formula for a Murder
I frati rossi see The Red Monks
Frozen Terror see Macabre
Fuga dalla morte see Luna di sangue

The Gates of Hell see City of the Living Dead
Un gatto nel cervello (I volti del terrore) see Nightmare Concert
Il gatto nero see The Black Cat (1981)
Il gatto nero see The Black Cat (1989)
Ghosthouse 2 see Witchcraft
Il gioco see The School of Fear
Gore in Venice see Giallo a Venezia
The Great Alligator River see The Great Alligator
The Great White see The Last Shark
The Grim Reaper see Anthropophagous
The Grim Reaper 2 see Absurd
Guardian of Hell see The Other Hell

Hell of the Living Death see Hell of the Living Dead
Holocausto Porno see Porno Holocaust
The House at the Edge of the Park see The House on the Edge of the Park

Incuba sulla città contaminata see Nightmare City
Inferno dei morti viventi see Hell of the Living Dead

Inferno in diretta see Cut and Run
Invasion of the Flesh Eaters see Cannibal Apocalypse
L'isola degli uomini pesce see The Island of the Fishmen
The Island of the Dead see Erotic Nights of the Living Dead
Island of the Living Dead see Zombie
Island of the Mutations see The Island of the Fishmen

The Killing Violin see Paganini Horror

Leviatán see Monster Dog

Macabro see Macabre
Il maestro del terrore see The Prince of Terror
Make Them Die Slowly see Cannibal ferox
The Malicious Whore see Malabimba
The Man Beast see Anthropophagous
Mangiati vivi! see Eaten Alive!
La maschera del demonio see The Devil's Veil
Midnight Horror see You'll Die at Midnight
Midnight Killer see You'll Die at Midnight
Il miele del diavolo see Dangerous Obsession
Minaccia d'amore see Dial: Help
Misteria see Body Puzzle
Mondo Cannibale see Cannibals
Monster Hunter see Absurd
Morirai a mezzanotte see You'll Die at Midnight
Murder in an Etruscan Cemetery see The Scorpion with Two Tails
Murder Obsession see Fear
Murderock–Uccide a passo di danza see Murder-Rock Dancing Death
Mystere see Dagger Eyes
Mystery in Venice see Giallo a Venezia

Nel nido del serpente see Bloody Psycho
Il nido del ragno see Spider Labyrinth
Nightmare Beach see Welcome to Spring Break
Night of the Zombies see Erotic Nights of the Living Dead
Night of the Zombies see Hell of the Living Dead
The Nights of Terror see Burial Ground
Non aver paura della zia Marta see The Murder Secret
Non si serviziana e bambini see Hansel e Gretel

Nosferatu a Venezia see Vampire in Venice
Nosferatu in Venice see Vampire in Venice
Le notti del terrore see Burial Ground
Le notte erotiche dei morti viventi see Erotic Nights of the Living Dead
Nudo e selvaggio see Massacre in Dinosaur Valley

Of Death and Love see Dellamorte dellamore
Off Balance see Phantom of Death
The Ogre: Demons 3 see The Ogre
Oltre la morte — Zombi 4 see After Death
L'ossessione che uccide see Fear

Patrick Is Still Alive see Patrick Still Lives
Patrick viva ancora see Patrick Still Lives
Paura nel buio see Hitcher in the Dark
Paura nella città dei morti viventi see City of the Living Dead
Per sempre see Until Death
Le photo di Gioia see Delirium
Photos of Joy see Delirium
Piranha paura see Piranha II: The Spawning
Piranha II: Flying Killers see Piranha II: The Spawning
Le porte dell'inferno see Hell's Gates
Le porte del silenzio see The Door to Silence
Possessed see Manhattan Baby
Possession of a Teenager see Malabimba
Presa tenace see Evil Clutch

Quando Alice ruppe lo specchio see The Touch of Death
Queen of the Cannibals see Zombie Holocaust
Quella villa accanto nel cimiterio see The House by the Cemetery
Quella villa in fondo al parco see The Ratman

Ragno gelido see Dial: Help
Raptors see Killing Birds
Rats — notte di terrore see Rats: Night of Terror
Red Ocean see Monster Shark
La regina dei cannibali see Zombie Holocaust
Revenge of the Dead see Zeder
The Ripper on the Edge see The House on the Edge of the Park
Rosso sangue see Absurd

Satan's Altar see Fear
The Savage Island see Anthropophagous
Schiave bianche: violenzia in Amazzonia see Amazonia
Screamers see The Island of the Fishmen
La setta see The Sect
The Seven Doors of Death see The Beyond
7 Hyden Park: La casa maledetta see Formula for a Murder
Sexy Nights of the Dead see Erotic Nights of the Living Dead
Sexy Nights of the Living Dead see Erotic Nights of the Living Dead
Shadow see Tenebrae
Shark (rosso nell'oceano) see Monster Shark
Il signore dei cani see Monster Dog
The Snake House see Bloody Psycho
Sodoma's Ghosts see Ghosts of Sodom
Something Waits in the Dark see The Island of the Fishmen
Sotto gli occhi dell'assassino see Tenebrae
Sotto il vestito niente see Nothing Underneath
La spaggia del terrore see Welcome to Spring Break
Spettri see Specters
Lo squartatore di New York see The New York Ripper
Stage Fright–Aquarius see Stagefright
Stranded in Dinosaur Valley see Massacre in Dinosaur Valley
Streghe see Witch Story
Stridulum see The Visitor

Tenebre see Tenebrae
Terror at the Opera see Opera
Testimone oculare see Eyewitness
Thrilling in Venice see Giallo a Venezia
There Was a Little Girl see Madhouse
Toxic Spawn see Contamination
Trolli see Troll 2
Trolls see Troll 2

L'ultimo squallo see The Last Shark
Una notte nel cimitero see Graveyard Disturbance
Un delitto poco commune see Phantom of Death
Unsane see Tenebrae
L'uomo che non voleva morire see The Man Who Wouldn't Die
Urla dal profondo see Voices from Beyond

Il violino che uccide see Paganini Horror
Virus see Cannibal Apocalypse
Virus see Hell of the Living Dead
Voci dal profondo see Voices from Beyond
Vortice mortale see The Washing Machine

The Wailing see Fear
When Alice Broke the Mirror see The Touch of Death
White Cannibal Queen see Cannibals
White Slave see Amazonia
Witchery see Witchcraft
Woman From Deep River see Cannibal ferox

Zeder: Voices from Beyond see Zeder
Zeder: Voices from the Beyond see Zeder
Zeder: Voices from the Darkness see Zeder
Zombi Holocaust see Zombie Holocaust
Zombi 2 see Zombie
Zombi 3 see Zombie 3
Zombi 3: Le notti del terrore see Burial Ground
Zombie 3 see Burial Ground
Zombie 4 see After Death
Zombie 5 Killing Birds see Killing Birds
Zombie 6: Monster Hunter see Absurd
Zombie Creeping Flesh see Hell of the Living Dead
The Zombie Dead see Burial Ground
Zombie Flesh Eaters see Zombie
Zombie Flesh Eaters 2 see Zombie 3
Zombie Flesh Eaters 3 see After Death

Index of Pseudonyms

Dorio, Daniela see Doria, Daniela

Eastman, George see Montefiore, Luigi

Fani, Leonora see Cristofani, Eleonora
Ferranti, Pino see Ferranti, Giuseppe
Fleming, Mag see Maglione, Maria Fiamma
Floyd, Drago see Fragrasso, Claudio
Foster, Robert see Mayans, Antonio
Fulci, Louis see Fulci, Lucio
Funari, Dirce see Funari, Patrizia

Gandus, Robert see Gandus, Roberto
Garfield, Frank see Garofalo, Franco
Garko, John see Garko, Gianni
Garrett, Roy see Gariazzo, Mario
Gelardi, John see Massacessi, Aristide
Goodwin, Fred see Prosperi, Federico
Goren, Annj see Napoletano, Annamaria
Gould, Jimmy see Sacchetti, Dardano

Hamilton, Cindy see De Carolis, Cinzia
Hampton, Robert see Freda, Riccardo
Herbert, Martin see De Martino, Alberto
Humbert, Humphrey see Lenzi, Umberto

Kamma, Loes see Kamsteeg, Louise
Keller, Sarah, see Monreale, Cinzia
Kennedy, Pluto see Giombini, Marcello
Kerova, Zora see Keslerova, Zora
Kinski, Debora see Caproglio, Deborah
Kirkpatrick, Harry see Lenzi, Umberto
Kittay, H. Simon see Fulci, Lucio

Lang, Melissa see Longo, Malisa
Lemick, Michele E. see Tarantini, Michele Massimo
Lloyd, Walter see Lucchini, Walter
Lombardo, Tony see Lombardi, Fausto
Louis, Larry see Bava, Lamberto

McKay, Julia see Cavalli, Marina Giulia
MacColl, Katherine see MacColl, Catriona
MacColl, Katriona see MacColl, Catriona
Madison, Jerry see Fulci, Lucio
Maglione, Budy see Maglione, Maria Fiamma
Mancini, Charles see Mancini, Claudio
Mann, Leonard see Manzella, Leonardo
Manner, Jeff see Franco, Jésus
Martin, Frank see Girolami, Marino
Martin, Robert see Bianchi, Mario
Matthew, Maurice see De Angelis, Fabrizio
McBride, Alex see Vanni, Massimo
Michelsen, Katrine see Michelsen, Trine
Milliken, Claude see Lattanzi, Claudio
Monty, Mike see O'Donahue, Michael
Moor, Peter see Tenoglio, Pietro
Moore, Jessica see Ottaviani, Luciana
Morghen, John see Radice, Giovanni Lombardo

Newton, Margit Evelyn see Gansbacher, Margit
Newton, Peter see Massacessi, Aristide

Oblowsky, Stefan see Mattei, Bruno
Old Jr., John see Bava, Lamberto

Paisner, Luca see Venantini, Luca
Parker Jr., David see Sacchetti, Dardano
Pignatelli, Mickey see Pignatelli, Micaela
Plummer, Christian see Martino, Sergio
Powder, Steve see Stelvio Cipriani

Ray, Andrew see Aureli, Andrea
Raymond, Richard see Dell'Acqua, Ottavio
Redford, Bryan see Mattei, Danilo
Rexon, Bert see Pisano, Berto
Ross, Daniel see Stroppa, Daniele
Ross, Howard see Rossini, Renato
Rossi, Gino De see De Rossi, Giannetto
Russell, Frank see Ruffini, Franco

Footnotes

[1] The different spelling—Emanuelle instead of Emmanuelle—is intentional. D'Amato's sequels were unofficial, so the 'm' was dropped to avoid legal complications.

[2] *The Psychotronic Video Guide*, p. 84 (Titan Books, 1996)

[3] Listed as 'The Goblins,' this particular incarnation consisted of bassist Fabio Pignatelli, drummer Agostino Marangolo and two other musicians. Claudio Simonetti and Massimo Morante were not present, having left the year before.

[4] *Cannibal Holocaust and the Savage Cinema of Ruggero Deodato*, by Harvey Fenton, Julian Grainger & Gian Luca Castoldi (FABPress, 1999), p. 16.

[5] Coincidentally (of course), the Japanese name for the computer game *Resident Evil* is also *Biohazard*.

[6] Soavi had previously been 2nd unit director on Gilliam's big-budget flop, *The Adventures of Baron Munchausen* (1988).

Index

De Masi, Francesco 101, 146, 147

De Mejo, Carlo 68, 70, 113, 136, 158, 159

Demonia (1990) 83

Demons (1985) 9, 27, 48, 68, 80, 85-88, 98, 133, 154, 157, 165, 209

Demons 2 (1986) 9, 87, 88, 133, 157, 169, 192

De Nava, Giovanni 37, 113

Deodato, Ruggero 9, 20, 35, 55, 56, 60, 62-65, 74, 75, 91, 95, 120, 121, 150, 162, 163, 196, 197, 211

De Palma, Brian 31

De Ponti, Cinzia 136, 143, 147

De Quincey, Thomas 24

De Rita, Massimo 51, 89, 99

De Rose, Francesco 115

De Rossi, Barbara 193

De Rossi, Massimo 176

De Rossi, Giannetto 37, 38, 56, 57, 59, 61-63, 68, 97, 113, 166, 167, 204, 206-210

De Sando, Giuseppe 192

De Sando, Stefano 173

De Selle, Lorraine 61, 120

De Sica, Manuel 81

De Simone, Ria 151, 185

Desire (1990) 112

De Toth, Nicholas 198

Devil Men From Space, The (1965) 15

Devil's Veil, The (1989) 89, 90

Devoti, Laura 89

Diakun, Alex 52

Dial: Help (1988) 91, 197

Didio, Tony 78

Di Girolami, Franco 32-34, 45, 146, 148, 208, 209

Di Giulio, Gabriele 120

Di Lazzaro, Dalila 164

Dinner With A Vampire (1988) 92, 154

Di Nunzio, Franco 63, 120

Diogene, Franco 180

Dionisio, Silvio 99

Di Salvio, Mario 55

Di Stefano, Marco 53, 185

Django (1966) 14

D'Obici, Valeria 202

Dobrin, Ronald 78

Dobtcheff, Alexander Vernon 180

Donaggio, Pino 45, 46, 74, 153, 162, 175, 186, 188, 190

Donati, Donatella 29, 40, 179

Donati, Sergio 124

Donatone, Mario 164

Donnelly, Margaret 36

Donner, Richard 19

Don't Look Now (1973) 160

Door to Silence (1991) 93, 94

Doria, Daniela 45, 68, 69, 113, 114, 147

Douglas, Kirk 19

Dourif, Brad 187

Druant, Pascal 83, 169

Dr Goldfoot and the Girl Bombs (1966) 15

Drudi, Rossella 32, 40

Ducros, Gabrielle 141

Duvivier, Moune 171

Eaten Alive! (1980) 75, 94, 95

Edmonds, Don 22

Eggar, Samantha 112

Egon, Robert 104, 138, 151

Elias, Cyrus 141, 153

Elmi, Nicoletta 85

Emanuelle and the Last Cannibals (1977) 20

Emanuelle in America (1977) 42

Emerson, Keith 67, 122, 123, 144, 145

Emmanuelle (1972) 20, 23, 150

Engelhardt, Christina 83

Eno, Brian 155

Eno, Roger 155

Erotic Nights of the Living Dead, The (1980) 96, 97, 168

Espositi, Danny Degli 138

Espositi, Gianni 145

Everett, Rupert 81, 82

Everly, Trish 133

Evil Clutch (1988) 97, 98, 157

Evil Dead, The (1982) 41, 98, 103

Evil Eye, The (1963) 15

Exorcist, The (1973) 18, 19, 57, 137, 194

Eye of the Black Cat (1972) 17

Eyewitness (1990) 99

Fabbri, Otavio 41, 42

Faceless Monster, The (1965) 22

Falchi, Anna 81, 82

Falcone, Patrizia 138

Fantasia, Franco 94

Farmer, Mimsy 45, 55

Farr, Jamie 73, 74

Farron, Nicola 55

Farrow, Tisa 36, 204, 206

Fassari, Antonello 141

Fatal Frames (1996) 33

Faulkner, Brendan 212

Faulkner, William 41

Fear (1980) 26, 99, 100

Feldman, Marty 93

Fenech, Edwige 162, 163

Ferrandi, Giancarlo 189

Ferrante, Giuseppe 30, 53, 61, 83, 109-111, 115, 116, 119, 120, 138, 143, 145, 148, 150, 151, 171, 180, 185, 195

Ferrara, Ranieri 113

Ferrario, Cesario 128

Ferrario, Enea 203

Ferrer, Mel 18, 94, 107, 108, 125, 148, 150, 194

Ferreri, Giorgio 130

Ferrini, Franco 67, 85, 87, 91, 92, 153, 155, 164, 186, 190

Festa, Al 32, 33

Fidenco, Nico 168, 210

Field, Richard 79

Fields of the Nephilim 89

Figura, Kashia 196

Filmirage 40, 41, 189, 201

Fincher, David 188

Fiore, Don 179

Fishmen And Their Queen, The (1995) 125

Fisichella, Enzo 108, 135

Fitzsimmons, John 151

Five Days of Milan, The (1973) 16

Five Dolls for an August Moon (1970) 17

Five Graves for a Medium (1965) 14

Flees, Anthony 37

Flesh for Frankenstein (1973) 24

Flora Films 32, 33

Fogacci, Gianluigi 116

Fonoll, Luis 110

Fontana, Agnese 97

Ford, Glenn 194

Forest, Andy J 119

Formica, Fabiana 81

Formula for a Murder (1985) 52, 100, 101

Forrest, Frederic 187

Forte, Paolo 97

Forte, Valentina 55, 56, 74

For Your Eyes Only (1981) 76

**If you enjoyed
this book,
visit our website
www.midmar.com
or write, call or e-mail
for a free catalog
Midnight Marquee Press, Inc.
9721 Britinay Lane
Baltimore, MD 21234
410-665-1198**

Printed in Great Britain
by Amazon

45168782R00145

Introduction to Italian Horror

Riccardo Freda

The Italian horror film arrived to little applause in 1957 with the release of Riccardo Freda's *I Vampiri* (*The Vampires*). At the time Freda was best known for directing historical adventures on a shoestring budget, but together with his friend Mario Bava—a respected cameraman and special effects technician—he resolved to create the first Italian horror film of the sound era. However, Freda walked off the set after disputes with the producers, leaving Bava to complete the work, which he managed to do, shooting the remaining half of the film in just two days. Nonetheless, *I Vampiri* was a commercial flop, ignored by critics and moviegoers alike.

Freda and Bava attempted another horror film—*Caltiki, The Immortal Monster* (1959), in which an ancient blob monster terrorizes archaeologists—but the director walked out, again leaving Bava to complete the film. This time, the film was a success, perhaps because Freda and Bava worked under English-sounding pseudonyms in the belief that Italian audiences wouldn't watch a horror film made by an Italian. Whatever the truth, *Caltiki* introduced the commercial potential of the Italian horror film.

It was Mario Bava who capitalized on the success of *Caltiki, The Immortal Monster*; however, after two abortive attempts Freda had lost patience with horror and turned to the sword-and-sandal *peplums* that were becoming popular. After stepping in to complete a troubled Jacques Tourneur film (*The Giant of Marathon*, 1959, starring Steve Reeves), Bava was rewarded with the opportunity to direct a film of his own. He chose to direct *La maschera del demonio* (*Black Sunday*), a Gothic horror movie based on a tale by Nikolai Gogol. The film's main asset was an excellent central performance from Barbara Steele, a young English actress with a porcelain complexion and captivating eyes. With Bava's gift for atmosphere and Steele's icy charms, *Black Sunday*